MARK BUNTING'S
VIRTUAL POWER

USING YOUR PC TO REALIZE THE LIFE OF YOUR DREAMS

Mark Bunting
with Mark Seal

SIMON & SCHUSTER

SIMON & SCHUSTER
Rockefeller Center
1230 Avenue of the Americas
New York, NY 10020

Designed by Irving Perkins Associates, Inc.

Manufactured in the United States of America

1 3 5 7 9 10 8 6 4 2

Library of Congress Cataloging-in-Publication Data
Bunting, Mark
Mark Bunting's virtual power : using your PC to realize the life
of your dreams / Mark Bunting with Mark Seal.
p. cm.
1. Microcomputers. 2. Internet (Computer network) I. Seal,
Mark, 1953– .II. Title.
QA76.5B8183 1997
646.7′00285′416—dc21 97-1706 CIP
ISBN 0-684-81482-X

Contents

Chapter One	Facing Your Fears	15
Chapter Two	Breaking Free and Heading Home	32
Chapter Three	Purchasing the Computer	56
Chapter Four	Entering the Internet	76
Chapter Five	Finding Success through Failure	108
Chapter Six	The Human Connection	134
Chapter Seven	The Five Secrets of Virtual Power	157
Chapter Eight	Going Portable, Getting Free	182
Chapter Nine	Ten Ways to Keep Pace with the Revolution	206
Chapter Ten	Turn It On!	239
	Index	245

Note on Text

Throughout each chapter, testimonial quotes have been set apart from the main copy in an "e-mail style" format, ideally giving the reader the sense of reading these quotes as if they'd come to him or her via e-mail on the computer.

Acknowledgments

This book would have never been possible were it not for the efforts of many people.

My special thanks to my mentor Rick Davis. A greater example of integrity in business I have never known.

To Tom Hoitsma, the best business partner and friend I could have.

To my brother, Kyle, my friend and salesman par excellence.

To my family, beginning with my wife, Kelly, whose dedication and support never wavered (even when mine did).

To my mother. Thanks for everything. There is too much to list!

To all of my staff at Guy TV, especially Kristen Painter, my resourceful and loyal assistant.

To my agent, Jan Miller, and her team, and to Bob Asahina, for his direction and vision.

Lastly, to Mark Seal. Without your collaboration and all your wonderful efforts, this book would have been impossible.

To my father, Jim Bunting

Thanks for your support, encouragement,
and uncompromising character.
You are a terrific role model.

The treasure which you think not worth taking trouble and pains to find, this one alone is the real treasure you are longing for all your life. The glittering treasure you are hunting for day and night lies buried on the other side of that hill yonder.

—B. Traven,
The Treasure of the Sierra Madre

CHAPTER ONE

Facing Your Fears

I was a computer idiot, a technological illiterate, a complete rank amateur.

I wasn't merely inept when I sat down before the unblinking eye of a computer screen.

I was afraid.

And that fear grew into hatred.

I hated the computer culture, the cyberspeak, the bits and bytes, the jargon of a world obsessed with itself. Armies of computer nerds, the dudes with the thick black glasses and calculators on their belts, invaded my dreams and disrupted my sleep. Walking into a computer store was an invitation to a panic attack. And the mere thought of deciphering a computer software program kick-started my brain into instant scream mode.

This fear haunted my life, because computers were my livelihood, my career. As an advertising salesman for *The Wall Street Journal,* my territory was the high-tech industry. Based in Silicon Valley, California, ground zero of the personal computer revolution, my customer base consisted exclusively of high-technology accounts: Compaq, IBM, Intel, Hewlett-Packard, and many more.

And I had a secret, a deep, dark, nasty secret.

Here I was, a twenty-eight-year-old, $100,000-a-year ad salesman, sitting in strategy meetings with executives in the highest echelons of the computer industry, discussing multimillion-dollar marketing advertising campaigns . . . and everyone assumed I was a computer expert! Yes, I learned the lingo. Yes, I could speak with you in detail about the transistor count on the 386 processor. But it was all a sham. I was merely an actor reciting a part. Personally I had never even *touched* a computer keyboard. Hell, I couldn't even figure out how to work a VCR, much less a computer. But here I was in Silicon Valley in its heyday, nodding my head at meetings where everyone is speaking cyberspeak, ever-intense and exclaiming, "Yes! Excellent! *I understand!*"

If you think it's humiliating being at work where everyone knows how to use a computer except you, if you think it's humiliating being the digitally deficient father of computer-literate children, try being in the heart of Silicon Valley calling on the biggest names in the business, executives who live and breathe technology ten hours a day, when you've *never even touched a keyboard!*

Do you blame me for hating computers? Hating them with a passion? I was the quintessential sales guy. You know the type. "Computers? That's for the backroom boys. I'm too busy out doin' business!"

How did computers set me free? How did I go from computer illiterate to running my own $20 million computer television company within the short span of thirty-six months? How did I move from sharing a ratty apartment on the Upper West Side of Manhattan with my business partner—living hand-to-mouth, unable to support my wife, much less an empowering lifestyle—to my present home, a 13,000-square-foot Dallas mansion? How did I conquer the fear of touching a keyboard and go on to run every aspect of my life with one? How did I go from computer shame to appearing on my nationally syndicated television programs, which are essentially tools to show people how easy it is to plug in to the computer revolution?

When people ask me these questions, I point to the blinking computer screen that resides in 36 percent of America's households. I point to that screen and say, honestly and without one ounce of exaggeration, "The answer is in that box."

Like many people caught in the crossfire of the technological revolution, I was driven out of one job by computers, only to be delivered salvation in another. Disillusioned with my advertising career, I was soon asking myself the age-old question: "What am I supposed to do with my life?"

Then, one day, I just hit the brakes. I quit my job. I bade good-bye to Silicon Valley with a celebratory helicopter lunch over the region with one of my best customers. Then I grabbed a backpack and split for South America. For three months I hung out with my best buddy and did some real soul-searching.

When I returned to my adopted hometown of Houston, a stockbroker friend of mine sat down with me and said, "You know, Mark, it's absolutely absurd that you've made your living in the computer business for all these years and you don't even know how to turn one on. It's really a terrible waste. You gotta get on-line. Let me show you this new computer on-line service called Prodigy."

Prodigy was perfect. Here was this nice, fun, easy-to-use program, a simple way to communicate with the everyday, grass-roots computer world. It wasn't a word processor or a spreadsheet or something boring. It was a totally exciting, graphics-driven communications program.

When I say easy, I mean elementary school easy. *Because I didn't even know how to type!* I had to hunt and peck out the keys, one finger at a time. Still, before I knew it, the screen lit up with colorful graphics and I was on-line. I was chatting with other users around the world. I was accessing my local supermarket and walking down virtual shopping aisles, picking out the items I wanted, and the grocery store would actually deliver the groceries to my home. I was accessing the weather and playing games. It wasn't scary. It wasn't something only a programmer who spoke the foreign language of cyberspeak could do. It was something *anyone* could comprehend.

The author Graham Greene wrote that in every life there is a moment when a window opens and the future rushes in. This was my moment. Something extraordinary "clicked" within me. When I looked up from that screen, I felt absolute exhilaration. It was like jumping out of an airplane and realizing that the chute actually opens and you're going to be safe on the ground. I felt this incredible rush of relief.

"I can do this!" I practically shrieked.

It was the coolest experience of my life, a major turning point, a personal revolution—so much of a revolution, in fact, that I quit my job search and threw myself into the computer full-time. I had taken my first step through the window, the first step of a journey from which I would never return.

I was hooked.

For weeks I raced back and forth to my stockbroker friend's office to spend the day playing with his computer. Finally I spent $2,000 on my own system, a no-name PC clone, and the computer consumed my life. I was unemployed. My wife was making $2,000 a month working as a special education teacher. But for the next eight or nine months I did nothing but sit, unbathed and unshaven in shorts and T-shirt, in a tiny loft of our cramped town house and jam on my computer all day long and deep into the night.

I was totally obsessed! My mission in life had been distilled into one simple statement: "I gotta learn this thing. I gotta crack the code!"

My computer proficiency multiplied with the time I invested. Soon I was loading software, taking the box apart and putting it back together again, teaching myself everything about my wondrous new window on the world.

Did it take a toll on my personal life? You bet it did! I went from being a rather gregarious social person who worked out five days a week to being an unshaven, pale-faced recluse comfortable only in the blue light of the computer screen.

I had become my worst nightmare. I had become a backroom computer nerd!

I was so consumed with the infinite possibilities at my fingertips—the cutting edge of a dramatic revolution—that I decided to make computers my life's work, my personal mission. I longed to help other people get started, just as my stockbroker friend had helped me.

"There's a business in this!" I was soon proclaiming.

Even my best friends thought I had lost my mind. My former associates at *The Wall Street Journal* urged me to visit a shrink—quick! "You quit a $100,000-a-year job to disappear into a bedroom with a computer?" they'd exclaim. "You've gone *crazy!*" What else could they think? My former boss called and said, "I hear you've hit the skids, so if you want to come back . . ."

But for the first time in my life, I had become *obsessed* with learning. This was all the more thrilling in light of my past educational accomplishments. Academically I had always been a marginal success at best. Out of 554 people in my high school graduating class, I was 538th, the bottom of the bottom 2 percent. I barely squeaked by in college, where I took a really monster curriculum in . . . *advertising,* which definitely isn't rocket science.

When I lost myself in that computer, I experienced the sheer joy of learning. For the first time I felt a sense of intellectual self-esteem. When I emerged from that bedroom, I was absolutely evangelical about the new frontier of personal technology and the profound effect it could have in every facet of every person's life. I had become connected with the paradigm shift, to borrow Dr. Stephen Covey's phrase, the irreversible sea change that was rocking the world in the era of the information society.

I didn't merely want to go out and spread the gospel. I wanted to scream, *"Folks, you gotta wake up here!"*

The call was so strong, I bought a flight attendant's rolling luggage cart, used bungee cords to strap a personal computer system and a box full of software onto its back, and rolled the load onto the streets of Houston.

Now, even my family thought I was ready for the straitjacket.

I created the world's first door-to-door computer sales company. My sales technique? The polar opposite of the Silicon Valley blind-'em-with-technology approach. I called my new business the Computer Howse Company. I wanted to show customers *how*—therefore the H-O-W-s-e—to plug in, turn on, and actually use a computer, enabling everyday people to climb aboard the computer revolution.

Every night I'd push my rack through the middle-class neighborhoods of southwest Houston and literally start knocking on doors. The door would creak open and there would be some hapless suburbanite staring through the screen, struggling to discern exactly which salesman or scoundrel had the gall to interrupt his or her dinnertime.

If they didn't slam the door in my face, they'd bark or groan, *"Yes? Can I help you?"*

I couldn't be dissuaded.

"Hi, I'm Mark Bunting, and I'm with the Computer Howse Company, and I don't know if you folks have a home computer or not, but if you don't, I'd be delighted to come in and plug this one in, give you a free in-home demonstration, and show you just how easy it is to get started in this computer revolution."

One of two things would happen: either the door would close immediately or it would open a crack farther, followed by something like "Honey, there's some, uh . . . guy out here who wants to know if we want to buy a computer."

It was the most uncomfortable thing I'd ever done in my life. I was accustomed to doing million-dollar deals for *The Wall Street Journal,* and here I was going door-to-door? But when those doors opened, I learned the most valuable lesson of my career: People are absolutely *hungry* to learn about new technology! Just like me, they had heard the endlessly confusing cyberspeak about the computer revolution, and just like me, they had no idea about how to get on board. And here was somebody literally at their doorstep, eager to explain in everyday terms about the force that could change their lives forever.

So when the doors swung open and my demo computer was unleashed from its bungee cords and plugged into the prospective customer's electrical and telephone outlets, and the Prodigy program flickered across the screen and the customer could see the possibilities firsthand . . . well, I witnessed a thousand miracles. Over countless lasagna dinners in countless homes, I'd heard the agonized cry of a world literally crying out to plug into the computer revolution: "Oh, yeah, we've been thinking about getting one, but we had no idea how to get started."

What drove me out of Silicon Valley was exactly what was driving these people away from technology: the cyberspeak, the bespectacled nerds speaking technoese. Going door-to-door, I took the exact opposite approach.

"Look, forget about the numbers," I'd say. "A 386, 486 processor? All the numbers don't matter. Let me put it in simple terms: The computer processor is the engine, okay? And you need a good engine. You wanna get a six-cylinder instead of a four-cylinder. And you want to use the engine to get you somewhere."

People related to that. I sold a lot of computers, then, almost overnight, a *phenomenal* amount of computers. I hired a salesman and then another salesman, then another. And when I looked up at the end of our first year, the Computer Howse Company had grossed $1 million in door-to-door sales.

Today, on television, I'm still going door-to-door, preaching the same message:

If I can do it, you can, too.

That's my mission with this book. I want to instill in you that same excitement, that same evangelical fever, that I experienced in those endless hours with my computer in that apartment loft. I want to knock on your door, interrupt your dinner, and take you by the hand for a walk through this Brave New World. I want to show you how computers can change your life forever.

Once again, I can already hear doors slamming by the skeptics among you.

"Oh, no, Brave New World," you're probably saying. "I've heard all that before."

Sure, it's an overused term, but it really tells the story better than anything else. It really is a Brave New World when you start looking at the ways in which technology is changing our lives. It's already altered the fundamental way in which we work, turning the entire structure of our economy upside-down, creating a downsized employment culture where behind every automatic teller machine are the bones of three laid-off tellers and behind every computerized corporation is a breadline of pink slips and shattered dreams.

We are under siege, my friends, with news of the job market moving from the classifieds to the front pages of newspapers like *The New York Times,* where the statistics read like obituaries: forty-three million U.S. jobs eradicated since 1979, the majority of them white-collar careers, with more jobs dying daily; three-quarters of all American families experiencing layoffs firsthand since 1980; roughly 50 percent more Americans being the victims of layoffs than those suffering violent crime, with no police force or antidote in sight.

The job security apocalypse has arrived in America, creating "the most acute job security crisis since the Depression," wrote the *Times.* "The job apprehension has intruded everywhere: diluting self-worth, splintering families, fragmenting communities, altering the chemistry of workplaces, roiling political agendas and rubbing salt on the very soul of the country."

But there is another statistic, one that offers some salvation: literally millions of new jobs have been created in America since 1979, enough jobs to absorb some of the laid-off workers plus accommodate new arrivals to the job market. Getting to these jobs usually requires a radical reshuffling of both job skills and, most important, personal mind-set. I've discovered that the best way to enter the new economic millennium is to fight fire with fire: we must unleash the technology that is displacing us to launch ourselves into the Brave New World.

This book is going to show you how.

But first let's examine this Brave New World, a place where the computer is changing every facet of our lives. If you want to talk about a Brave New World, just wait until the year 2000. Or wait until the country is wired with optical fiber, the fastest link for two-way communications, and a hair-size fiber can deliver every issue ever printed of *The Wall Street Journal* in less than a second, making every American home an information kingdom. The idea of employees burning gas to gather in high-rent offices will be as antiquated as cave dwellings. Wait until you have speech recognition in computers, when technology is voice-activated. Wait until that same microprocessor technology that organizes your office finds its way into consumer electronic items. You're going to be telling your appliances how brown to toast your bread; how hot to heat your water; how far to fax your résumé.

This is not the *The Jetsons* or *Star Trek.* This is real-life, everyday technology that will be here *tomorrow.*

Still, I know what you're thinking: Talking to my toaster is a nice concept . . . but what's this Brave New World going to do for me?

What if I told you this computer, this plastic box of bits and chips, can help you become more physically fit? What if I told you this box can help you find financial self-sufficiency? That it can free you from the shackles of that nine-to-five job you hate and enable you to earn your same salary—or even more money—by working at home, with the added dividend of more time for yourself and your family? What if I told you that this box could help you find your spiritual self?

You're thinking I'm a little bit wacky, aren't you? I hear you:

"You're telling me, Mark, that this computer is going to help me find fitness and spirituality? It's going to help me find personal wealth, or at least financial self-sufficiency? *C'mon!"*

But I am promising all this and more. Allow me to take it one step further. What if I told you this box can dramatically improve your relationship with your spouse or your significant other?

"How the hell is it going to do that? It's a *@#! computer!"

But this computer can set you free in one crucial way: it can buy you a tremendous amount of life's most precious resource: *time.* You can accomplish things with this box that in days past took hours, if not days, to accomplish. What I'm saying is that computers can bring you *happiness.*

"What?" Maria Shriver asked me recently on an NBC television special devoted to America's search for happiness. "You're telling me that a computer can bring you happiness? C'mon!"

Yes, I told her, computers can bring you happiness. Not by themselves, of course. There's not a magical force inside this box that's going to tap-dance out and improve your life with a simple keystroke. But I can show you how to use a computer to download happiness. Because everything that brings us happiness—whether it's in our personal, professional, or spiritual lives—is a function and an element of *time.*

Wait . . . there's more. The computer can allow you to reshuffle time, to trade the nine-to-five and the twice-daily commute for an empowering new life that focuses on *people* instead of the conventional *process* of employment. Technology has afforded us not only the power to accomplish ordinarily complex tasks in a fraction of the time it took before, but equal opportunity access to resources that allow us—downsized, pink-slipped, or fired—to rise from the scorched earth of unemployment and reinvent ourselves as independent entrepreneurs with our own computer-driven *home-based business.*

That's how a computer can help you find happiness.

> *The ancient dream of civilized workers had been to escape the pit of toil. The Industrial Revolution answered that dream with machines that made human strength obsolete. The modern dream is to escape the office where workers have been trapped by those machines—to reclaim their days and make time their own. The information revolution is starting to make that happen.*
>
> —*Laurence Gonzales,*
> Men's Journal *magazine*

How do you join the revolution to reclaim your days? By following the steps that others have taken in their own journeys of computer empowerment. Through a series of real-life testimonials, I am going to take you from the rank amateur who overcomes the initial fear of purchasing and plugging in that first computer to the breakthroughs of individuals who have completely reshuffled and radically redesigned their lives. We are going to hear the stories of everyone from the single mother starting her own home-based business to the multitudes of business executives who left the daily grind to create thriving entrepreneurial concerns in living rooms across America and how the computer was the integral tool that propelled each of their dreams into realities. In their stories we can glimpse the heart and soul of the computer revolution, centered around a powerful tool that, properly deployed, can absolutely set you free.

The subjects of these disparate testimonials cut across all lines of class, career, and income level. What they had in common is the recognition of what I call the four fundamental keys to unlock the doors of the technological revolution:

1. They Awakened to the Future!

Imagine the year 2025.

Workerless factories produce our nation's goods and farm out marking and distribution duties to small entrepreneurial firms. U.S. corporations, having reduced upward of two million jobs annually since 1995, have made conventional "labor" practically extinct. Computers, robots, and other technological contraptions have dehumanized the assembly line. Voice-activated computers have replaced the conventional secretary and middle manager. Electronic bar codes and touch-sensitive menu screens have made the restaurant "waitperson" obsolete. The electronic Home Shopping Network has cleared the malls of employment opportunities.

The scenario presented above is not some sci-fi fantasy, but a reality predicted by several authorities and publications to be only twenty-five years away. Imagine! In the time it took television to switch from Johnny Carson to Jay Leno and politics from Richard Nixon to Bill Clinton, the computer will have invaded virtually every area of our lives.

"We are being swept into a technological revolution that will set off a great social transformation unlike any in history," wrote Jerry Rifkin in his book *The End of Work: The Decline of the Global Labor Force and the Dawn of the Post Market Era.* "It is time to prepare ourselves and our institutions for a world that will phase out mass employment."

Where will you stand? I am here to tell you that the key to whether you'll be standing in a breadline or dipping into a breadbasket is staring you in the face.

Infinite power is at your fingertips! When you stare into that computer screen, realize that it holds all of the tools for personal and professional fulfillment. If you can determine your skill sets, passions, and desires, you can harness an awesome amount of technological power to propel you toward your dreams. This book will show you how to harness that power—to unlock the seemingly nebulous world of cyberspace—and bring it into your living room.

All you have to do is determine your passion. Ask yourself, "What inspires me and motivates me? What do I absolutely love to do?" The answer to this question is your key to your home-based business future. The sky is truly the limit. Just like the revolution that brought down the walls of Eastern Europe, the technological revolution is bringing down the walls of convention around the world. It doesn't matter whether you are college or high school educated, whether you live in a major urban or rural area. Access to technology no longer depends on your geography or social status. With a touch of a keyboard you can communicate with people around the world, immediately access everything from the Library of Congress to the Home Shopping Network, market your goods and services to millions of potential clients whom heretofore only corporate giants could afford to reach.

You can discover the keys to your own rebirth.

When Henry Ford invented the Model T in 1908, he explained that it would allow people "to get out of the shells in which they had been living." When Steven P. Jobs founded Apple Computer almost seventy years later, Jobs said, "As the bicycle extends muscle power, allowing human beings to go farther and faster, so the computer extends the mind, allowing us to learn more, know more."

It took Henry Ford a decade to sell one million Model T's. But in the next five years he sold *ten* million. "The home computer is right now where the automobile was in 1919," wrote the *Los Angeles Times,* "on the verge of a takeoff that will make it a familiar product in 80 percent of American homes within five years and a necessity of life within a decade."

Don't be the last to get on-line in the revolution.

2. They Conquered Cyberphobia!

Throughout history invention has always been met with common reactions: doubt, confusion, and fear. People called Oliver Evans "crazy" when he designed the steam engine and predicted that someday people would cross the country in steam-powered stagecoaches, called trains. The naysayers neighed when Henry Ford predicted that the automobile would someday replace the reliable horse. The Wright brothers were known as "the Loony Yankees" before they proved that steel could fly.

But no force has been as misunderstood, or as feared, as the computer.

Cyberphobia. Are you among the afflicted? Its symptoms are easy to spot. If the idea of buying a computer and plugging it in leaves you shaking, if the mere word "computer" lights a bonfire in your brain, if the thought of deciphering a computer program conjures up visions of an army of backroom computer nerds coming to drag you away, you're among the legions of would-be computer users plagued by cyberphobia.

You are not alone.

Consider the cyperphobic case presented in a daily newspaper concerning C. Potter, a sixty-six-year-old retired midwestern librarian applying for a part-time job last year, who was stumped by an interviewer who asked if she "knew DOS," the standard operating system for personal computers. When a befuddled Potter replied, "No," she was out the door in a heartbeat. "I felt that computers had humiliated a person who had always felt pretty intelligent," said Potter.

Things were worse at home. She could no longer speak to her children.

"They'd talk about RAM and ROM, megabytes, CPUs—it meant nothing to me," she remembered. "I couldn't follow their conversation."

Sound familiar? It sure does to me. Bits and bytes, RAM and ROM, gigabytes and megahertz, pixels and pointing devices. Is it any wonder that 55 percent of all U.S. consumers profess a fear of computers, that 49 percent of U.S. executives resist new technology, that a recent MCI-Gallup survey of three hundred entrepreneurs discovered that 46 percent claimed to be cyberphobic? Is it any wonder that the titles of the most popular computer books on the market include the words "dummies" and "idiots"?

You are not an idiot! It's the other way around. It's the computer revolution that has failed miserably in taking its message to the masses.

So how do you get through the maze of misinformation? As they say in the Nike ads, *Just do it!* Touch the keys, play with the machine, get started on any program that's available. The computer doesn't bite, and you're not going to break it. Just . . . get . . . going! Choose the simplest program you can find—a simple interface like America Online, or a game, a simple piece of cooking software—and get comfortable. Just get accustomed to interfacing with the equipment. Because computer literacy simply means being able to accomplish what you need to do. The old defensive posture—"This is just one more thing to complicate my life, who needs it?"—no longer works.

I am going to show you how to join the revolution at its street-level depot: those giant, grocery-style computer super stores that have popped up like beige bunkers all across America. At the front there will invariably be a row of shopping carts, in which you can pile boxes of computer components as simply as stacking a sack of potatoes. The aisles are as easy to navigate as a grocery: systems here, software there, and, if you get stuck, service agents everywhere.

Walk proudly down these aisles. Demand assistance! And if you get some techno-weenie, speaking in the cyberspeak of bits and bytes, ask him or her to stop, take a deep breath, and talk like a human being instead of an android. This is your gateway to the Brave New World. The days of backroom computer nerd dominance of the computer industry are *over!* Research, discover, and, above all, purchase.

How can you conquer cyberphobia? First of all, realize that it's a myth. The computer screen is like looking in a mirror. Act cool and it'll welcome you with open arms. Be afraid and it will serve as your house of horrors.

This book is going to help you break the bond of cyberphobia forever by taking you step by step through the process of becoming computer literate, from the moment you open the box to accessing the incredible power at your fingertips.

3. They Acknowledged Virtual Power!

Karen is a $20,000-a-year legal secretary with two young children. Her husband is an accountant with an annual salary of $40,000. Karen's daily routine is exhausting—even before she gets to work. Mornings are absolutely manic. Awaken at five, dress quickly, prepare breakfast, outfit the children for their eight hours at day care center, drop off the kids, and begin the forty-five-minute commute to work. At five P.M. the routine begins anew, this time backward: freeway, day care, more freeway, prepare dinner, eat dinner, collapse in bed, then jolt awake with the blast of the five A.M. bell to start the cycle anew. Sadly, Karen is not the exception; she's the norm. There are millions of men and women just like her in our increasingly hectic world.

The years rush by like a film on fast-forward. What happened to the so-called juice of life? The magic of love? The joy of family? The necessity of exercise? The experience of art and culture? The ingredients of a fruitful, satisfying life always take a backseat to routine when you're a slave to the nine-to-five.

When the smoke clears at the end of the month, what Karen spends on her children's day care, on her nice, professional working wardrobe, on her gasoline and quick lunches—not to mention the emotional toll of leaving the kids at a day care center and working for some troll of a boss in the middle of a crime-riddled downtown—whittles away more than half of her $20,000 salary. Side benefits include emotional and physical exhaustion.

Would she prefer to work from home? Would she like to win the lottery? Who wouldn't? But while the lottery's a crapshoot, working at home is a reality. It doesn't take much math to figure out that if she stayed at home and kept her own kids—which is where her heart is, anyway—Karen would save probably fifty cents on the dollar. But the benefits far exceed that.

Imagine a life where the car is used only for neighborhood jaunts, where the children are raised at home by their parents, where life is centered in the living room and the community, instead of in cold skyscrapers full of strangers. If Karen could exorcise the devil commute from her life, what might she be able to accomplish with that time? Could she spend more time exercising? Discovering her spiritual self? Could she focus on her relationship with her husband and children? In each of these diverse areas, fulfillment is merely a function of time. Time invested is in direct proportion to benefits reached.

The day of deliverance has arrived, my friend. For the computer can become your partner in creating a business that can forever alter every aspect of your life. I call it the Power of One.

The home-based business.

Ford, Apple Computer, Hallmark Cards, Hewlett-Packard, Nike, Borland, International . . . These giant corporations share more than changing the face of their various fields and bringing their shareholders tremendous dividends.

All were businesses that started in homes.

Today 7.6 million people are working by telecommuting from home, an army that is growing 15 percent annually, estimated at topping 15 million by 2002. Productivity studies show that telecommuters outperform conventional office employees by 16 percent. With as little as a $2,000 investment in a personal computer and another $500 for software and assorted peripherals, a home-based business can be started for 75 percent less than a conventional storefront start-up, according to a recent study. The scope of these businesses span the spectrum of commerce. Home-based business people run everything from secretarial services to farms to mail-order empires from the comfort of their own homes. Every aspect of business—mailing lists, client correspondence, billing, marketing, research—is all accomplished by computer.

With the computer, the home-based entrepreneur is never alone. I call it my "staff in a box." My computer is not just my secretary, ever-ready to send electronic letters faster than I could lick a stamp and keep track of my schedule with more accuracy than a full-scale executive assistant. It's also my airplane, my train, my car, allowing me to hold conferences, both electronically and visually, without ever leaving my keyboard. My computer's desktop publishing program can create brochures slick enough to compete against any corporate giant's multimillion-dollar printing budget. It allows me to collaborate with distributors from Texas to Taiwan. I can send e-mail messages across the hall or around the world. I can jump on the Internet and immediately access information that would've taken a month in a conventional library to retrieve and instantly reach an Internet marketplace of three million users, a market that would have previously cost a fortune to address.

David has become Goliath. Information is power, and the computer has enabled the home-based business as much access to as much information as any monolithic corporation. This equal opportunity access hasn't only leveled the playing field of business; it's also changed the way corporations regard the small-business owner. Just about every rule about how business is conducted, and every barrier once inherent in entering the game, has been broken by the computer revolution. Now, that's not to say that you forgo fundamental practices of accounting, hiring, and basic good business principles in starting a new venture. But what once was a corporate game, a virtual lockout for small, especially home-based businesses, has now become an equal opportunity arena.

Consider the revolution from the field:

Xerox recently launched a "virtual office" program, giving its sales reps computer equipment, training, and a shove out the door.

Philadelphia-based Bell Atlantic has made telecommuting available to all of its sixteen thousand company managers.

AT&T, which recently unveiled a wireless data system that allows employees roving the globe to use laptop computers and to work together as easily as if they were physically sharing the same office, predicts that 15 percent of its workforce will telecommute from home by the year 2000.

Big business is sending its soldiers home, outsourcing much of its work to small, frequently home-based, subcontractors. No longer considered inferior, home-based businesses are, in many cases, deemed *superior* to conventional staff. Hiring home-based entrepreneurs to outsource jobs that previously required tremendous staff, expenses, and overhead offers corporations substantial financial incentives. This drastic change in corporate ideology—called the outsourcing revolution—is one of the key reasons for our downsized employment culture.

So if you've been laid off by technology, understand this: What laid you off can set you free! Layoffs have historically been a result of computerization and mechanization. If you're a factory worker displaced by automation, robotics, and mechanization of the assembly-line process, realize that the same technology, if you'll learn to master it, can enable you to take your skill sets and create an independent business that can give you not only personal satisfaction, but financial independence that would have been inconceivable before.

This book is going to show you how.

4. The Map Is at Your Fingertips!

So let me take you door-to-door, business to business, life to life, to discover the world of personal computing from a new, yet incredibly basic, perspective: from the everyday miracle of transformed lives.

My goal is to present you with the ultimate, easy-to-read road map to computer mastery. I can promise you this: By the time you finish this book, you will not only have the desire to go out and conquer this Brave New World, you will know how to do it. If you follow the lessons and testimonials in this book you, too, can find your own road to financial freedom, to more time in your own life, to improving every area, from physical fitness to relationships to spirituality. If you will take this leap of faith and follow some simple steps, I will show you how you, too, can unleash the power of the computer to find happiness and radical personal growth.

Let's take our first step through this amazing window. . . .

CHAPTER TWO

Breaking Free and Heading Home

America was built on the concept of the frontier. We carved a nation out of the wilderness, using as tools enthusiasm, adolescent energy, and an unwillingness to recognize limitations. But we are running out of recognized frontiers. We are getting older and stodgier and losing our historic advantage in the process. In contrast, the Personal Computer business is its own frontier, created inside the box by inward-looking nerds who could find no acceptable challenge in the adult world. Like any other true pioneers, they don't care about what is possible or not possible; they are dissatisfied with the present and excited about the future.

—Accidental Empires,
by Robert X. Cringely

`[Maureen Schaak:] My philosophy is best said in the acronym for JOB: just over broke!`

She was careening toward her forties with two kids, a professionally dissatisfied husband, and an unfulfilling future in law enforcement. As a probation counselor and parole officer, she worked in a prerelease program for both the Montana and U.S. federal prison systems. But Maureen Schaak felt as imprisoned as the prisoners she counseled, locked within the confines of convention, behind the bars of nine-to-five, deep in the wilds of Billings, Montana.

Ask her to list her job's shortcomings and Maureen will unleash a litany—the manifesto of millions who have been shortchanged and displaced by the traditional workplace:

> Bureaucrats; limited creativity; high stress; low pay; low to no success rate; a job that's too highly structured, leaving no room for your own common sense, ''robotizing'' the workaday individual. I wanted the freedom to work as late as needed to complete a project and when that project was completed—especially when it took a thirty-six-hour stretch to complete—to be free to take a day off before I turned to the next crisis. But my bosses didn't see things that way.
>
> I suppose I've always been a relative nonconformist, and the criminal justice system is not the place for that personality type. I also have a problem with low-paying jobs and taking orders from people who operate on an intelligence level of about 89.

This is the voice of a revolution, of hardworking men and women who, preparing for their golden years, have discovered that they have invested their lives in lead. It's the voice of young people taking their first tentative step into the job market, only to find that the door to their destiny has been slammed in their face. Their careers were supposed to be as strong as Fort Knox, an investment of years that could eventually be cashed out for security, prosperity, a dependable future. But in the face of corporate downsizing and the technological revolution, they've found themselves trapped in a future that frequently holds nothing but a pink slip and a hollow thanks-for-the-effort spiel, then a slow, torturous slide into the grave.

Want a recipe for job insecurity? Take the debt-riddled crazy eighties, where corporate takeovers devoured pension plans. Add the S&L crisis. Then mix in the technological revolution. The legacy of all this is an employment culture that's upside-down. Long gone are the days of corporate loyalty and one job for life. It's estimated that today's college graduates will change jobs ten times in their working lifetime.

"The social contract has been sundered," warned *Fortune* magazine. "Corporate fealty has become a fool's errand. The days of linear advancement—the 30-year progression from subaltern bean counter to department supervisor to division head, for example—are pretty much over. . . . [Everyone knows] their bosses won't commit to anything—not to job security or a guaranteed annual raise or a company-funded pension."

If you think it's tough to be professionally unsettled in your twenties or thirties, imagine how it feels to crash into the dead end of Career Street in middle age. But that's what happened to Maureen and Dale Schaak. She told me her story via e-mail:

> My husband, Dale, was a rancher, but, faced with grim ranching prospects in the seventies, we sold the family spread and he went to work as a grounds foreman at Rocky Mountain College in Billings. He worked there for twelve years. In that time, his annual salary was increased by approximately $4,000. He didn't receive raises for nine of the twelve years because the college administrator said, "Contrary to projections, there just wasn't enough money for raises to staff." When he resigned he was given a plaque to commemorate his service. Guess he didn't stay long enough for the watch and the speech.

Maureen and Dale knew there had to be more. But what separated them from the hordes of the dissatisfied was their willingness to do *whatever it took* to get what they were lacking. They were sick and tired of being sick and tired, so deeply dissatisfied with their current situation that they had no other option than to find something new.

> I just always knew there had to be a way out of this insane delusion of job security. My philosophy is best said in the acronym for JOB: just over broke! So I kept looking and steering my own progress toward owning my own business

and operating from my home. People say that bronc and bull riders are crazy, but I know better. Because starting a home-based business is like riding a bull. It's like taking hold of a suitcase and jumping off a twenty-story building. If you've never done it, you've got to understand: the complete exhilaration of the ride, the leap, is exactly what keeps bull riders coming back again and again. Even if you get bucked off, it's not the pain or humiliation you remember; it's the experience of the ride. So I say, ''Pull in your belt, do some careful planning, then take a hold of the suitcase handle and step over the edge.

So the Schaaks took the leap. They followed their passion, and it led them into a dramatically different business frontier—marketing log cabin homes via computer—and Maureen and Dale Schaak reinvented their lives and recast their future by running their business from their home. Their combined annual income increased from $35,000 in their previous jobs to $60,000 in their first home-based year to a projected $150,000 this year.

The mechanics of how they accomplished all of this—the bits and bytes, the hardware and software—are not important to understand at this juncture. What is important in this testimonial is that the new frontier of personal computing awaited beneath Maureen and Dale Schaak's feet. But it wasn't until they escaped the prison of nine-to-five that they could embark upon the empowering new path that awaited them no farther than their living room.

What do I get from being home-based?

1. Absolute freedom.
2. A sense of personal pride and accomplishment.
3. No structured workplace, aside from how I design it. I live by *my* rules, not someone else's!

4. Money. Not that money means everything, but it certainly gives people the ability to achieve all of their other dreams and desires.
5. Self-confidence and self-esteem.
6. An opportunity to work with people, but with the added ability to define the parameters. I work with whom I want to work, not with whom I have to. I work when I want to (or need to), not when someone else tells me to. I don't answer to anyone, aside from my own standards and those of my partner/husband.

My old cowboy daddy always told me, ''You'll never make a dime on another man's payroll.'' If you place any value on yourself, your abilities, and your talent, stop wasting them working for someone else.

Arriving at this powerful, self-directed state is among life's most satisfying personal achievements. But as with any real achievement, getting there is damned hard work.

So how do you begin?

As Maureen Schaak discovered, the first step to becoming a home-based entrepreneur is to acknowledge *dissatisfaction* in your current situation. There is no greater motivation, no greater call to action, than dissatisfaction. The people who have the most difficult time getting started are those sitting on the fence. *They're just happy enough.* Corporate America has always done a great job of giving us just enough to be happy about: a little more money, a little more security, a little more satisfaction.

But a little happiness can be a lifetime prison.

Dissatisfaction, turmoil, dread—these are the emotions that can set you free! These emotions leave us without the option of *inaction.* If you are truly unhappy, then you cannot afford not to make a decision, you can't afford not to get started.

Remember that 60 percent of your life awake is spent at your job.

If that 60 percent is spent doing something that doesn't bring you *absolute* joy, what a miserable waste of a lifetime! Would you trash 60 percent of your years on this planet? At an average age of eighty, you're talking about forty-eight years! Would you be happy dying at thirty-two? Not if you could live to be eighty! But that's what you're giving up—60 percent of your waking hours—if you're not totally impassioned about your life from nine to five.

We aren't just talking about money here. No amount of cash will bring you as much fulfillment as being *truly* excited about what you do every day. So if you're dissatisfied in your current situation, don't waste that dissatisfaction on depression. Use it as a motivation to propel you into a new and greater life.

You have riches and freedom here, but I feel no sense of faith or direction. You have so many computers, why don't you use them in the search for love?

—Lech Walesa

The personal computer industry is a business built on serendipity by a gang of postadolescent California nerds who Dumpster-dove for spare parts to assemble the first PC in a two-car suburban garage. Their invention was a crude machine that conquered the majors merely by whit of its size, simplicity, and speed, and the industry that sprang up around it was equally fast and unconventional. It's an industry led by young coupon-clipping billionaires and blue jean–clad buccaneers who began with no business experience and no concrete goals. Like many an explorer before them, they were fueled by passion, and that passion, combined with the ignorance of what was impossible, led them into the new frontier.

That same spirit of discovery has become the key to propelling many a home-based entrepreneur into the Brave New World of prosperity and personal freedom. But in today's competitive market, passion is most effective when combined with a concrete *plan.*

So do not buy one piece of computer equipment.

Not yet. Not until you know precisely what business arena you're going to enter. Those who exult, *"Eureka!* I'm gonna start my own home-based business!" and then rush out like mad prospectors and immediately buy a computer are doing themselves a terrible disservice. Here they are, loading up with thousands of dollars' worth of computer hardware before they have any idea of what kind of business they're going to get into.

No, no, no! *Wrong!*

Computers are as different—and in some respects as complicated—as cars. You wouldn't want to be in the construction business driving a Dodge Dart instead of a pickup truck. The same analogy applies to buying a computer. You must first determine the business field you're going to enter.

To do this, you have to delve into the software of your brain.

How?

Begin with the end in mind.

This is really a very simple philosophy of basic life planning, something that far too few of us actually do. I know I didn't. Like most of us, I took life as it came. I had been taught that this was a *positive* practice. We wish, instead of plan, believing that dreaming is tantamount to achieving, that if we hope hard enough, we'll find that ephemeral pot of gold at the end of the rainbow.

We live in the language of the laid-back:

"Roll with the punches."

"Take life as it comes."

"Live one day at a time."

Those are nice, neat slogans. But it is goals, not wishes, that come true. This whole kick-back and chill-out mentality, of "taking things in stride," is a surefire ticket to eventual unfulfillment. Taking things in stride—not giving, not creating, but *taking*—puts us in a passive mind-set with regard to life planning.

So take a proactive approach to life. Quit hoping and start doing. Changing your current direction in life is as simple as changing your direction in driving. First you must stop, then turn around. You must make a change. And the first step to doing that in driving terms is, of course, to have a "destination."

What is your destination in your personal journey?

Sit down and imagine it. Picture yourself five years into the future, ten years into the future, and ask yourself, "Okay, where do I want to be?"

I'm asking you to forget about limits for a moment and picture yourself at your optimal best in the five most important areas of life: career, relationships, finances, health, personal fulfillment. Make the scene come alive. Paint all of the details in your mind—give yourself the optimum job, spouse, bank account, health, emotional fulfillment—and write down the descriptions without editing from pessimism.

If you get stuck, ask yourself a few basic questions:

"What kind of home would I be living in if there were absolutely no limits?"

"What's the optimal career path I can imagine?"

"What lifestyle would be my dream?"

"If I could do anything, what would it be?"

> *I've never had a fantasy in my life. I don't believe in fantasies. . . . I believe, if you want something, you go after it. You don't sit around and dream. You make it happen.*
>
> —*Dallas Cowboys owner Jerry Jones*

The next step is the hardest: to jump or not to jump? This is the dilemma of every fledgling home-based entrepreneur. When I was sitting on the fence, wondering whether to quit my *Wall Street Journal* JOB for an uncertain future, I devised a quick gut-check technology to make my future come into focus as clearly as if I were staring into a crystal ball. I wrote out a detailed accounting of my optimal goals in the major areas of my life and, beside each, analyzed whether my current occupation could transport me to the desired destination:

Relationship: A family was paramount. I envisioned my wife and me living in a big house with several children with plenty of time to build real, lasting intimacy. Our home would be our rock, the indestructible base for all of our dreams and desires. But as I was conjuring up the picket fence, the mailbox blocked the view. It was stuffed with bills: clothing, cars, college tuition. I did the math: college tuition in eighteen years for a child born today comes to roughly $175,000 in today's dollars. Then I flashed back to my recent abodes: a succession of drab apartments. My job at *The Wall Street Journal,* where the average tour of duty is two years per market, had already pushed me onto the treadmill of constant movement. I was headed toward a life of promotion, move, promotion, move. . . . My marriage was starting to suffer from the stress of constant movement, and we hadn't had the time even to think about building a family. I stared up from my writing. What kind of support system was I building for a family?

Finances: While wealth was an important motivation, I wanted to spend my life doing more than acquiring money and material possessions. Money alone doesn't solve problems. But financial independence buys freedom, which returns us to a recurring theme in this book: finding the time to pursue the things that truly matter. But to arrive at the point where I could pursue my aspirations, I had to achieve a significant financial base. I didn't want to have to go to work every day simply to make money. But that's exactly what I was doing in my current job.

Career: Before I first stared into the computer and realized what the machine could accomplish, I had merely aspirations regarding my career. I dreamed of becoming part of something important, something in which I could have a profound and positive impact on others. I realized that very few businesses actually change the world, and while I didn't expect to reinvent the light bulb, I nonetheless needed an emotional attachment to stir my professional passion. I desperately wanted a career that acted as my alarm clock every morning. Selling advertising for a national newspaper was a job, not a quest.

Health: Physical fitness is key in my life. Exercise was my salvation, transforming me from a frail-framed, skinny teenager to a physically fit young man. The summer before my senior year, I suffered a botched appendicitis operation, spending eight weeks in the hospital and emerging at a horrific 118 pounds. I began a weight training program that continues today. The self-esteem I received from my physical health was incalculable, and I vowed never to waver from my regimen. But I looked around my workplace and saw young men slowly dying: booze, junk food, cigarettes, and stressed-out twelve-hour days with a one-hour commute tagged onto each end. The daily workout? Trying to beat the guy down the hall. I envisioned myself waking up one morning in the not-too-distant future, staring in the mirror to find a sad, beaten old man staring back.

Personal Fulfillment: Adding up all of the above with the additional dividend of keeping my own hours and selling my own goods left me no doubt that a new path would lead me toward the goal of personal fulfillment. Could I have any doubts of my destiny? Could there be *any* question that my current occupation would not, *could not,* be the vehicle to transport me toward my dreams? I took the leap. Soon after quitting my job, I experienced the second step integral for success as a home-based entrepreneur: defining my passion.

I connected with the computer and felt such a rush of confidence and absolute optimism that I made the most audacious bet of my life. I wrote it out on a cocktail napkin in a Mexican restaurant in Houston in 1992. I had just begun selling computers door-to-door, and my wife, Kelly, and I were out for dinner and drinks. The topic turned serious when we were at the bar. We had just finished our first margarita when I scrawled it out in black and white:

"In eighteen months, I'll either have become a millionaire or, failing that, I'll pronounce my quest ill-fated and get into something else."

It's usually the ultrarich and the ultrapoor who find the most flexibility in life. I can speak from experience: I was definitely at the lower end of the spectrum. I was absolutely broke and professionally unencumbered but found ultimate freedom and ultimate enthusiasm in this setting. I felt as if for the first time in my professional life I were totally free to create whatever I could in the purest entrepreneurial terms possible. I found incredible power in the knowledge that whatever I did, whatever I created, would be completely and totally of my own doing. I wouldn't be dependent on anyone but myself. The sky was truly the limit. That's one of the premises on which this country was founded, and to step out and take the reins of that power is both liberating and empowering.

For the first time in my life I was confident of my destiny. I had begun with my passion—to create a business helping others plug into the personal computer revolution—and I was absolutely clear on the goals I wanted to achieve. I knew that with my total spiritual, emotional, and financial commitment into my newfound company, at the end of eighteen months I'd either have untold wealth or absolute assurance that I was going in the wrong direction.

Once you've come to the realization that you're not getting where you want to go with your current course, you must determine which path will take you toward self-fulfillment. The first step? Determining your passion. This is the stuff on which to best build a home-based business.

Men are not prisoners of fate, but only prisoners of their own minds.

—Franklin Delano Roosevelt

Dick Grove loved the wide-open spaces, the open road, the wind in his hair. But he was cooped up in a conventional skyscraper, running his Prime Time Publicity and Media, which was floundering, partly because of Grove's discontent. So Grove took the leap of faith. He created one of the world's first virtual offices, equipping his sixteen associates with PCs, cellular phones, and client lists and allowing them to work from their homes across the country. Grove moved his office to a thirty-acre Kansas ranch and began running his business while touring the country on his Harley-Davidson motorcycle with a laptop computer and cellular phone in his leather saddlebags. Prime Time's operating costs plummeted, profits soared. Grove credits the virtual office from saving his company from ruin and propelling it into a bright new future. "I invest in people and technology, not fancy offices," he says.

Richard "Zap" Zoppo, a longtime rock guitarist, harbored a lifelong dream of becoming a record producer. But he was stuck in Piscataway, New Jersey, in a conventional job as an insect exterminator. One day he saw his future in a computer store. With an initial investment of $4,000 he purchased the requisite computer equipment to set up a recording studio in his garage, which he began calling "the Digital Dungeon." Now his Zap Records is more lucrative than his extermination business. Soon he'll be able to leave the bugs forever.

Scott Olson loved the way his newfangled roller skates performed. But while his skates were as fast as lightning, his attempt to license his invention was as slow as molasses. Sick of doors slamming in his face, Olson returned to his home in Waconia, Minnesota, where he equipped a spare bedroom with two Macintosh computers and a fax machine and created a home-based company to market his idea. "The rest," he says, "is history." You might have heard of Olson's product, the biggest deal on wheels: Rollerblade.™

What do these three people have in common? Each of their personal salvations lay in defining their *passion* and then following that passion into empowering new careers. If you can search your soul to discover exactly what you most want to do with your life, this book can show you how to unleash the power of the computer to achieve your dreams.

> *Adventures don't begin until you get into the forest. That first step is an act of faith.*
>
> *—Mickey Hart, drummer,*
> *The Grateful Dead*

Spurred on by my confidence, and perhaps the tequila, I added a kicker to my bet on the cocktail napkin: If I hadn't made my first million dollars in eighteen months, my wife and I would reward ourselves for all of our time and effort. If we failed, we'd take the last of our money and treat ourselves to eighteen days in Rio de Janeiro. Then we'd return to Houston and start all over again. If we couldn't find financial success, we would at least get a nice trip out of it.

So it was eighteen months to a million dollars or eighteen months to eighteen days in Brazil.

[Beverley Williams:] Eight years ago I quit my job managing somebody else's pet store. I'd been promised profit sharing, a piece of the action, and, finally, the chance to buy out the business—none of which came about. I worked there for thirteen years, averaging ten to thirteen hours a day, six or seven days a week. Every day included an eight-mile, half-hour drive to and from work through the traffic. I was tied to a time schedule and had responsibility for all employees; if someone didn't show up, I had to work their shift. On weekends, and many week nights, the burglar alarm would go off and I'd have to go down and make sure there wasn't a break-in. There I'd be past midnight with a caged menagerie of barking dogs and burly policemen, seeking signs of burglars. My family and I were constantly interrupted by the pet store in every aspect of our lives.

As I was racing my own eighteen-month deadline, hundreds of thousands of other home-based business entrepreneurs were on their own race for professional and personal fulfillment. Just like me, they had become dissatisfied with the conventional workplace or had been laid off or cut back. It wasn't just major corporations displacing and disappointing employees. It was happening every day in every conceivable small business setting, in settings as seemingly innocent as a neighborhood pet shop.

For thirteen years Beverley Williams, forty-nine, of Rockville, Maryland, was the manager of such an innocent pet shop, one of a million perfect examples of men and women who discovered that their investment of body and soul in their jobs was ultimately not going to pay off:

Along with everything else, I hated going out and driving in traffic every day. It left me frustrated before I'd get to work and then before I'd get home at night. I was stuck in a rut. I was one of the highest-paid managers in the pet shop industry. But I've never been one to define success as money. What was more important was satisfaction in having the freedom to do what I wanted to do, in a way that I wanted to do it. Edgy, dissatisfied, feeling lost, I didn't like the lack of direction that my life was taking.

Did Beverley Williams hear the call of dissatisfaction? You bet she did. She became so dissatisfied, she had no choice but to take her destiny into her own hands. She'd always had lots of job offers within her industry. But after a bit of soul-searching she decided that she didn't want to work for somebody else. She had obviously been successful managing the pet store. So if she could run a business so well for somebody else, she figured, why not run a business for herself?

Her dreams were twofold: first, to accomplish something as an entrepreneur; second, to be able to accomplish it from her home. Now, all she needed was to define her passion. What did she love most? Beverley Williams absolutely loved to write.

At the same time I was becoming disgruntled over working so many hours, I was using an electric typewriter to write an employee manual. A friend of mine saw me revising it for about the hundredth time and said, ''You really oughta use a computer.''

''I don't know how,'' I replied.

My friend brought a computer over to the house that she borrowed from her office. It was a little intimidating. I was so afraid that I didn't know enough about it, that I was going to do something to hurt it or break it. But my friend sat me down and said, ''You will learn.''

She showed me how to turn it on and how to use a word-processing program called WordPerfect. I got so excited! I discovered that I could write as fast as I could think. This had always been a struggle for me. In typing classes I'd make a lot of mistakes, not because I didn't know how to type, but because my mind would always go faster than my fingers. I became mesmerized by the computer, to the point that I found myself staying up until three or four o'clock in the morning typing. And suddenly what was about an eleven-page manual turned out to be more than sixty pages. I just kept writing.

The incredible thing about the computer was that I could lose myself in it. I would be working along and all of the sudden realize that hours had gone by when I was thinking it had only been minutes. It was always amazing to me. It just opened up a whole new world. I felt so productive being able to get before the computer and letting it all come out.

My friend told me about desktop publishing, which she defined as the ability to mass-produce printed materials of the same high quality as any professional printing company at an incredibly low price, using a personal computer and a relatively inexpensive publishing software program.

A light bulb went on in my head!

At the pet shop, I had been trying to develop information sheets for people who would buy a thirty-five-cent goldfish and didn't want to spend another $2 on a book on how to care for this cheap fish. I would try to tell the customer all of the information he or she needed, but by the time they got home with the fish they'd forgotten everything. I wanted something the customers could take home with them, just to give them the fundamentals of taking care of whatever animal they bought. On the typewriter, I had been typing and retyping endless information sheets about all of the different pets. But I thought I could do them a lot better and quicker on the computer.

It was so apparent that desktop publishing could handle these tasks a lot better, and far easier, without spending a lot of money.

This is it: her "a-ha moment," that incredible instant of complete clarity, when the door opens and the future storms in, when the road to your destiny stretches out before you in one clear, easy line.

When your passion, the computer, and your home-based business path become one.

It's one exhilarating moment. Fear and intimidation vanish and you can see and feel the absolute power of the unlimited potential of what this "box" can accomplish. What led Beverley Williams to her epiphany? Simply, solving a problem: cheap publishing for small businesses. At the time, she didn't realize that desktop publishing is one of the fastest-growing home-based business fields. What business couldn't use this service? Beverley Williams saw an opportunity, one of the endless opportunities that surround us constantly, popping up as "problems," just waiting to be noticed—and solved. Beverley Williams realized that if she was sick of endlessly retyping instruction sheets, others must be tired of typing, too.

How often during the day at your job do you run into inefficiencies, problems, begging for solutions? The question to ask yourself is, "Is there a business opportunity around the solution?" Consider the solution, always the solution. This is the trailhead of many an entrepreneurial path. If there is a need, fill it. If there is a problem, solve it. Find the solution, then consider how that solution might help others in similar straits.

So like Bette Nesmith, the twenty-seven-year-old Forth, Texas, secretary who painted over errors she made in her bosses' correspondence and typed over corrections, thus inventing the secretarial salvation (and future multimillion-dollar corporation) called Liquid Paper, Beverley Williams had hit upon an incredibly obvious solution to a common problem. It was so obvious, in fact, she had to ask herself why no one had thought of it before.

My friend loaned me a copy of Ventura Publisher, a desktop publishing program, and I loved it. It allowed me to do all kinds of things I'd never been able to do before: word processing with commands that allowed me to automatically format into different typefaces. It gave me the same capabilities as a lot of the traditional print houses. I'd been approached by a local author who was writing a book who wanted me to typeset it for her. The money I made from that job helped cover the $450 cost of the program.

This is the essence of the computer revolution. For $450 Beverley Williams was able to mobilize an instant staff, which in years past would've required a significant, and probably insurmountable, cash outlay. She would have been dependent upon typesetters, graphic artists, paste-up personnel, darkroom technicians, and more. All of the expensive elements once required to enter the professional publishing business had now been compressed into a $450 software package.

You couldn't do that five years ago, let alone fifteen or twenty years ago. After teaching herself how to use the desktop publishing program, she was ready to roll.

> Excitedly, I told the pet shop owner about my plans.
>
> He said, ''It's a nice idea, but not worth the time and money.''
>
> Typical attitude: it's not broken, why fix it? It was this attitude that made me realize it was time to leave the pet store and do something different. I wasn't allowed to be creative and grow.
>
> I told my husband, ''I don't know what I'm going to do, but I want out of this.'' I don't advise others doing this. If you've got to pay bills, keep your job and investigate your options. Otherwise it's extremely hard.
>
> But I handled things differently.

She had reached the crossroads. Dissatisfaction had propelled her to this point. She had defined her passion, determined a home-based business that she could become truly passionate about, and reached the crossroads of whether to stay in her old JOB or reinvent herself as a home-based entrepreneur. Now she had to take the leap.

Sky divers remark on the euphoria that they experience at the end of their first jump, that moment when they finally touch ground. That experience is rarely, if ever, equaled. After the absolute terror of the leap comes the blissful euphoria of the realization, Hey, I'm not gonna die! If you're still on the lip of your own professional cavern, desperately clutching the tree limbs with both fists, I have a very simple question to push you forward: Could there be any greater loss, any greater cost, that you could experience than inaction?

Finally, I decided that if I was going to work that hard, I was going to put the profit in my pocket, not somebody else's. I went into the owner's office and said, ''It's time for me to move on.''

How long might Beverley Williams have had to wait for another opportunity to come along? Ten years? Twenty? I only need to encourage you to think about the consequences of *inaction.* If you are unhappy, if you are dissatisfied, you can be absolutely certain of one thing: nothing will change if you don't take action. With that as a downside, can there be any greater failure than refusal to act? Whatever failure may lie before you, it's not going to be anywhere near the failure you will experience as a result of doing nothing.

If you don't know who needs something, why are you doing it? If you don't know what the chances are of success, why are you doing it? If you don't know how much it's going to cost—not just in resources, but in years of your life—why are you doing it? You ought to know all three things! This is a way of looking at the world—the ability to look at the larger context—and you don't get that by using a No. 2 pencil between two vertical dotted lines. You gotta come up for air.

—Dr. Arno Penzias,
Astrophysicist and
Nobel Prize winner

[Beverley Williams:] I started talking to potential clients about desktop publishing, helping them understand what it's all about, telling them how I could help them design their brochures and advertising materials cheaply. Several of my friends in business—a lawyer, the director of a special services agency in county government, the pastor of my own church—all said they'd be interested in using my services. That was my market research!

So you've become dissatisfied with your current career. You've written down your optimal goals in the four major areas of your life and determined that your current job cannot propel you toward your dreams. You've defined your passion and determined a home-based business field that you're absolutely passionate about. Now you must become a detective, investigating the answer to the first of four simple questions: "Is there a basic need for the service that I want to provide?"

The best information is going to come from your own investigation. Interview other people who are already running existing businesses similar to yours, clients who use these services, members of special-interest groups in your field, and, finally, prospective clients. Tread lightly when dealing with the latter group. Ask, don't tell. Approach a prospective client for your home-based business and ask them straight out, "What do you need? How can I create more value for you?"

This is music to a manager, who is all too accustomed to the know-it-all blare. Of all potential salespeople, 99.9 percent open up a presentation or an inquiry by talking about what they have to offer.

"Let me tell you what's better about *my* service," they stress.

"Let me tell you why *my* company is best," they chorus.

As a businessman, I'm insulted when people begin by telling me about *their* product or *their* service before they have the decency to ask me questions about mine. How dare you profess to know what I need as a company? How dare you tell me how you can help me when you haven't bothered to ask, "Excuse me, sir, how can I help you?"

Reverse your order. Ask the dumb questions: "How could my service help you in what you do day-to-day?"

This may sound like basic logic, but unfortunately most people don't go through these elementary steps to simply ask the easy questions, to solicit information from people in similar fields.

Second question: "What kind of competition already exists in this field?"

Is your chosen field so crowded that you're going to have a battle even entering the market? I think of the example of a dry cleaner. Not that you can't start a dry-cleaning business today, but you're talking about a mature market where there is a tremendous amount of competition. Margins are very, very low. That's a difficult business to break into. Mature businesses, with low profit margins, are going to be far more difficult places in which to hammer out a living.

Third question: "Is there an overbearing cost of entry?"

Is it a business that you can realistically get into with a computer and your skill sets, or does it require exorbitant capital, equipment, and employees?

Fourth question. "Can this business be run effectively from the home?" Can it be contained in a residential space, or is it so industrially oriented that a warehouse is required to house vital equipment? Are you able to communicate with clients via modem and fax, without them physically coming into the office? Do your neighborhood zoning ordinances allow your type of business? Or is it so truck and personnel intensive that your neighbors are going to picket your home? Are you going to be able to work from home without constant interruption from domestic duties, children, and spouse? Finally, are you motivated and disciplined enough not to be distracted by the television, refrigerator, and isolation?

Success boils down to two simple words: total commitment. If you're going to launch your own home-based business, total commitment is more imperative than computer equipment. We're talking about radically redefining the way you earn a living and live your life. You can't expect massive changes with profound effects by putting out the same level of effort that you did in your old nine-to-five. There is no shortcut, no big secret, except this: hard work and total commitment.

There are a lot of people who fantasize about working at home but, quite frankly, don't have the internal self-discipline to work efficiently, without supervision. The idea of not having an immediate supervisor or boss sounds like the greatest thing in the world. The reality is that a lot of people can't function without that structure and without that discipline. Listen to the testimonial of Beverley Williams:

> I had no real business background, no idea of what I was doing, nor how to go about doing it. The local paper was hiring freelance writers,

and I decided the best way to learn about home-based businesses was to do an article about it. Somebody was teaching a course on home-based businesses at the local community college. I asked the teacher if I could sit in on a few classes and interview her afterward.

I discovered that I wasn't alone: a lot of people were working from home. Primarily, what this course focused on was how to start a home-based business: how to set up your office and set your prices, more small-business techniques than anything else.

Sure, there was part of me that said, ''Wait a minute. You don't have any training. How do you know that you're doing it right?'' There was a real problem of self-confidence. But then I got involved with the computer program and everything snapped into place.

I decided to become a sole proprietor, and I went down to the county courthouse and registered a name: Williams Associates Desk Top Publishing. Instantly I became a home-based business owner.

Note the plural in "Associates." Beverley Williams was working out of her home alone. So who were the associates in her sole proprietorship?

In addition to the "staff in a box" that came with the $450 desktop printing program, the "Associates" were the infinite roles immediately assumed by Beverley Williams. Overnight she became everything from her new company's CEO to secretary to janitor. She was her accounting department, her secretarial pool, her personal administrator, her financial planner, her marketing department—all roles reporting to and organized by Beverley Williams, personal computer operator. All of the essential components of a traditional business are available to entrepreneurs with the touch of a keystroke. You have the brainpower, the horsepower, to accomplish things that once required a staff or a battery of specialists.

Business came to Beverley Williams quickly, everything from publishing business cards to books. Every job added up to referrals for others, until eventually she had built up a clientele: associations, nonprofit agencies, brochures and advertising materials, mailers.

> I celebrated tremendously when I was a success at anything. When I'd get a new client I'd be riding high for days. The knowledge that I could do something on my own—in my own definition of success—was a high that I didn't get working for someone else.
>
> Primarily I was a lot more satisfied.
>
> I found a need and filled it.

Think about the revolution that occurred in this middle-aged woman's life. She went from cleaning out birdcages and removing hairballs from kittens' throats to running her own potentially nationwide business, a business with no limits. Her financial return has been tremendous; her personal lifestyle has become a platform that can support her dreams. But none of this would have occurred had she not found dissatisfaction in her current situation, realized an opportunity, and—most important—acted on it.

> Soon after, I discovered there was a need for people to have more information about home-based business, so they could become home-based business owners themselves. Since I'd been through it, I started offering advice. The woman I interviewed for that article quit teaching the community college class. I was asked to teach the home business course.
>
> This isn't the wave of the future. This is the here and now. My husband, John, fifty-seven, was with IBM for thirty-one years and had planned on being there until he reached retirement age. But he got downsized, laid off. Although he was able to take a full retirement, in order to live the lifestyle we want and put

money away for our retirement, he's started his own home-based business. It's called Rent-a-Husband-Handyman Service. His office is in the upstairs spare bedroom. His slogan is, ''I'll do your honey-do list for you.'' It's home repairs, minor projects, all the little odd things when you never know whom to call. Call Rent-a-Husband.

If we didn't have home-based businesses, we'd have to change our lifestyle, and we're in a period of our lives where we want to have the freedom, both financially and timewise, to spend time with our children and grandchildren. Thanks to our home-based businesses, we have money and flexibility to do the things we want to do.

Beverley Williams became so committed to the home-based business as the wave of the future, she founded the American Association of Home-Based Businesses, which now has one hundred chapters either existing or in development across the United States, representing everything from home-based consultants to home-based craftsmen to home-based attorneys.

As for her former employer, the pet shop owner who resisted new technology with the age-old pessimist's cry, "It's not worth the expense"? Well, he might have found it necessary to set up a new cage in his shop and climb in under a sign reading DINOSAUR. . . .

If he were still in business.

The pet shop went out of business within two years after I left.

No matter what your business, you can't afford not to be computer literate in the next millennium. Because the reality is that there's a pet shop right down the street whose owner is going to be on-line, who is doing light desktop publishing and creating added value for his or her customers.

If you're a reluctant business owner, don't consider yourself immune. Because when you finally awaken to tomorrow, the computer is going to be as commonplace as the telephone—and yours will be the only one on the block that's not ringing.

Now, let me show you how to plug in to the technological revolution, whose awesome power can propel you toward your dreams. . . .

CHAPTER THREE

Purchasing the Computer

Of course, purchasing a computer can be confusing, which is why at this time we are going to answer your questions, using a question-and-answer format.

Which model of computer should I get?

The best computer for your specific needs is the one that will come on the market immediately after you purchase some other model. This is the key to computer ownership. There is always a newer, swoopier one coming out, and you need that one. . . .

What, specifically, should I look for when shopping for a computer?

You should look for a "Pentium"-style computer, containing numerous "megs of RAM."

What do these things mean?

Nobody has any idea, but everybody agrees that they are very desirable. You should stress them when dealing with the computer salesperson, so he or she will know that you're a knowledgeable consumer and not just some random idiot.

—Dave Barry,
Humor columnist

If you don't already own your first computer, dear Reader, the moment of truth has arrived. Time to ante up a few thousand dollars to open the doorway to your dreams.

Time to buy the Computer.

First step? Take a deep breath. Relax. It's relatively easy these days to buy the perfect computer for your purposes, and I want to give you a hit list to enable you to purchase exactly what you need. But before I do that, let me give you a brief history of the hell of buying computers, beginning with how it was in the computer store stone age, back in 1991. . . .

The air thickened, the lights dimmed, and the salesman seemed almost satanic. He stared me down like some crazy professor addressing an inconsequential idiot, tongue-lashing me with endless indecipherable lectures about motherboards and chip sets and the inner bowels of the Pandora's boxes that filled his shelves.

Red-faced, I felt like bolting from the store, a no-name, mom-and-pop clone shop that built and sold their own computers in Houston. But if I left, I knew a worse fate awaited me: not being able to work on a computer at all. Having worn out my welcome with daily sabbaticals on my stockbroker's machine, I had to buy my own computer—or be forced to go cold turkey. But instead of finding helpful salespeople in a bright, clearly organized sales dealership, I landed at the gates of hell: a computer store owned and operated by computer nerds.

The owners were Middle Eastern, which was not uncommon in the early nineties. Foreign entrepreneurs were at the forefront of cloning name-brand computers and selling them at discounts. But while the prices were right, communication and customer service were nonexistent. Prospective buyers walked into a triple maelstrom of woe: we couldn't understand the shop owners' very broken English, their highly technical computerspeak, or, even, their products. Because the computers were almost all DOS- (not Windows-) based at the time, they weren't graphical. So they sat cramped on steel shelves, flashing command prompts like blinking eyes from some other world.

I was so eager to get on-line, I would've walked through a field of broken glass if there was a computer at the other end. But that little clone shop was torture enough. At least, when you go to buy a car, you know what they're talking about when they throw all that overhead-cam-V-8 technology at you. I don't know what an overhead cam is, but I know when I get behind the wheel of the car whether or not it's right for me. So if I like the car's style and drive and can handle the down payment, I'll drive it off the lot.

With a computer, added to all that terminology you don't understand is the fact that you really don't get the opportunity to hop on-line and drive it. So a computer isn't something you can truly experience on the showroom floor.

Worst of all, computerspeak is still a foreign tongue.

Fast-forward three years to the age of the computer superstore. As in the Jurassic era, giants walk the earth. Some of the mom-and-pop clone shops remain, like remnants of an earlier epoch, but they sit in the shadow of these mammoth outlets. Into these bunkers stroll droves of average Joes and Marys, who, the store designers hope, can navigate the aisles with the same ease of rolling through a grocery store. Pushing carts over acres of linoleum, prospective computer consumers encounter a dramatic terrain. The stores are pretty! The aisles are easy to navigate! The computers all run Windows programs with pleasing graphics and vivid colors!

But problems persist. Most of the people on the floor are under thirty years old, whereas most of the customers are over thirty. If you're a woman, there is also a gender gap; most of the sales personnel are men. The language barrier still exists as well. Because technology is changing so fast, most of the sales staff can't keep track of the constantly upgraded models. So they're stuck expounding in bits and bytes, expelling the same confusion of the mom-and-pop clone shop era. The best computer for your purposes? As Dave Barry cracked, "The one that will come on the market immediately after you purchase some other model."

The third outlet, the mail-order house—offering computer equipment at a discount over 800-numbers, Internet Web sites, and mail-order catalogs—is even more difficult to navigate. Although some of these outlets produce and sell exceptional products (Dell and Gateway, for instance, which sell their own computers best and cheapest, if you know exactly what you need), they offer absolutely no hand-holding along the way. If you're starting from ground zero, this is absolutely not the way to buy a computer, unless, of course, you've had adequate consultation from someone who can tell you exactly what you need for your specific purposes.

So buying a computer is easy. Buying the computer that is perfect for your individual purposes is extremely hard.

The answer? First of all, find a consultant. Chances are you can locate one literally on your own block. Simply ask your neighbors,

"Who's the computer person on our street?" You don't need to pay someone to advise you. I'll bet you that someone across the street or on either side of your home is already computer proficient. Somebody helped them. If you'll ask, you'll be surprised at how willing they are to help you. If you can't turn to friends or neighbors, try one of the local computer users groups that have sprung up around the world. These organizations have members who either donate their time or, for a very low hourly fee, will train you on a variety of computers with a wide spectrum of software.

The main thing to remember is this: Do not try to go it alone.

You have to raise a white flag and scream, *"Help!"*

Listen to the lament of Jan Herrick, who cried for computer assistance and received it, even though she lives in a trailer in the middle of nowhere on a 167-acre ranch in the timberlands of Oregon. At five feet nine inches and 280 pounds, Jan describes herself as a "queen-size lady." But if pressed for a definition, she'll answer, "I'm fat." Like millions of Americans, she was a divorced career woman in her forties who thought she was on the way up, when actually she was forever going sideways, as a manager in an international marketing job in sunny Santa Clara, California.

> I started out as a secretary and worked my way up to manager's level. Along the way, I grew to dislike much of what I saw in the corporate world. So much politics! I didn't like the way I was treated as a woman. I was a manager, but I was still treated, basically, as ''the girl.'' If someone needed something typed and the secretary wasn't there, it was always, ''Oh, Jan, you do this.'' I was excluded from meetings. I never knew what was going on.

Then came the day when her bosses couldn't hide: the company, which produced video games, was being forced out of business. They had tried to diversify into other products, but it was too little effort, much too late. Jan Herrick got laid off just before the ship sank. It was 1985. An excellent typist, she took a succession of temporary secretarial and paralegal jobs, then began managing her own vending machines and pay telephones.

But something was percolating in the back of Jan Herrick's brain, a call that grew louder every time a child laughed or a waiter snickered or a prospective employer—many of whom, she says, "see fat people as fat, lazy blobs and worse insurance risks"—paused in mid-sentence. She knew all too well of the discrimination and humiliation fat people experience in today's thin-obsessed society. How it's more difficult for fat people to find jobs. How they're routinely paid less than their thin counterparts. She was sick and tired of turning on the television to find comics, who wouldn't dare single out minorities, routinely dumping on fat people . . . and listening to the audience howl.

It was a mission calling, a mission that had been sitting right under her nose: if Jan Herrick, a former large-size model, couldn't find clothing or dates or support systems or, even, catalogs designed for and devoted to fat people, other fat people must need these services, too.

She had determined her passion, realized a need, and devised a plan. Jan Herrick founded Vendredi (French for Friday, the traditional market day) Enterprises, publishing catalogs that offer everything from clothing resources to dating services to dieting programs for heavies like herself. Her comprehensive resource guide, *Royal Resources,* "the Yellow Pages of the fat world," has 1,200 sources in fifty categories. Her singles publication, *Love Handles,* a magazine with personal ads for large singles and those who love them, attracts 5,000 listings a month.

She is able to run her business from a three-bedroom trailer in the wilds of Oregon because of one essential tool, a machine that unleashed her from convention and allowed her to fly: her computer. But her journey from computer illiterate to computer maven was as rough as adolescence.

Years ago, I considered myself an unacceptable human being because I was not thin. This is before I got accepted in the Size Acceptance Movement. Then, another revolution took place in my life. I decided I didn't have to work in an office in a city. It had been coming for some time: I did not want to be working for someone else. And just out of the blue one night, I decided to start this information directory for large-size people. I decided I had trouble finding large sizes, so I figured others must, too.

It was like opening the door and having a tornado blast through. Jan Herrick's directory took off. But success was soon running her ragged. Her fingers were numb from typing—and retyping and retyping—her directory, her subscription lists, her correspondence. Her life was full of cutting and pasting and more cutting and pasting . . . She had left the drudgery of nine-to-five only to find even more drudgery at home.

It was obvious that I was either going to hire someone to help me or I was going to have to buy a computer. And the computer won because it was a lot cheaper than hiring another person. I was also concerned about the physical appearance of my products, my ads, and my catalog. . . . I needed a much more professional representation of my company if I was going to survive and grow. It came to the point where it was time to ''grow up and become a real company.'' I wanted a professional appearance to my product and advertisements. As long as things are just typed, you look like a flunky company, somebody who hasn't quite made it yet.

So Jan climbed into her old Ford pickup truck and clambered down Raccoon Road and onto the highway, driving twenty miles to the nearest town, Roseburg, Oregon (pop. 16,000). After parking in front of a computer store called PC Solutions, she strode confidently into the Brave New World. She was hard to miss: five feet nine, 280 pounds, blond hair to her waist, wearing a tight T-shirt, jeans, and cowboy boots. "I can stop traffic," she says.

But inside PC Solutions, Jan was the one who got stopped in her tracks. On the low-pile, gray tweed carpet, she grew dizzy with confusion.

What kind of store was this?

Young men in matching cotton Dockers slacks and button-down shirts assisted seemingly know-it-all customers in a fluorescent-lit room full of gray cubicles, each displaying complete computer systems, their screens swirling with colorful software programs. Signs screamed each machine's attributes in jargon only a nerd could comprehend.

Boxes of software filled shelves. A "Communications Section" sported little boxy modems, which connect computers, via the telephone line, to the outside world. There was a section for accessories and supplies, another for computer games, and another for computer books like *The Complete Idiot's Guide to Computers* and *DOS For Dummies,* as well as for scholarly tomes like *Upgrading and Repairing PCs.* A far counter was stacked high with defective computers being repaired by three harried technicians.

But then . . . absolutely nothing. Not one salesman rushed to Jan Herrick's side. Not one customer offered advice. Jan was lost in computer limboland, a place where nothing ever happens until you scream for help.

And Jan Herrick screamed. Boy, did she scream.

Part of me wanted to turn and run. But something kept me. I wanted a daddy figure to say, ''Okay, this is what to do and we'll help you.'' But nobody came. So I walked up to the counter and laid it out plain:

''I'm a total computer idiot!'' I screamed. ''I know nothing! *Help!*''

You could have heard a pin drop. A salesman rushed over. I deposited my package of materials I needed to produce on the computer—my information directory, *Royal Resources;* my singles publication, *Love Handles.* I wanted both publications to look much nicer than they did, which wouldn't be hard considering I was typing them. I showed the salesman my mailers and my advertisements—and said, ''This is what I need to produce.'' I told him about my extreme space limitations, that my home office

> was in one of my trailer's three bedrooms. I'm not five hundred pounds, but it was very, very crowded.
>
> Finally I said, ''I have $3,000 from my logging work. Tell me what I need.''
>
> He huddled with another salesman and they began writing up an order. They'd tell me what they were writing and I just kept nodding, saying, ''Fine, fine, if you say so. Fine.'' I had no idea what I was ordering! Even when I got it I didn't know what it was. The bill came to exactly $3,000. They made his sale, to the penny.

Could there be any better or more effective way to deal with a computer geek? Simply march into the computer store and scream, *"Help!"*

The louder, the better.

It's not the subtle approach. But, believe me, it works.

Jan Herrick got lucky. The young man who heeded her screams, Stan Welch, thirty, turned out to be a pretty proficient computer salesman. He's seen a hundred Jan Herricks in his six years on the job: men and women seeking to fill the beds of their pickups with cutting-edge technology and absolutely no idea of how to proceed.

Jan was different, he says, in one refreshing way: she admitted ignorance.

"Most people try to act as though they know more than they do," says Welch. "And we've found they have no idea. They'll shop in catalogs, find certain prices, and come in and start blurting out industry terms. But it's obvious that they have no idea what they're talking about. They'll ask about CD-RAM, when it's CD-ROM, and talking about getting 8 megabytes of ROM, when they mean RAM."

Why the ruse?

"They're intimidated by the salespeople and scared they'll be taken advantage of if they admit they don't know what they're talking about. It's true—we could give them a lesser discount, which could be merited. The person who doesn't know as much is probably going to need more ongoing help from us before and after they buy the computer.

But standard industry margins are only 10 to 20 percent on hardware. So there's really not much of a discount you can get."

Welch sees his mission as simple. While most computer salesmen try to tell the customer what they need, basing their advice on the most frequent requests, Welch first asks: "What do you want to accomplish with your computer?"

"Lots of times, the people need to use a particular piece of software —perhaps a database for particular business," he says. "For example, the owner of a local tuxedo rental company needed software to track his tuxedo rentals. I did some research and discovered the right software. And once I found the software, I could determine exactly what kind of computer hardware they needed to best run that software."

Why don't most computer purchases go this smoothly? Welch says it's the customers, not the dealers, with the communications problem. He's a frequently misunderstood soldier in the computer revolution, he complains.

"Computer dealers are people, too," he says. "Just like customers expect to be treated straightforwardly and honestly, the computer dealers expect to be treated honestly, too."

So here it is, straight from the computer nerd's mouth: Stan Welch's Five Rules for Dealing with Your Neighborhood Computer Salesperson:

1. Admit ignorance.
2. Don't be so concerned about the financial aspects of the sale that you're not totally honest with your salesperson as far as your concerns about pricing and ongoing service.
3. Seek out the salesperson who's willing to listen to your needs, and, conversely, be willing to listen with an open mind to what the salesperson recommends.
4. Don't merely look at the system, but study the service that backs it up. "We're an authorized service center for the systems we sell and, therefore, don't have to ship them four hours away to Portland or even halfway across the country to the factory for repair, which can leave the customer without the tool that they've learned to rely upon for weeks at a time," says Welch.
5. Finally, Welch's Golden Rule when connecting the computer's parts at home: "Each cord can only go one way. So don't worry: it's impossible to plug anything into the wrong place."

A few weeks after writing the check for $3,000 to PC Solutions, Jan Herrick once again made the long drive into Roseburg to pick up her equipment. It filled up most of her truck bed: an upright computer central processing unit preloaded with word-processing, database, and desktop publishing software; a Magnavox VGA black-and-white monitor; an Okidata OL-400 laser printer, and a tangle of cords and paper and software books and paraphernalia . . . and not one word of practical instruction on how to set any of it up.

It wasn't a pretty sight when Jan brought her mother lode into the trailer's tiniest bedroom, which serves as her home-based office.

Try to visualize the dimensions of that room. It was about seven feet wide and eight feet long. The only place where I could put my butt was on the floor! I lugged all of the equipment inside and took everything out of the boxes and started stacking it around the floor. Today, I know what it all is, but back then I could only think, Oh, my God, what have I done? I couldn't even plug in the cables. I was so afraid the whole thing would explode if I did something wrong.

I sat on that floor and I began to cry . . . and cry and cry.

I had such unreal expectations! I thought the computer would help me immediately. I didn't realize what the learning curve would be. I thought, Oh, my God, I've spent $3,000 and I'll never be able to do anything!

Ten minutes later I picked myself up, packed up all the gear, loaded it back into the truck, and drove the twenty miles back to Roseburg. If you thought I stood out before, you should've seen me then: arms full of computer boxes, shouting, "I have absolutely no idea what to do with any of this!"

The salesmen patted me on the head and said, "It'll be okay."

They told me exactly how to set it up. They told me the cables can only go one place. I had a notebook and I wrote down their words, exactly. They gave me paint-by-numbers directions on how to set up everything. They were right about one thing: the cables can only go one place.

She was up and running by midnight. She booted up her database and began adding the names of her customers. What a revelation it was! She could call up any name in an instant. For three days she worked patiently, until the database contained several thousand names. Then, one bleary-eyed midnight, she pulled out the tray that held her keyboard . . . and it broke from its casing and crashed to the floor. The screen went blank. Jan turned the computer off, then on again, and . . . *nothing!* She couldn't even get the computer to work, much less retrieve her database.

Her system had crashed.

I sat back on the floor, and now I *really* cried.

The next dawn I packed up everything except the printer, loaded it up on my pickup truck, drove back down to Roseburg, and once again screamed, *''Help!''*

They reloaded all of the software, because everything was lost. After they had done that I had to go back home and start from scratch, typing in all these names again.

I gradually started learning all of the software programs. I learned very, very slowly. Every once in a while there would be what I consider a breakthrough. Something would work and it would absolutely seem like a miracle. To find one name in a database of twelve thousand names, which had previously been typewritten, to find that name in a split second—well, that was incredible to me.

I've survived since 1987, working on basically the same $3,000 computer hardware, with some added peripherals, doing everything, from desktop publishing to accounting to financial planning, on my computer. Last year I brought in over $30,000 just from my business, which was substantially more than when I'd last worked for other people. But the best thing is I get to live on a ranch, without the hassles of the nine-to-five world. Even more than that are the awards and letters I've received about the lives that have changed because of the work I do. That's what's most rewarding, and I couldn't even begin to do half of it without the computer.

Man is a tool-using animal. Without tools he is nothing, with tools he is all.

—*Thomas Carlyle*

I want to give you a hit list of terms that you need to understand to go out and buy your first machine. But as soon as you buy the machine, I want you to forget everything I've told you. Because getting too hung up on the jargon of technology all too often causes people to become computer nerds instead of computer users. Notice the distinction: computer nerds talk incessantly about computers; computer users use them to realize their dreams.

There are a gillion and one "how to buy your first computer" books, most full of agate type and endless cyberspeak. But once you buy your computer, these names and numbers will mean absolutely nothing to you. And considering that computer hardware technology is advancing and improving by the millisecond, these names and numbers will be worthless six months from now because everything will have changed.

Don't get so focused on the minute parts of the engine that you don't get to drive the car.

For now, here's what you need:

1. A Pentium-based computer, not a Macintosh. That will enrage all the Mac users out there. I'm sorry, but ninety-three out of one

hundred machines are PC-based, meaning they operate on the Windows operating system, not Apple's. Macs are great, and there are some situations where I do recommend them, but for the beginner, ninety-five out of one hundred times you're going to need a PC to further your cause. Ask for an Intel Pentium processor, but don't ask me or the salesman to explain how it works. You don't need—or particularly want—to know what it took to make the sausage to enjoy eating one.

2. In your Pentium-based PC, you want a five hundred-megabyte hard drive or larger if you have the budget. The hard drive is where your programs are stored, and you need plenty of space to store enough programs. And five hundred megabytes is a lot of space.
3. RAM: random access memory. This is the size of your computer's brain, and the bigger the better. You need a minimum of sixteen megabytes of RAM. With the Windows 95 program and all of the new multimedia stuff that's out there, sixteen megabytes will function better than eight. You'll pay about $30 per megabyte, so we're talking about $250 extra to go from eight to sixteen.
4. Modem, short for "modulator-demodulator." Again, don't worry about what that means. Your modem simply allows your computer to talk to other computers through the telephone line. It comes in different speeds or sizes, from 14.4 on up. You need at least a 28.8. The numbers are irrelevant.
5. Monitor. This is your window on the world, the television-style screen on which the computer shows you its soul, and you want the biggest, most colorful window you can afford. While twelve- and thirteen-inch monitors used to be acceptable, their days are over. Now you need at least a seventeen-inch monitor. Anything smaller is just not enough real estate to accomplish some of the things that you're going to want to do. The great thing about Windows 95—the Microsoft operating program that all of the non-Mac PCs come preloaded with today—is it lets you open different programs at the same time. So you can work on a spreadsheet on one part of the screen and work on another program on another screen section. Working on a monitor of less than seventeen inches just doesn't afford you enough physical room to have all of the multiple windows open. So make sure you get at least a seventeen-inch monitor.

6. CD-ROM drive. This is exactly like a compact disc unit in a stereo, but instead of playing only music (which it also plays), it runs computer programs that come on compact discs. Most of today's computers come preloaded with CD-ROM drives. They come in different speeds. I recommend at least an 8X CD-ROM drive, if your budget allows. Again, don't ask me what the numbers mean. This is what you need for peak performance.
7. Finally, buy the best and most expandable computer you can afford. But beware of ads that tell you that you can have it all now. You may not need to spend the money for everything now. Buy things as you can afford them. You may not be able to afford a CD-ROM now, but buy a computer with a slot to add the CD-ROM later.

Once you purchase your computer equipment, it's time to set up your home-based office. What's the best way to proceed? I call it the "whatever it takes" theory of home-based office management.

Let me show you how it works.

In December 1991 the time had come to move from my small, hermitic bedroom into the only other available quarters in my tiny Houston town house, the barely bigger downstairs basement. Six months of hibernation in that bedroom—six months of staring into that computer window—would now end with me flying like some enlightened butterfly into . . . the basement.

With more space and easier access, the basement move represented a step up, even if I was heading down. But I knew I couldn't make the move alone. All home-based business entrepreneurs eventually need to seek help in their mission, and I was no different from the rest. I needed an employee, a cheap employee, someone I could trust implicitly. So, naturally, I turned first to my younger brother, Kyle, then twenty-three. He was smart, energetic, just graduated from the University of Texas. He would be the perfect first employee.

But there was a problem.

Kyle had a JOB.

He had landed a rather cushy job (considering his age) with a major management-type consulting firm. The firm was based in Houston, and Kyle had come to meet with his new bosses to inspect his new offices in a sleek glass skyscraper, the exact opposite of my digital dungeon. He was supposed to start in a week.

Luckily I got to him first.

"I was walkin' into Cush City," Kyle remembers. "I'm all set up and then Mark starts in. 'You gotta come join me, man. You gotta come join me.' Mark was so passionate. He was so excited! Telling me how people were crawling around on floors in Sugarland, a Houston suburb, just dying to buy their first computer."

I regaled him with stories of the revolution thundering beneath our feet: how over in Austin a college kid named Michael Dell had created Dell Computer, a soon-to-be multibillion-dollar operation out of his dorm room; how right in our hometown of Houston, a couple of entrepreneurs had created the lean giant Compaq Computer on the premise of producing quality machines at affordable prices.

"We're going to create the next Dell Computer, the next Compaq Computer!" I exclaimed. "Computers are going to invade every home in America, yet most people are scared to death to get started! We're going to turn the marketing of computers upside-down. We're going to conquer the world by selling computers door-to-door!"

Lesser men might have laughed in my face. But my brother Kyle stared at me with the evangelic conviction of an aspiring choirboy who's just heard "Rock of Ages" for the first time and voiced the magic word of 1990s assent:

"Cool!"

After thinking it over for a day, Kyle marched into his nice new cushy offices and told his high-ranking future bosses that he'd had a change of heart. He was going to join his brother in "the Computer Cave," as it was affectionately called, where we created the first home office of the Computer Howse Company.

Our home office furniture consisted of a rickety bed and a particle-board desk. To this I added my 386 clone system, a dot matrix Panasonic printer, and a box of assorted software. From the vantage point of my computer desk, I could survey my terrain, and it was gloomy. The basement looked more like a storage room than an office. The walls were white cinder blocks. There were no windows. No air-conditioning. No heat. No ventilation. It was 140 square feet of constant pressure.

It was a mess—but a completely functional mess. Best of all, the rent was cheap. The telephone was connected. The marketplace was eager. Within a couple of weeks I had hired two more salesmen and a secretary, all working out of that dank and dusty basement.

As I discovered, the first rule of the home-based business person is "Whatever it takes." But if you can plan, there is a right and a wrong way to physically arrange your home-based office. Beverley Williams at the American Association of Home-Based Business says to follow the "look, hear, and smell" principle.

Because associates or potential customers will invariably find their way to your door, pay special attention to what your client will see (are you trailing them through the house or past the laundry room?), what they hear (that washing machine might be music to you, but it will scream "Amateur!" to your client), and, finally, what they smell (offices near kitchens or cat boxes, which you may have grown accustomed to, won't be so endearing to your clients or employees).

Remember: You're trying to project a professional image, both for yourself and for others.

Susan Sharp, who survived a divorce and near financial ruin by moving her design agency from a standard office complex to her Rockville, Maryland, home, where she now grosses $1 million annually, says the first imperative for the home-based business entrepreneur is to think of yourself as a professional, especially in the confines of your own home.

The first step? Get dressed for work. And when you walk into your home-based office, consider it an office, not an adjunct of your living room.

Says Susan Sharp:

> I have a business that just happens to be in a home, rather than a home-based business. My business is a corporation and I'm an employee. I've always paid myself rent. I get up every day and I get dressed, most times, in a suit. You have to make that distinction.
>
> I take a salary, what I need to live on, and toward the end of the year, I give myself a bonus. It would never occur to me to say, ''Oh, I need a new dress. I'll go dip in here and take twenty or seventy.'' I have to manage on a salary just like anybody else.
>
> People say to me, ''God, you have your business at home, so I guess you could bake

> cakes during the day.'' I sort of looked at that person squirrelly. It would never occur to me to go upstairs and cook during the day. The other day someone came over and started laughing, saying, ''That's so funny. You have your purse in your office with you, like you're at work.'' And I said, ''I am at work.'' I don't leave things upstairs. There are two completely separate lives in my home.

Equally important is to consider the other lives in your household—especially your spouse. Having a house full of people is not the best prescription for marital bliss. Often, employees arrive at dawn and frequently work through the night—and in my case, my brother decided to move in with us full-time so he could work around the clock. Combine this scene with my own total, tunnel vision commitment to a personal mission, and you've got a recipe for marital disaster, which, luckily, my wife and I survived.

So when you start considering your own home-based business, direct your first question to your spouse or significant other. Make sure you are on the same page as far as your mutual objectives and that he or she understands the stresses that are going to be strolling through the door. Kelly and I had been married for eighteen months when my home-based business began. You can imagine what a household of six or seven strangers around the clock could do to a just married couple's sense of privacy. The alarm clock quickly drowned out the sound of the wedding bells. We had to set some rules and establish some guidelines. You do, too.

As far as equipping your office, don't rush out and buy new furniture. That's not necessary and, unless you've got a substantial nest egg, usually not practical. Buy your desk and other furniture at auctions and consignment stores. Going-out-of-business sales are, sadly, prevalent in today's downsized economy. Take advantage of them. Beverley Williams found a beautiful oak desk at an auction for $40. The out-of-business entrepreneur who had paid $1,200 literally cried when she took it out of the room. You'll be amazed at what you can find if you take the time to look.

I don't advise you to scrimp on two things, however: your computer and your computer chair. You'll be spending a lot of time in both. So save your money to buy the best computer and a good "ergonomic" chair.

The physical layout of your office depends on your business and personality. Most homes weren't built with adequate office lighting. So you're likely to require additional sources of light. Look at halogen lamps that reflect off the ceiling. Another common problem is not enough electrical outlets. The best advice: Buy the best power strips with surge protectors. Your computer is going to require at least four to six outlets. You don't want to be constantly plugging and unplugging your components.

Because you'll be working alone, it's nice to have some background noise to break the monotony: some people like music (but only if you won't get too involved in it); others prefer the television on low. (But for most, TV spells disaster. So turn it on *only* if you won't watch the programs.) It's background sounds we're seeking, not active entertainment.

In my case, the sound of the burgeoning Computer Howse business was loud enough. Desk to desk we sat, like underpaid garment workers in a sweatshop, sweltering in summer and freezing in winter, all to the beat of a constantly jangling telephone.

If you'd called that office, however, you'd have thought you'd reached a major corporation.

Because we did voices.

Pay particular attention, all you wannabe home office cyberentrepreneurs. If you want to survive, much less thrive, in the lean and hungry years of your business, you've gotta learn to do voices.

Selling computers door-to-door, we felt it was imperative that our customers feel secure. We wanted them to have confidence that they were dealing with a solid, reputable firm. They were, after all, investing $3,000 with us for a computer—usually a household's third most expensive investment, just behind the house and the car. We certainly didn't want our customers even to consider that they were dealing with a months-old shoestring working out of the owner's shabby basement, with infinitely more ambition than assets.

So we did voices. Multiple voices.

If you called the Computer Howse Company, a secretary/assistant/

receptionist greeted you with a chirpy, "Good morning, Computer Howse!"

If you were seeking the owner—namely *moi*—she would put you on hold for precisely two seconds, then return with her second voice, full of cool, East-Side-of-Manhattan-front-office professional attitude. "Mark Bunting's office. How may I help you?"

Because the bulk of my crew consisted of sales staff, that left only me in the office, fielding the myriad calls as the heads of the various departments, each with his own distinctive voice. I had a different voice for the accounting department, for shipping and receiving, for customer service . . . so many voices that by the end of the working day I was not only hoarse, but completely discombobulated.

I do not recommend that fledgling home-based entrepreneurs deceive their customers, and I'm not necessarily proud of some of my own early practices. But I was so convinced that we could get the job done—which we always did—that I was willing to do whatever it took to pass along that confidence to our customers.

Of course, without a conductor, a dozen voices becomes a scream, not a choir. And the Computer Howse had an excellent conductor in—what else?—our computer. In days past, fake voices wouldn't have kept back the dam waters of a small staff and low overhead. But the computer made all the voices legitimate; it backed up their bravado. Fake voices couldn't have covered the myriad functions of shipping and receiving, customer service, and accounting. But the computer allowed the Computer Howse, and millions of fledgling companies just like it, to run like a real business and function with infinitely fewer people than a regular start-up would have required in the pre–computer age.

So when the voice answers the phone on the Kinko's copies television ad with, "I'll put my team on it," and then the lone operator stares into the blinking screen of a computer, that's the power of a real team.

For this is what America is all about. It is the uncrossed desert and the unclimbed ridge. It is the star that is not reached and the harvest that is sleeping in the unplowed ground.

—Lyndon Johnson,
January 20, 1965

The team at the fledgling Computer Howse was impressive, both for its ability and its efficiency. Our accounting department was our easy-to-use, all-purpose financial software, the $89.99 Quick Books program. Our Graphic Arts Department was a relatively inexpensive PageMaker program on our 386 computer that designed brochures and fliers that would have taken thousands of dollars to produce at a conventional printing firm. Our Shipping and Receiving Department was nothing more than a very basic $119.99 software package called Excel. Our database, which inventoried our purchases of distressed and discounted bulk-rate machines as they made the journey from our house to our customers, was a $189.99 ACT program. Our Marketing Department was a database of mailing lists organized by zip code, allowing our sales staff to cold-call prospective customers and check on existing ones.

All of these functions would have required such suffocating staff and insurmountable research that the overhead would've been suicide for our fledgling company. Through our computer, we could accomplish with a staff of six what, only a few years back, would have certainly required a staff of twenty-five! So when I walked into prospective customers' homes, plugged in the computer, dialed up Prodigy, and connected to the local Gerland's Grocery Store, allowing those customers to walk down the aisles and pick up their groceries, then e-mail their order to the store and have the bags on their doorsteps before I'd finished my demonstration, their "Wow's" and exclamations of "Sign me up!" did not go unfulfilled. Within the week each new computer was home-delivered just as quickly as the groceries had been, and the Computer Howse had more satisfied customers.

The company grew to eight people within the first year. We became approximately a $1 million company in twelve months.

But while we were out busily knocking on doors, something began pounding louder and louder on our own. It was the incessant banging of computer progress, the arrival of the most important technological development since the invention of the PC, a force that would soon be invading every home and empowering lives throughout the world. Blasting through the phone lines, it was the force of a zillion voices and a million dreams: the coming of age of the Internet.

CHAPTER FOUR

Entering the Internet

A year ago I was the original Dummy. . . . Then, while I was on vacation, a colleague ran some telephone wire into the back of my computer, loaded a communications package, and left me a note about how to launch the operation.

Readers, that note is now framed in my office. Eventually, that telephone wire led to the Internet and the single most amazing, entertaining, and educational experience of my career.

Quite simply, the Internet has revolutionized the way I interact with the outside world, altered my work habits, and burst the bubble around my PC. It has also changed my thinking about the future of personal communications technology. And I believe that sooner—rather than later—those changes will be mapped onto society as a whole.

Consider this: My $1,000 PC is now a personal broadcasting system that reaches more people than the CBS affiliate in Washington, D.C. I can get more local viewers with a single e-mail posting to the Internet than Sally Jessy Raphael can get in a sweeps month.

—*Paul McCloskey,*
Executive Editor,
Federal Computer Week,
in the introduction to
The Internet for Dummies

Henry just pointed with his gun and said, "That way, out on Highway 61."

—Bob Dylan

Trying to describe the Internet to someone who's never seen it is like attempting to describe the night sky. Like the sky, the Internet's size is infinite, changing by the millisecond, old stars dying and new stars constantly being born. But unlike the constellations, we have a ladder to enter the Internet, a way to actually work and play among the stars.

In the most basic terms, the Internet is the information superhighway that's getting all the play in the media, the mother lode of information that computer visionaries like Microsoft's Bill Gates have called the site of the new Gold Rush. Through the Internet your computer is connected to millions and millions of other computers. In the same way that you can pick up your telephone and call anywhere from Harrisburg to Hong Kong and speak with your party instantly, so can you make instant contact via the Internet. An infrastructure of access, the Internet allows you to go out and communicate in typed, video, and multimedia language. Instead of calling someone in Tokyo on your telephone, you can use your computer to call them, either by e-mail, through videoconferencing, or on their Web site.

But for the home-based entrepreneur, the Internet's greatest strength is its ability to retrieve information. If information is power, then the Internet, like its predecessors, from the printing press to television, is a revolutionary tool that allows the user to bring that information home. By offering equal opportunity access to information, the Internet has radically—and irrevocably—leveled the playing field between the home-based entrepreneur and the monolithic corporation. According to an in-depth report by International Data Corp., $100 billion in business will be done via the World Wide Web in the year 2000, with access by 163 million people (compared to 16 million in 1995).

I was trying to explain all of this to my father-in-law, Doyle Winters, after dinner the other night. He's a retired banker seeking to open his own little business. And since his passion is golf, the business he most often dreams of opening is a driving range.

"Hey, Mark, how would you find information about opening and running a driving range?" he asked me.

I grabbed my laptop computer. "Well, why don't we put the Internet to the test," I said.

He didn't immediately jump for joy. "Look, I'm learning the computer," said Doyle. "Do I really need to get on the Internet, too?"

Any acquiescence on my part would have been his loss, not mine.

"Being on your computer and not surfing the Internet is like having a black-and-white TV that only gets the big three channels, okay?" I said. "You know how much fun it is to have that remote control in your hand and go from channel to channel and check out all kinds of things? Multiply that times *gadzillion!* That's what you get when you surf the Net."

He expelled oxygen in a moan of surrender, then voiced the mantra of Missouri.

"Okay, Mark, show me," he said.

We sat in front of the computer. Before beginning, I offered a bit of introduction:

"There are many ways in which the Internet connects the personal computer to the outside world," I said. "The most popular are on-line services like America Online and CompuServe, which allow the user to access news, send and receive e-mail, join chat lines, and correspond with users around the world. But the Internet's most powerful function is the World Wide Web, the graphics- and text-driven application that is only one part of the massive Internet. The WWW, called 'the Web,' comprises 'pages' (which appear on your screen in a combination of text, graphics, photographs, and multimedia), on which individuals, organizations, and companies post highly personalized information. Like the Gold Rush days, land—or home pages—on the WWW is cheap. You can set up your own home page, your personal electronic log cabin, and invite the world to visit, just as easily as you can visit the entire universe of home pages. . . ."

My father-in-law looked a little confused. So I clicked on the browser (the name for the software used to navigate the Internet) called Netscape and began to "surf" (or browse) the World Wide Web. When the Netscape search engine (the blank you fill in to find things) asked me to enter a topic, I simply typed in the words "Driving Ranges Golf" and hit the "return" key.

The screen went blank for a second, and then an index of possible leads (one or two sentences that, when clicked, open up the corresponding pages) filled the screen, with a dozen more pages immediately accessible by clicking on an icon labeled "More Documents." There were *hundreds* of sites on the topic of golf and driving ranges. There were sites posted by people seeking advice on opening driving ranges, sites on driving ranges in states and countries around the world, sites about the current "action" on driving ranges in Connecticut, sites listing the equipment required to open a driving range, sites on "today's development opportunities" . . . page after page of everything the driving range entrepreneur needs to go out and open his business.

As a sample, I chose one entitled "Looking for Info re: Starting a Driving Range," moved my cursor on top of the sentence, and clicked once. The screen went blank, while the strip at the bottom of the screen advised us of the search progress, first advising "Host Contacted," then "Waiting for Reply," then "Transferring Data," and finally, "Document Received."

The screen came alive in a burst of text, graphics, and color. It was the highly personalized page of one Whit Potter, a golfer in the Midwest, and included "links" (highlighted words that become interactive connections when clicked, offering instant access to related pages) to various golf sites and, of course, a place to click on Whit Potter's name and send him e-mail.

At the top of the page, Potter had typed: "I'm interested in starting a driving range and looking for any information that might be used in the process."

At the bottom of the page, there was a number, indicating the number of "hits," or visits, the page had received thus far in the first six months of the year: 1,029.

My father-in-law was getting the picture: 1,029 people had visited Whit Potter's home page, leaving him advice and information on starting his own driving range.

"How long would it take you to speak with 1,029 people by telephone?" I asked Doyle. "And this is only one example. Let's say you're considering adding a wing onto your house."

I typed the word "Construction" into the search engine and a hundred entries relating to home repair ran down page after page. I typed in "Automobile Repair," and the listings ran so many pages that I scrolled through ten and had the feeling I had only begun. I typed "Zoological Research," and the sites ran down the pages like a thousand zebra stripes.

"These are very basic examples, but the point is clear: As you're starting your own home-based business, exploring opportunities, or merely trying to grow the opportunity you've already chosen as your home-based business field, you have a tool in your computer to access information that has never been available before," I said.

Then I kicked in a quote from Kevin Kelly, whose book *Out of Control* is one of the bibles of the new information society:

> *Computers, in themselves, don't change lives. Communicators change lives, which is what computers have become.*
>
> —*Kevin Kelly*

"While your computer can provide some pretty basic functions, from writing your letters to handling your accounting to storing your database, these functions pale in comparison with what the computer can do as a communications device," I said. "As a tool that can go forth and retrieve information on just about any subject in the world."

I stared into the busy screen.

"In days past, what would you have to do to access this information?" I asked. "You would jump in your car and drive down to your local library, usually downtown, and you would trundle over to the card catalog. You would have to spend hours—or days!—looking up books and thumbing through them, if they weren't already checked out by like-minded seekers. What a miserably inefficient system!"

Like a trusted hunting dog, I told Doyle, this computer can go out and fetch information anywhere in the world. As proof, I began typing in topic after topic, and the computer responded with pages and pages of lists of sources: from aboriginal studies to beer brewing to cryptology to design to finance to languages to museums to paranormal phenomena to recipes to spirituality to sports to wine to yeasts to zoos.

The wealth of the entire planet is at our fingertips! There are sites for everything from the Library of Congress to the corner drugstore! We can shop for anything from stocks and bonds to houses and house shoes! We can call up every issue of *The Wall Street Journal* ever printed and immediately access current and back issues of favorite magazines! We can get the TV news by the second from all three networks! We can call up the home page of the White House and take a virtual tour with the president or access Roger Ebert and read instant movie reviews! We can track down old friends and have e-mail conversations with relatives halfway round the globe. And all it costs is the monthly charge from your local Internet connection company, called a "service provider," which usually runs about $10 a month.

I glanced over at my father-in-law. Now, he looked, well, *overwhelmed.* . . . Perhaps I was giving him too much information too quickly. Maybe I needed to show him, not tell him about the Internet. I had the greatest teaching tool ever invented at my disposal. All I had to do was get on-line and drive.

"Are you ready to surf the Net?" I asked my father-in-law.

He nodded tentative assent.

I clicked on Netscape and typed in my topic of interest, calling it, for lack of a better term, "Internet How-To," and pages of possible leads immediately popped up on the screen.

I scrolled through the list. There were Internet facts, Internet tutorials, Internet glossaries, lists of the best Internet books, personal diaries from Internet surfers. I clicked on a site called "Future of the Net," presented by an information provider called C/NET. The screen filled with a combination of multi-colored text and vivid graphics. My father-in-law read the text, written by Dan Ruby, aloud:

> In Internet years, the future is now. Events are moving so quickly that the Net equivalent of a few days has already elapsed since you clicked on this article. The Net is bursting with dazzling multi-media displays, increasingly secure commerce, and mainstream publishing. Every major corporate player in the computer, communications, media, and entertainment industries has devised an Internet strategy. . . .

The page included links to comments about the Internet from everybody from Bill Gates to President Clinton. I moved the mouse over to the president's name, and my cursor, which usually looks like an arrow turned into a tiny index finger above the president's name, indicating a live link. I clicked it on, and Clinton's face and printed comments filled the screen:

> I challenge business and local governments throughout our country to make a commitment of time and resources so that by the year 2000 every classroom in America will be connected [to the Internet]. . . . I want to get the children of America hooked on education through computers. Computers give us a world where people are judged not by the color of their skin or their gender or their family's income, but by their minds—how well they can express themselves on those screens.

A nice overview, but I wanted something more basic. So I clicked on another site entitled "Introduction Internet," with a summary that proclaimed, "The Internet Pilot's Home Page. Class Notes." A long list of possible pages appeared. I chose one entitled "Introduction to Internet by Professor Jimmy Lin," and the information was basic but extremely enlightening:

> Almost everywhere you turn today, you read, watch, or hear something about the Internet. If you are in Education, Government, or Business and use a computer, you probably have been asked the following question, ''What is your Internet address?''
>
> Let's take a moment and consider the following questions:
>
> What is the Internet?
> Did this global network suddenly appear overnight?
> How many people are on the Internet?
> Where is the Internet heading?
>
> The Internet is the largest electronic network in the world. It is really a global network of networks. Some sources estimate the Internet

currently interconnects over 11,000 different networks in over 100+ countries. It is believed that over 1.7 million computer hosts take part in the Internet and provide service for between 15 to 25 million users worldwide.

It is very hard to pin down actual numbers to describe how large the Internet really is. No one runs the Internet. There is no central office that you sign up with. There is no regulatory body making up rules with the power to enforce them. Also the Internet is growing at an ever-increasing rate. It is easier to talk about how much the Internet has grown in the years since its introduction than it is to put solid numbers to its current growth.

The beginning of the Internet dates back to the year 1969. A network was developed by Bolt, Beranek, and Newman (BBN) for the Advanced Research Projects Agency of the U.S. Department of Defense. This network became known as ARPANET. This new network connected university, military, and defense contractors who were working on ARPA projects. The intent was to allow researchers at these organizations to share information. From this early research network the Internet traces its history.

In 1973, ARPA, renamed DARPA for Defense Advanced Research Projects Agency, started a program called the Internetting Project. This project was to study how to link various packet networks to each other. This Internetting Project evolved into what is known today simply as the Internet.

Here is how fast the Internet has grown.

In 1985, there were only 100 networks within the Internet.

Four years later, in 1989, the number of networks had risen to over 500.

The Defense Data Network Information Center reported 2,218 networks were connected by January of 1990.

The National Science Foundation's Network Information Center estimated over 4,000 networks were connected by June of 1991.

Using these figures, the Internet is growing at a rate of better than 15% a month. . . . If that growth rate continues, the Internet would top 100 million by 1998.

Okay, what this means is the Internet is a LOT of computers interconnecting LOTS of users into what has been called the first truly global electronic village. Still, this information only makes way for a new set of questions. . . .

"Questions," repeated my father-in-law. "This is all very exciting, but they're certainly right about that."

"Well," I began to explain, then returned to my Internet how-to search pages. "Let's find something even more basic."

I scrolled down to an entry that sounded perfect:

Basic Internet Help
Summary: Yahoo's Page for Over 70 Beginner's Guides to the Internet

I clicked, the screen went blank, and two tiny green highway signs reading "Welcome to the Internet" popped onto the screen, framing the words "Basic Internet Help." Below, there were thirty or more links with titles ranging from "Internet Training Manual" to "Thar's Gold in Them Thar Links!" I selected one called "Surfing the Internet" and was soon staring at the home page of Jean Amour Polly, a Cleveland, Ohio, librarian, offering her impressions of surfing the Net:

> Today I'll travel to Minnesota, Texas, California, Cleveland, New Zealand, Sweden, and England. I'm not frantically packing, and I won't pick up any frequent flyer mileage. In fact, I'm sipping cocoa at my Macintosh. My trips will be electronic, using the computer on my desk, communications software, a modem, and a standard phone line.
>
> I'll be using the Internet, the global network of computers and their interconnections, which lets me skip like a stone across oceans and continents and control computers at remote sites. I haven't ''visited'' Antarctica yet, but it is only a matter of time before a host computer becomes available there!
>
> On my electronic adventure I browsed the online catalog at the University Library in Liverpool England, leaving some ''Hi, there . . .'' mail for the librarian.
>
> I downloaded some new Macintosh anti-virus software from Stanford's SUMEX archive.
>
> Then I checked a few databases for information needed for this article, and scanned today's news stories.
>
> I looked at the weather forecast for here in the East and for the San Francisco Bay area, forwarding that information to a friend in San

Jose who would read it when he woke up. The Internet never closes!

After that I read some electronic mail from other librarians in Israel, Korea, England, Australia and all over the U.S. We're exchanging information about how to keep viruses off public computers, how to network CD-ROMS, and how to re-ink ink-jet printer cartridges, among other things.

I monitor about twelve discussion groups. Mail sent to the group address is distributed to all other ''subscribers.'' It's similar to a round-robin discussion. These are known variously as mailing lists, discussion groups, deflectors, aliases, or listservs, depending on what type they are and how they are driven. Subscriptions are free.

This, of course, was the key. The "why" of the Internet—the bits and bytes and minute interworkings—aren't what's important; what is important is the what of the Internet: what can you do with it?

I hit the "back" key on the Netscape page to return to the directory, and pages of possibilities once again filled the screen. There was the entire text of the landmark 1993 paper "The Whole Internet User's Guide and Catalogue." I called it up so my father-in-law could read one particularly inspired paragraph, which puts the Internet into proper perspective:

What Does This Mean for Me?

The concept that the Internet is not a network, but a collection of networks, means little to the end user. You want to do something useful: run a program, or access some unique data. You shouldn't have to worry about how it's all stuck together. Consider the telephone system—it's an Internet, too. Pacific

Bell, AT&T, MCI, British Telephony, Telefonos de Mexico, and so on, are all separate corporations that run pieces of the telephone system. They worry about how to make it all work together; all you have to do is dial.

If you ignore cost and commercials, you shouldn't care if you are dealing with MCI, AT&T, or Sprint. Dial the number and it works.

Once again, you don't have to be a computer nerd to reap the benefits of the wired world. Still, I wanted my father-in-law to have a brief glossary of Internet terms. So I clicked on a line titled "ILC Glossary of Internet Terms," and when a half dozen pages of terms appeared on the screen, I pointed out the highlights:

Bandwidth—How much ''stuff'' you can send through a connection. Usually measured in bits-per-second. A full page of English text is about 16,000 bits. A fast modem can move about 15,000 bits in one second. Full-motion full-screen video would require roughly 10,000,000 bits-per-second, depending on compression.

Baud—In common usage the ''baud rate'' of a modem is how many bits it can send or receive per second. Technically, ''baud'' is the number of times per second that the carrier signal shifts value—so a 2,400 bit-per-second modem actually runs at 600 baud, but it moves 4 bits per baud (4 x 600 = 2,400 bits per second).

Browser—A client program (software) that is used for looking at various kinds of Internet resources.

Cyberspace—Term originated by author William Gibson in his novel *Neuromancer*, the word

Cyberspace is currently used to describe the whole range of information resources available through computer networks.

URL (Uniform Resource Locator)—The standard way to give the address of any resource on the Internet that is part of the World Wide Web (WWW). A URL looks like this:

http://www.matisse.net/seminars.html
or telnet://well.sf.ca.us
or news:new.newusers.questions

The most common way to use a URL is to enter into a WWW browser program, such as Netscape or Lynx.

E-mail—Messages, usually text, sent from one person to another via computer. E-mail can also be sent automatically to a large number of addresses. . . .

Doyle's hand shot up into the air.

"Hold it there," he said. "I'd like to know more about that."

I hit the "back" key and returned to the list and selected a file that discussed e-mail. The Internet answered the question better than I ever could have:

''Electronic mail (e-mail) is the most basic and popular form of communication over the Internet. E-mail is similar to postal mail (referred to on the Internet as ''snail mail''), because you send the mail to a particular address, and it must be delivered there (usually by your Internet provider's mail server). You also must check your mail to see if you receive any. If you don't know somebody's e-mail address, you won't be able to mail to them, but there are many ways of finding someone's email address on the Internet (asking the person is still the easiest way). If someone doesn't have an e-mail address, you won't be able to e-mail them, but more people are getting e-mail addresses every day.

But, e-mail is better than postal mail in several ways. The main advantage is speed. E-mail sent over the Internet should arrive in hours, minutes, or seconds depending upon where it's sent from and to (some servers and connections are slower than others). E-mail is also usually free when you establish an account with an Internet service provider (although a few service providers do charge for individual messages). You can mail the same message to several people easily with most e-mail programs and there are also many mailing lists on the Internet you can join to get information on topics you're interested in delivered to you via e-mail. Most people with e-mail accounts gain access to other Internet services as well, but if all you have is e-mail, some Internet services such as ftp can still be done via e-mail.

Internet Service Provider—An institution that provides access to the Internet in some form, usually for money.

After hitting the "forward" key, we returned to our glossary:

Netscape—A WWW Browser and the name of a company. The Netscape (TM) browser was originally based on the Mosaic program developed at the National Center for Supercomputing Applications (NCSA). Netscape has grown in features rapidly and is widely

> recognized as the best and most popular Web browser. . . . The main author of Netscape, Mark Andreessen, was hired away from the NCSA by Jim Clark, and they founded a company called Mosaic Communications and soon changed the name to Netscape Communications Corporation.

Now my father-in-law was waving his arms as if he were trying to flag down a taxi. He'd read about the twenty-four-year-old whiz kid Mark Andreessen, of course. He'd recently been featured on the cover of *Time,* which detailed his $58 million overnight windfall the day his company went public and its price soared through the roof. Pretty amazing for a company whose first incarnation was the Mosaic program Andreessen helped develop for $6.85 an hour while an undergraduate student at the University of Illinois at Urbana-Champaign.

"Let's see more about this guy Andreessen!" my father-in-law exclaimed.

I returned to the search engine and typed in Mark Andreessen's name. We were instantly transported to Andreessen World, staring down a seemingly endless list of leads, everything from the Mark Andreessen Home Page to pages relating news and views of the twenty-four-year-old wunderkind. I clicked on an entry called "Netscape Visionary Surfs to Fame and Fortune," and the screen was immediately ablaze in Andreessen pictures and text, including an interview with him from the C/Net content provider. It began with a comment from a journalist named Hart:

> You might think that a guy who co-founded a company valued at more than $5 billion would have a little more attitude. Especially if you knew he was 24 years old—and that his stake in the company, last we checked, was worth around $250 million. . . .

The interview followed:

> HART: In four or five years, will people watch television over the Internet?

ANDREESSEN: ''Maybe, but that's one of a hundred thousand different applications that people will be doing at that point. If you want to watch TV, you will be able to, but you probably wouldn't want to spend that much time in front of your PC watching TV—simply because you'd have a hundred thousand other things you could be doing with your time that would be more interesting.''

HART: Comment about the technology of the Web. What does the Web do better than other media?

ANDREESSEN: ''One of the things it does better is that it completely knocks out the traditional distribution bottlenecks. All the different media—television, radio, publishing—have had these huge distribution bottlenecks that have shaped how the business works. There's only a certain number of TV channels or shows that can actually move through the channels—or books or magazines that can actually find shelf space. The Web knocks that down so anybody can publish—and, in fact, in the long run, everybody does. The Web does that really well. It lets anybody put content up, and over time that content can be any kind of content you want, up to and including video. That's exciting.''

"*Anybody* can put content up?" asked my father-in-law.

"Anybody," I replied. "Anybody from the Pentagon to *Playboy* magazine."

As proof, I accessed up a popular home page called "Jason's Notes from the Underground," a popular site written by a twenty-year-old Swarthmore College student named Justin Hall. His home page flashed on-screen, and Doyle and I read Justin's writings together:

I look at the Net as a neighborhood.

I want to live in a neighborhood with funky houses, neighbors who greet me on the street and have something to say. Not amidst office sky-disgracers, plastered with useless billboards and littered with forgotten glossy fliers. I want my house to have a warm glow, like people really live there. I have given my online space a human feel with honest and revealing material, publishing even the painful parts, because cyberspace will only be funky if it reflects all our joys and sorrows. Anything else is sanitized, alienating and just not any fun at all. Computers teach us that we can build our world, construct a reality according to our vision.

Jason had certainly succeeded. His page was undeniably funky. Titled "Computopia," it was a compendium of his hopes, dreams, interests, and personality. There are links to stories ("I recently came down off an erratic intense relationship"), links to his favorite Web site and home pages, reports from friends' weddings, even reports from a child in Sarajevo named Alma Duran, which, Jason says, offered him the scoop on the war-torn region better than any newscast ever could:

Everyday life in Sarajevo is awful. We do not have enough electricity, gas, water or heating. Sometimes we do not have it at all. Right now, it is snowing heavily and the gas and heating systems are out of order, so when I go back home I will be freezing to death. Since the war has been going on here for three years, people stopped working and so they do not have any salary. Because of that they can not pay for this gas, water, electricity, etc. . . .

Finally, there is Justin's manifesto for the home-based economy, his take on a world heading home:

Each office I have worked in has sucked up hours of my day. Dealing with other people's crises, lounging by the coffee machine, pointless meetings, getting from one place to the other. Home working, the time you waste is your own, around your family and friends. . . . When culture, work and humanity can be found in part through a computer, the home and the neighborhood will come into focus as the center of life. No more midmorning headlight caterpillar crawl between suburbs and cities, we can live in houses in the country with big gardens and still enjoy the connectedness of living in a city. . . .

If we abandon the concept of the inner city office workplace, we can begin to unpave this country. The ugliness and blight that is skyscrapers and highways can be stripped for houses and forestry. No longer will towers of glass and steel house the most vital aspects of our economy—people will be rooted in their local communities while maintaining global presence. . . .

I've been working largely full time on the Internet since January 1994. Many hours a day bent over the keyboard, staring into the glow, building and exploring virtual new worlds. At first I was solely fascinated with commenting on what I saw on-line, recounting cool places to visit and strange slices of Internet life. As I spent more time there, holding a mirror up to the Net began to inspire me less. Recently, I've been putting my life online, telling stories about the people I know, the things that happen to me.

I have fun telling stories on the Internet. I have made pages about my family members, my friends, the places I've worked and learned, the trips I've taken. . . . People I haven't spoken to in years, as well as people I have never met, take the time to write me and share their impressions, or their stories in return.

I liked this kid Jason, felt that I knew him, even though we had never met face-to-face.

"Would you like to create your own home page?" I asked Doyle. "You could start your own 'Official Doyle Winters Driving Range Home Page,' have your customers register for their time on-line, learn about new happenings at your range, and offer suggestions for improvement. When you're ready to go global with 'Official Doyle Winters International Driving Ranges,' your home page could serve as a nexus to access developers and potential customers around the globe."

He was sold.

"How do I set up a home page?" he asked.

I hit the "back" key and returned to my search engine, typing the words "World Wide Web Home Pages." From the list of leads, I selected one called "An Overview of the World Wide Web" and its summary, "It's Not Just for Scientists Anymore." A page appeared with a quote from the scientist Isaac Asimov at the top:

I do not fear computers. I fear lack of them.
—Isaac Asimov

Simply put, the World Wide Web is a way to share resources with many people at the same time, even if some of those resources are located at opposite ends of the world. If you think of it as a research paper that lets each footnote take you right to the original source, then you've got the basic idea.<P>

What began as a research tool has blossomed into something unexpected and much more fun. With the introduction of Mosaic and other graphical Web browsers, the Web has become a

```
communications tool for a much wider
audience.<P>

Web pages can include text information,
pictures, sounds, video, FTP links for
downloading software, and much more. You can
create living documents that are updated
weekly, daily, or even hourly to give Web
surfers a different experience every time they
visit your pages. As the technology develops,
even more amazing applications will be
possible.
```

"Can I set up a home page now?" asked my father-in-law.

"Sure!" I replied. "Fortune 500 companies spend thousands, sometimes hundreds of thousands, of dollars to create Madison Avenue–slick home pages. But the home-based entrepreneur on a shoestring can create a perfectly respectable and frequently downright dazzling home page, too. The same technologies that Fortune 500 companies use on their pages—audio greetings, video clips, hyperlinks to related sites—are available to you, too. All you have to do is first find a service provider, a company that will house your home page for a monthly fee ranging upward of $15 a month. Then, all you have to do is design your page, either by hiring a professional or by doing it yourself. You can list your site on a half dozen Internet search indexes for free."

My father-in-law paled. "I couldn't design a home page!"

There are a hundred how-to books on the subject, I started to tell him. But then I stopped and let the Internet show him how easy designing a home page can be. I returned to the directory and found an entry containing the summary, "How to Create a Home Page."

We sat back as the file loaded onto our screen, a conglomeration of graphics and colors, a doorway for anyone to instantly create a home page.

```
 Welcome to the ''Create A Homepage'' section
of The-Inter.net's World Wide Web server. This
form will automatically generate a homepage for
```

```
you that you can upload to your Internet
provider's World Wide Web server for everyone
to see. Please note however that the homepage
created will not be as intricate as other
homepages you may see online. This system was
developed to create a homepage for those who
are a novice at HTML programming. Simply fill
in the blanks with your information and our
system will create the source for you. You
might want to check out a A HREF=''sample.html''
sample that was created by the Homepage Creator
System or look at the A HREF=''temp/index.htm''
last homepage that was created.
  This service is to use and you can make as
many homepages as you would like. If you offer
products on the Web you might want to consider
A HREF=''http://the-inter.net/www/future21/
adver.html'' advertising on our site to
increase traffic.
```

What followed was a simple question-and-answer path:

```
General Homepage Design & Colors

Backgrounds are placed behind your homepage.
Examples are available for you to see.

Please select your background:

  None
  lgback.gif
  radbarb.jpg
  grey.gif
  radtex2.jpg
  radtex3.jpg
  radwav1.jpg
  ragglow.jpg
  ragjewl.jpg
```

```
  ridges.jpg
  greywh.gif
  star.gif

Please select your text color. Please note, if
you selected a dark background (i.e. blue),
make sure you select a light colored text
color.

Please select your text color:

  1. Black
  2. Blue
  3. Green
  4. Red
  5. Yellow
  6. White
  7. Light Grey
  8. Dark Grey
```

The list went on until, when all questions were answered, the user had created a rudimentary home page instantly—without spending a dime or leaving the comfort of home. Of course, a sophisticated home page for a business is best produced by a professional, not a do-it-yourself software program. But my father-in-law grasped the concept: *anyone* can set up a home on the Net, cheaply and quickly.

He stared into the tube. The grin that had washed across his face a half hour ago had widened. His eyes blazed.

I think he might have been experiencing his "a-ha moment."

In golfing terms, he had struck a hole in one.

Suddenly he could see the world was at his fingertips.

But like any red-blooded son of America, he wanted to know how to bring this incredible database of information to the bank.

He wanted to know the answer to the big question: How can you make money on the Net?

"A Web page can be an entrepreneur's most effective sales tool," I said. "Think of it as an on-line, interactive catalog. It requires no shipping costs, has no minimum print run, and can be constantly updated with no additional charge. It's available to potential customers twenty-four hours a day. You can advertise your product in vivid color and get your message across in both type and audio. You can take orders instantly. If customers have questions after reading your material, they can e-mail you, a vastly more pleasurable method than having people who know little about your business call your 800-number with questions. Best of all, when potential customers call up your home page, they are there because they want to be, not because you've cold-called them during their dinner hour."

My father-in-law was getting the picture. To drive it home, I wanted to show him one particularly powerful page, the home page of Atlas Motorcycles, and the testimonial of its owner, a laid-off middle-aged middle manager in Chicago, Illinois: Joe Orlandino.

Orlandino told me his inspiring story via e-mail:

> I had felt my planned obsolescence building for almost one year. Being the regional Sales Manager for the 9th largest Cable Company in the world, my job was to report to the Regional Marketing Manager. For the bulk of my career in this position my boss was a self-educated, street smart, Texas cowboy cum Brooks Bros. Suit. This man knew his customers. Prior to him getting ''booted upstairs'' to corporate, he alluded to my throwing my hat in for his position. Never to succumb to the ''Peter Principle,'' I politely declined—I was a darn good SALES manager.
>
> Through power struggles, politics and many closed door sessions in our large office, white smoke finally billowed from the conference room. A new Marketing Manager emerges.
>
> Herein began my demise.
>
> Approximately 18 months after this changing of the guard I was called into my new bosses' office and asked for my resignation.
>
> Reason? I was told I was not a ''team'' player anymore.
>
> Exit: Middle aged, middle manager.

> I was confident of my Sales Skills and I had substantial reason to believe that one could make good money selling old motorcycles. But the real turning point came during my third night of research at the Chicago Public Library when I ran across a recently printed article from the Chicago *Tribune* ''Money'' section by Lesley Alderman of *MONEY* Magazine. The article was about investments in collectibles, wine, Italian glassware, artwork, etc. However, leading the list was ''Antique Motorcycles'' as one of the best investments. That's when I literally had the light bulb go off in my head.

His brother Jim, a computer programmer, had listened to Joe's lament for years: how he never wanted to "work for another neurotic again," how he dreamed of going into business for himself, how his passion was buying and selling antique motorcycles, and how, in a perfect world, his passion would be his life's mission.

Jim told his brother that there was a way for his dreams to come true. He could start an international antique motorcycle catalog on the Internet. Buyers and sellers around the world could click on the Orlandino motorcycle Web page, actually see color photographs and a live-action video of bikes for sale, read about their prices and attributes in one of a dozen languages, then place their order by typing in their credit card numbers. When a particularly beautiful bike came along, Joe could actually hold a live "auction" on-line, heating up the bidding by allowing potential buyers to see the glistening motorcycle and the alluring auctioneer on their computer screens, then send in their escalating bids via e-mail. All of this could be done via the Internet, promised Jim Orlandino.

"The . . . *what?*" Joe replied.

Even though he had used a computer in his business for years, he had never accessed the Internet and just couldn't grasp the concept. So Joe's brother decided to show him, instead of telling him, what the Internet was all about. He created a home page for Joe Orlandino Motorcycles, calling it Atlas Motor Vehicles, then equipped his brother with a modem, downloaded Netscape, and told him how to call up a certain Web site, where "a big surprise" would be waiting.

My brother, Jim, had downloaded Netscape into my hard drive and told me to ''Go surfing'' and that, if I had any questions, ''I'd figure it out.''

Younger brothers!

After passing the better part of a Sunday afternoon at this, he rings me up and gives me a URL (another damn acronym) http://atlasmv.com to log onto.

''Check this out,'' he says.

I typed the letters into my search engine and . . . BaBOOM!

There it was, clear as day on the computer screen, a design that I had sketched out a few days before. It was completely fleshed out by a professional graphic artist neighbor. A vintage, skirt-fendered Indian chief jumped off of my screen in blazing yellow against a velvet black background, encircling the earth . . . with the neatly typed words ''ATLAS MOTOR VEHICLE—Putting Buyers and Sellers of Vintage Cycles Together—From Around the World.''

YEAH!

I call Jim back and my mind is racing. I feel like a part of my creative mind was just turned on and the handle broke off!

''Jim, can I have customers click on flags for different languages?'' ''Jim, would it be possible to have icons of the various cycles to refer to?'' ''Jim. . . . blah, blah, blah. . . . ?''

Oh, but this euphoria lasts but a brief moment . . . seems like everyone has a Web site. There are now Cycle Sites galore.

That's for sure. There are now millions of Web sites on the World Wide Web. And the numbers are growing by the instant, for good reason.

Our Web site at www.worldwideTV.com gets over one hundred thousand hits—or accesses by users—every day. That's a rather dramatic figure. One hundred thousand people a day is more than most major market radio stations attract, even in their morning drive time. So we're talking about having the ability to reach masses and masses of people overnight and impacting them in ways that just would have been impossible before. A Web site is becoming one of the best ways to reach potential customers for the relatively low or frequently free price, as opposed to spending considerable money on radio or television advertising.

So with the birth of his home page, Joe Orlandino instantly joined the burgeoning Internet marketplace. But he couldn't merely hole up in his room and expect buyers and sellers to come to him. The Web page is a business tool, not a cure-all. He needed bikes to sell to begin his business. So with his laptop computer in hand, he climbed into his BMW and, wearing jeans and a blazer that made him stand out like a Civil War–era Union Army officer in Dixie, walked into the toughest biker bar in Chicago, determined to show the Harleys what he had to buy and sell.

> There were Stars and Bars on the wall (hey . . . this is Chicago), Harley slogans in abundance, and some veiled Nazi references here and there. These dudes could care less about selling their bikes ESPECIALLY to foreigners! But I was oblivious to this. All I knew was that I was armed with the greatest Cycle Trader in the world and everyone HAD to see it.
>
> The bar itself was filled with black T-shirts, leather vests, ZZ-top-style beards and smoke. Boy, was there smoke! I walked past the bar toward the pool table and asked the Polish matron if I might stick a poster up on her bulletin board. After giving me the O.K., I carefully (and proudly) placed my ATLAS MOTOR VEHICLE poster amidst the 3x5 cards looking for parts or selling bikes and faded, out of date road-rally flyers.

I sat down at the only unoccupied seat at the bar and ordered a Bud (bottle, longneck). There was more sweat under my arms and forming along my brow than there was on the beer bottle. I was scared to pull out my Mac 270C laptop for fear I wouldn't walk out with it. But then I began a light conversation with Eva, the Polish bar frau, about her unique tavern and clientele and asked her if she had ever seen a 1912 New Era motorcycle.

''No,'' she replied.

''Well, it just so happens . . .''

I convinced her to unplug her bar phone for about 20 minutes so I could go on-line, live. ''Trust me, Eva . . . it's a local call,'' I assured her. Once I was plugged in, I turned on the Mac 270c computer, dialed up the Atlas Web site, and antique motorcycles began filling the screen.

The crowd around me slowly took shape, and even though I wasn't in my ''target'' market, I think Tattooed Slim, Shaved-Head Bennie, Ditzy Dale, and Two-Bit Tammy were a few of the more intrigued viewers I would ever have.

''Hey, Mitch, get a load o' this!''

These were the first comments that came out of Curley's mouth when I booted up my computer at Eva's tavern. I actually thought by showing Eva, the owner, a full color graphic of a 1912 New Era motorcycle I could interest someone with an old knucklehead Harley to advertise their cycle in my catalogue.

Slim ambled over and gazed at the image slowly taking shape on my screen.

''Yeah. @#!&*!' computers,'' he said. ''Pretty soon we're all gonna be outta work.''

A slight tug pulled at my stomach lining. How extremely out of place I felt. Laptop computer, my BMW 325 parked neatly behind the row of Hogs on the street. I was in sales all of my life, but this was becoming one tough crowd.

''Y'know,'' I began, ''I got into this stuff cuz all my yuppie neighbors are buying up the good bikes, and they don't even ride.''

''That's the damn truth!'' the little bar crowd resounded.

''Lemme buy you guys a beer and show you this stuff,'' I said, sliding a ten spot over to Eva to buy a round of Buds.

We started playing Stump the Net.

''Call out a topic and let's see if we can find it!'' I dared the bikers.

Of course, the first thing that came up was, ''BABES!''

''Hey, guys, there's a lady here,'' I said, referring to Eva.

''Ahh, don't worry about it,'' said Eva.

I took this as a command. After perusing several X-rated sites and ordering a second round, we got over to ATLAS on-line.

And thus began my winning the hearts of the hard-core. We spent at least 45 minutes tying up Eva's phone!

Today, if you call up the Atlas Home Page, you'll be greeted by the same blazing motorcycle icon that first amazed Joe Orlandino, flags that allow the user to click which language they'd prefer to be displayed, a list of available bikes, and the following welcoming text:

The Global Gateway for Vintage and Collectible Vehicle Sales

Welcome to our Home Page! If you're interested in unique, collectible vehicles, you need only to select a category that interests you.

You will then experience a new method of bringing together sellers and buyers.

Consider being able to view a vehicle from numerous perspectives, or allowing the seller to provide close-up images to highlight specific details of interest to the collector.

No more quarter page ads!

No more 2 hour phone explanations!

Enter the 21st Century and acquire the vehicle of your choice through immediate and comprehensive visual information.

After information on "Current Merchandise" and "Live Auctions," there is an item that proclaims:

You are the 18880th person
to visit this page since November 21st, 1995

Pay special attention to that last figure: 18,880 people visited the Atlas home page in its first eight months of operation. That's more traffic than most conventional storefronts can expect in a lifetime.

But for Joe Orlandino, it's just a beginning.

I've been in several biker bars, but I now chose the more up-market clubs which cater to the antique and vintage crowd. I've started a Midwest chapter of the Antique MC of America (8,000 members nationally).

It has taken almost 8 months for a steady stream of advertisers to utilize my service. ATLAS is truly THE player on the WORLD WIDE WEB. Because we are the only catalogue that I have found that speaks to the world . . . in their language!

Only 20% of the Earth speaks English . . . why be a global trader and limit your marketplace by eighty percent ?

The ATLAS concept is still in lockstep with the World Wide Web . . . we truly market to the WORLD. All text in German, Japanese, Italian, Polish, and, of course, English. We're presently adding French, Spanish, and Portuguese. My approach is not one of a Cycle Magazine Publisher, but more of a broker who caters to Serious Collectors who are willing and able to '''play'' in the Global sandbox, as opposed to kicking back and reading the latest CYCLE WORLD. I mix in reading from WORLD TRADE, PRESIDENTS AND PRIME MINISTERS, EXPORT TODAY, and COLLECTOR. I spend time on-line monitoring motorcycle manufacturing stocks and I also try to keep up on the latest shipping issues for partial container loads (an expensive shipping cost can be a deal breaker). My goal is to not only put Buyers and Sellers together, but long term I would like ATLAS to be synonymous with classic motorcycles.

Plaid Shirts = L. L. Bean

Old Motorcycles = ATLAS MV

We're paying all of our bills and putting a few bucks back into the business (software, hardware, and personnel) . . . all without ANY advertising. Our advertisers are seeing the results they were hoping for. The biggest challenge is opening up the consumer's mind to Global Trading. The WEB, I believe, will be the greatest boon to this area of commerce. Nevertheless, my day is not marked by the hands on the clock anymore. It's usually punctuated with a dozen or so ''Jim . . . can we design a . . . ?''

The Internet will allow everyone with access

to a computer to take part in the most profound exchange of goods and information our planet has to offer. Whether it be motorcycles or menstrual cycles, philosophy or pornography. If you want it, here it is, come and get it.

Here it is, come and get it!

The Internet is waiting to welcome you on board.

All you have to do is follow a few simple guidelines, which Joe Orlandino voices perfectly:

1. The Internet allows you to interact with each potential customer on a personal basis. *Do it* or go back to licking stamps and folding paper. Get away from the ''target'' market concept. Build your customers based on what they need, individually. If you've lost sight of what that is, ask them.
2. Never, never, *never* send a shotgun e-mailing. Always *ask* if you can have a potential customer's permission to send some info about your product or service.
3. When you get a ''Yes,'' begin at this point to build a database on this customer. Include everything you can find out about him or her: kid's names, anniversaries, type of auto, job location . . . *Get personal!* This medium allows you to make friends as well as customers. Start tailoring your replies to that person. Do you talk to your mother the same way you talk to your mechanic? Is your wife concerned about the same issues as your parking lot attendant? Give your customers a life, treat them as people, and they will pay you back tenfold—if not in $$$$, then in the sense that you are truly providing a service. Be a Nordstrom's. Greet your customers at the

door. Use the potential of this means of human interaction to its fullest potential.

4. Do favors! Don't be so quick to ''charge'' for every little thing. You want a customer for life, not just a transaction. This person's gonna pay your electric bill every month someday . . . treat them right! In my business (motorcycle trading) there are over four thousand domestic cycle-related Web sites on the Internet. I want a contact to come back to me because it makes sense to him . . . on *every* level. If he views my Web site as a commodity, I might as well quit now and go pour coffee at Starbucks.

Eleanor Roosevelt once said, "The future belongs to those who believe in the beauty of their dreams."

Entrepreneurs like Joe Orlandino are proof that this dictum is still absolutely true. Believe in something strongly enough and the future has a way of finding you. No longer bound to a business suit or a downtown office, Orlandino has revived his once weary future and become the master of his life. His Internet motorcycle auctions are watched everywhere from biker bars to banker's houses, each hit from the cyberspace public one more vote of confidence for the viability of Joe Orlandino's dreams.

My father-in-law was soon reveling in the Internet's infinite possibilities, and we played on the Web until deep into the night. By midnight—fore!—a new driving range cyberentrepreneur was born. And he was eager to learn more about the future at his fingertips.

CHAPTER FIVE

Finding Success through Failure

Far better it is to dare mighty things, to win glorious triumphs, even though checkered by failure, than to take rank with those poor spirits who neither enjoy much nor suffer much, because they live in the gray twilight that knows not victory or defeat.

—Theodore Roosevelt

The secret of virtual power did not pop onto my computer screen with the ease of a new software program. It was a secret borne only in the depths of disillusionment, when all seemed lost. I had reached the point where the road back seemed infinitely more inviting than the path forward, and it was at this moment that I learned one of life's greatest secrets. Not until I learned to look at failure as opportunity, the virtual key to the Brave New World, could I access virtual power.

I'm not telling you to seek out failure. It can find you easily enough. But you'd best prepare yourself for it, especially in the beginning. Giving birth is never a pleasant experience—ask any mother!

Starting my home-based business made me think a lot about my father and the parallels between our searches for personal fulfillment. Both of us suffered financial losses in the beginning—such tremendous losses, our friends and families thought perhaps we'd lost our minds. My father quit his lucrative Houston manufacturing company job to move to South Carolina and open what he envisioned as "the first superstore Christian bookstore," and it put us through some extremely trying financial times while he was finding his way, both personally and professionally.

He scrambled around for a couple of years, trying to make ends meet. As a family we went through some very tough times while he found his professional independence. But my father had something that money and houses and social invitations cannot buy: a dream backed by faith and propelled by persistence. This force creates a tangible "power" more combustible than gasoline in the tank of a Ferrari.

It is not a force attained by committee. It is a force summoned up in the deepest recesses of the individual, literally virtual power.

Neither of us was motivated by layoffs. We merely heard and heeded the call to do something more, something on our own. The call became an obsession, something never understood by the general populace, whose mantra is always "moderation." But what great cause was won by moderation? Like the Nobel Prize–winning inventor of the telegraph, Guglielmo Marconi, whose family and friends had him incarcerated and psychologically examined when he ranted of how he'd invented a way to send long-wave radio signals across the Atlantic Ocean without wires, my father and I were thought by most people to be a couple of nuts.

Ultimately my father's business was incredibly successful. When he sold his company in December of 1994, it had become the largest Christian bookstore in the country, forty thousand square feet of Christian books, music, and gifts.

I tell you this story because it's important to realize that most of us share the same inner drive. Like wild beasts in the jungle, we value freedom as our first priority, and to find freedom we frequently must resort to flight. So "rephrase" your internal dialogue: you're not leaving security; you're finding freedom. You're not quitting a job, you're embarking upon a journey. Always remember the words of the anonymous prophet who said, "Man cannot discover new oceans until he has the courage to lose sight of the shore."

Erase the word "failure" from your mental vocabulary and replace it with "temporary setbacks," and the hills you have to climb on your way to the mountaintop of personal fulfillment won't seem so daunting.

To show you how seemingly impossible odds can be mastered

through sheer passion and persistence, I'd like to use part of this chapter to finish my own believe-it-or-not journey of empowerment: the improbable rise of a C student with absolutely no television experience who became the host of his own nationally syndicated television productions and the owner of a multimillion-dollar production firm.

The climb didn't really begin until I hit the wall of seemingly insurmountable obstacles. It started out promisingly enough, in the office of personal computer wunderkind Michael Dell, who founded what would become a billion-dollar company in the unlikeliest of home offices—his University of Texas dormitory room—all on the concept of selling discount clone computers by catalog. I'd sent Michael an introductory e-mail, telling what I was doing with door-to-door computer sales, and we started corresponding. As he asked questions and I gave him more details, he got very interested in the whole idea of my "outbound computer sales business," the Computer Howse.

After he invited me to visit him in Austin, I found myself standing before this mammoth high-rise building up in the Texas Hill Country, where barely twenty Michael Dell and his corporate staff held forth on the top floor. As I have a tendency to do, I got rather animated and excited about the prospects of what I thought a Dell-owned Computer Howse business could do.

Michael and I spoke for more than two hours in his conference room. All the while, I'm dancing on rainbows, thinking, Okay, so I sell my company to Dell as a new division, they're going to want me to be the guy running it, I'm going to get stock options . . .

In my mind I've already got the cigarette boat and the beach house and the Coppertone on my face.

Michael sent me down to meet his company's VP of marketing, and I was so amped up I was practically jumping out of my skin.

After considerable research on acquiring my door-to-door business—focus groups, ad agency testing, etc.—Dell decided to pass. It was the right decision. Shortly after our meetings in 1991, computer prices plummeted, making profit margins so small that you couldn't afford the cost of door-to-door delivery. Dell had the good sense to realize that my idea wouldn't work forever, despite my enthusiasm.

Somewhere in your make-up there lies sleeping, the seed to achievement, which, if aroused and put into action, would carry you to heights, such as you may never have hoped to attain.

—*Napoleon Hill,*
Think and Grow Rich

Looking at the Dell episode merely as a temporary setback and not a full-time failure, I wondered: What could lie sleeping in my own makeup that could carry me to heights I couldn't imagine? What would be my wildest dream in terms of taking my computer message to the greatest number of people?

The answer came as a single idea, something so simple that if I hadn't been alert, it could have flown through my brain as fast as a rare bird lists on a rose:

Wouldn't it be great to take my door-to-door computer sales service to a forum where I could knock on fifty thousand doors, one hundred thousand doors, even potentially millions of doors simultaneously? Wouldn't it be great to knock on doors through *television?*

In my old life I might have laughed it off: Sure, right, Mark Bunting on television? Hah! But instead I took my idea and ran with it. My first stop? An independent TV station that screened mostly infomercials. You know, the tummy tucker, the weight loss miracles, and magical emollients that will make you younger, prettier, and more successful after just one application. But for a door-to-door kid with absolutely no TV experience, Houston's Channel 39 was prime-time. Getting in the door was relatively easy. My wife's cousin's husband, Gary, ran the station. He at least had to "listen" to my idea. Right?

Hearing my pitch, Gary thought it had merit but not enough merit for the station to fund the show itself. But he said that if I wanted to "buy" time on the station, the station would be happy to assist me in producing a show.

Pay dirt frequently comes disguised as gravel and requires hard work and persistence to mine. I agreed to a price and set out to create my first show, if you could even call it a "show." It would actually consist of little thirty-second TV spots discussing different computer hardware and software—paid for by local computer stores—that were designed to look like news programming.

I wasn't thinking of myself as the on-camera host. However, I quickly learned that when you're planning a show that's only one step away from rank amateur cable, you've got to do everything yourself. I thought TV stations created shows and all I had to do was show up. Wrong again! Somebody has to come up with the ideas, somebody has to write the show, somebody has to produce it.

And that somebody was me.

I came on and introduced myself as "the Computer Man," and I would show you the different software and hardware and explain what it all meant. I did it all in very friendly, casual, layman's terms. I even had a coffee mug printed with the word "NERDS" with a circle and a slash through the word. (No Nerds!) So when my computer company guests would get too technical, I'd tap my coffee cup and say, "Now, Bill, Bill, wait, whoa, whoa, *whoa!* No nerds here! Back up and explain what you mean."

The guest would laugh uncomfortably, then explain it to me in terms any ordinary Jack or Jill like me could understand. The show was miserably hokey and as low budget as they come. But it was a beginning. Just as with my door-to-door job, people were incredibly receptive. The show actually started to get what's known as "a rating," meaning a respectable market share, even though its Sunday morning time slot put it in direct competition with *Meet the Press* and *Face the Nation.*

As poorly produced as the show was, and as inexperienced as I was on camera, the concept was absolutely on target. We didn't need a Nielsen rating to tell us that viewers were absolutely starved for easy-to-understand computer information.

Eight weeks after I started the TV show, I sold the Computer Howse Company and decided to put my effort into television full-time.

It was a little too early for the champagne and caviar.

I had sold the business and reaped a pretty significant chunk of change. But I'd also had to borrow an equally significant chunk of change to grow. When it was all said and done, I had about $80,000, which isn't bad. But fast-forward a few bill-laden months. Now, as fledgling TV entrepreneur I had come full circle.

I was flat broke.

So prepare yourself. It happens. You are going to work your tail off, and one morning there is the very real possibility that you'll wake up and find your coffers . . . empty. In my case, it was only the beginning of a real roller-coaster dip from which it didn't seem I'd ever surface. Trying to push my fledgling TV production to greater heights, I was sinking in unfamiliar waters, surrounded by people with barely more television experience than myself. I needed help, instruction, guidance. So I followed the gospel of every self-help prophet: find someone who's doing or has done what you want to do, then model—or pantomime—their actions.

I desperately needed to find my mentor.

When Edwin C. Barnes climbed down from the freight train in Orange, N.J., more than fifty years ago, he may have resembled a tramp, but his thoughts were those of a king!

As he made his way from the railroad tracks to Thomas A. Edison's office, his mind was at work. He saw himself standing in Edison's presence. He heard himself asking Mr. Edison for an opportunity to carry out the one consuming obsession of his life, a burning desire to become the business associate of the great inventor.

Barnes' desire was not a hope! It was not a wish! It was a keen, pulsating desire, which transcended everything else. It was definite.

A few years later, Edwin C. Barnes again stood before Edison, in the same office where he first met the inventor. This time his desire had been translated into reality. He was in business with Edison. The dominating dream of his life had become a reality.

Barnes succeeded because he chose a definite goal, placed all of his energy, all of his will power, all his effort, everything, back of that goal.

—*Napoleon Hill,*
Think and Grow Rich

I went to see Bob Vila. You know, the host of *This Old House,* the folksy how-to show about home repair and reconstruction? I kept thinking to myself, What a fabulous show! I didn't even own a house and I loved watching this guy. It's like voyeurism: you go to all these wonderful places, you meet interesting people, you visit great houses.

I knew I'd found my model for a how-to show on computers and technology.

I wanted to become the Bob Vila of home-based computers.

So I flew to the annual convention of the National Association of Television Producers and Executives (NATPE) to meet the master and ask him if he thought a how-to computer show could make it nationally. I found him in the convention hall, standing around with Martha Stewart and a couple of quasi cable celebrities, everybody schmoozing and shaking hands. I waited two hours before I could catch Vila alone. The minute I saw my opening, I darted over and said, "Hey, Bob, I don't want to bother you, but my name's Mark Bunting, and people call me the Computer Man, and let me tell you what I'm doing."

I was like our chapter 3 testimonial subject, Jan Herrick, when buying her first computer. I was literally screaming for help!

"Bob, I've got this show, *The Computer Man,* and I'm thinking we could sell our shows together: Bob Vila, the Home Repair Man, and Mark Bunting, the Computer Man. Whaddya think?"

You should have seen his face: paler than radish root.

"Listen, kid, I like your enthusiasm, but I don't know a thing about computers," he said at last. "What are you talking to me for?"

"Well, Bob, I know about computers, but I don't know a damn thing about TV," I replied. "I want to learn the inside story on how to get a show up and running."

Miracle of miracles, he became sort of a mentor to me. I made a couple of trips to New York to meet with Bob Vila and his producer, Michael Ferrone, and for a long time Bob actually considered having his production company represent the show and help me develop it. Ultimately he decided that he didn't have the time. But what he taught me turned out to be invaluable. He gave me ideas on how to structure the show, the importance of taking the show out of the studio and into the field.

I thought I could simply take this concept of *The Computer Man* show and syndicate it nationally, just as Bob Vila had syndicated *This Old House.* I just felt someday soon someone was going to do for computers what Bob Vila did for old homes, and I wanted to be that guy. I was nothing more than a glorified door-to-door computer salesman with a little local TV show in Houston, Texas. But now another door had opened—as doors to entrepreneurs frequently do—and through this door I could glimpse my future: to enter the homes of would-be computer users through the TV screen instead of the screen door.

Like Edwin C. Barnes, the tramp who became an associate of Edison totally on the power of persistence and drive, I was a pauper. But in my thoughts, I was a king.

So I began to learn everything about the TV business. My first lesson? TV time is expensive! I had to pay the Houston TV station for airtime and production facilities, then rush out to talk computer stores into running advertising spots to cover the cost of production and, hopefully, have something left over to live on.

Of course, there never was anything left.

I had to live on my wife's meager teacher paycheck. The $80,000 I had from selling my company was long gone. Only by the grace of credit cards was I keeping pace with the financial demands of TV production.

We've all heard the horror stories of home-based entrepreneurs living on their credit cards, charging up more than they can afford, then hoping their business clicks before their credit cards are canceled. It's not a method I recommend. But I believe in the "whatever it takes" rule, as long as it's legal and honest. I ran up more credit card debt than I could pay, however, and American Express canceled my plastic. My Visa was maxed out, too, as were my parents, who had generously loaned me $14,000 and finally said, "No more."

Eighteen months after launching my show, I went from having $80,000 in the bank to owing more than $80,000—a $160,000 reversal!

The show was still stumbling, experiencing what's known in the industry as "hick-ups." National syndication was the answer, but I couldn't get it sold at the NATPE convention in the fall of 1993, which meant I'd have to wait an entire year to try again. The lesson? Nothing is going to go according to schedule, especially when it comes to money. No matter what you think something is going to cost to launch, multiply it times three. Then do the same with the time you estimate it will take you to finish your project.

After almost two years of declaring my independence from nine-to-five, I was right back where I started: one man with one computer working alone in the tiny bedroom of a small Houston town house.

My employees were long gone. The telephone was deathly silent. My wife was supportive but, I could tell, wondering. My dream of turning a garage business into a major computer retailer had vanished.

I had arrived at the crossroads, where the road back seemed much easier than the path forward. In this moment I felt I had failed miserably. But then I switched on the computer, accessed the Internet, and typed the words "Individual Achievement" into the search engine. I was soon staring at a list of references of men and women who, armed with more aspirations than assets, accessed an inner power to bring their dreams to fruition.

One name kept repeating itself on the computer screen: Napoleon Hill. The author of *Think and Grow Rich,* published in 1937 as the first real motivational book, Hill, I learned, was a rough-and-tumble Horatio Alger character born in a one-room log cabin in the Blue Ridge Mountains in 1883, who suffered crushing business and personal failures before achieving such stunning success that he came to personify the term "perseverance." He became an adviser to two U.S. presidents and spent twenty years studying the secrets of achievement, which he passed on to more than seven million readers in *Think and Grow Rich.* The Internet, the newest motivational tool, allowed me to access *Think and Grow Rich,* and I ordered a copy of the book on-line.

My first awakening had involved accessing the astonishing power of the computer. Now I understood something else, something just as vital: a computer alone isn't the answer. Virtual power is the electricity generated when a viable idea, coupled with faith, drive, and persistence, connect with the computer.

I typed passages of *Think and Grow Rich* into my computer and programmed the passages to pop up on my screen as daily reminders, and my computer became a cheerleader to my cause.

Here is one of my favorites:

The Spur That Drives to Riches

A long while ago, a great warrior faced a situation which made it necessary for him to make a decision which insured his success on the battlefield. He was about to send his armies against a powerful foe, whose men out-numbered his own. He loaded his soldiers onto boats, sailed to the enemy's country, unloaded soldiers and equipment, then gave the order to burn the ships that had carried them. Addressing his men before the first battle, he said, "You see the boats going up in smoke. That means we cannot leave these shores alive unless we win! We no have no choice—we win—or we perish."

They won.

Every person who wins in any undertaking must be willing to burn his ships and cut all sources of retreat. Only by so doing can one be sure of maintaining that state of mind known as a burning desire to win, essential success.

Cut all sources of retreat.

I typed Hill's dictum onto my screen and it became the bedrock principle of virtual power. Reading on, I learned of Hill's belief that once a person decides that retreat is not an option, they soon experience a pivotal "turning point." It was outlined in a section of the book headed "How to Get Dreams off the Launching Pad":

A burning desire to be and to do is the starting point from which the dreamer must take off. Dreams are not born of indifference, laziness, or lack of ambition.

Remember that all who succeed in life get off to a bad start, and pass through many heartbreaking struggles before they "arrive." The turning point in the lives of those who succeed usually comes at the moment of some crisis, through which they are introduced to their "other selves."

Hill gave a host of examples of men and women who experienced crushing tragedy but through perseverance rose to find their "true selves" and greater victories than they could have ever imagined in their previous lives:

O. Henry discovered the genius which slept within his brain after he met with great misfortune, and was confined in a prison cell, in Columbus, Ohio. Being forced, through misfortune, to become acquainted with his "other self," and to use his imagination, he discovered himself to be a great author instead of a miserable criminal and outcast.

Using Hill's examples, I found a host of twenty-first-century counterparts, home-based, computer-driven entrepreneurs, who, having reached their nadir—the depths of misfortune—used the computer to rise above their strafed lives and soar to greater glory. I'll quote Hill's examples first, then present a corresponding twenty-first-century example:

Charles Dickens began by pasting labels on blacking pots. The tragedy of his first love penetrated the depths of his soul and converted him into one of the world's truly great authors. That tragedy produced, first, David Copperfield, then a succession of other works that made this a richer and better world for all who read his books.

Sandy Mooneyham was an ad agency/creative department manager at a conventional art firm in Houston, Texas, who left her job on maternity leave. When her baby boy was nine months old, she returned to work, and nine days after her return, a fire broke out at her babysitter's house, burning the child critically.

From age nine months to his twelfth birthday, the boy had thirty-six surgeries. Ms. Mooneyham's husband decided he "wasn't strong enough" to endure the ordeal and abandoned his family. But Sandy Mooneyham was determined to stay constantly at her son's side, pay all of his medical bills without government assistance, and spend every night with him in the hospital.

She wasn't able to report to a conventional office anymore, of course. But her office went with her in the form of three Macintosh computers, which Sandy calls "my other children," allowing her to run a lucrative graphic arts business from her home.

"Your product set me free," she wrote to Apple Computer. "It let me decide what was important to do with my life."

Helen Keller became deaf . . . and blind shortly after birth. Despite her great misfortune, she has written her name indelibly in the pages of the history of the great. Her entire life has served as evidence that no one ever is defeated until defeat has been accepted as a reality.

Larry Skutchan was twenty when he suffered a detached retina in his right eye. That was bad news for a hardworking laborer, a derrick man on a roustabout oil rig, a roughneck in air-conditioning repair. He hadn't yet found his niche in life. But when his left retina became detached, for reasons his doctors couldn't fully explain, and his twenty-twenty vision dimmed to total darkness, exploring the conventional job market was a luxury he could no longer afford.

Larry Skutchan was suddenly totally blind.

"I had no idea what I would do," he remembers. "I thought maybe long term I'd get a degree and maybe do some writing. I was living in Hope, Arkansas. I went to the University of Little Rock and got a degree in English. I was going to go to law school after that. Really, all you can do is just go on and make the best of it. Being blind is really more of a pain in the butt than anything else. I was over all the bitter stuff."

He had always thought of computers as a domain reserved for nerds. "I had the old picture of the science-fiction movies with the cold rooms and long white lab coats," he says. "I never thought I'd be interested in them."

But seeking some way to speed his writing work—endless hours of dictating his texts into a tape recorder, then editing with another tape recorder, then hiring someone to transcribe his voice onto paper—he talked the Little Rock rehab center for the blind into buying an Apple 2E and a printer. But to his disappointment, none of the off-the-shelf word-processing programs had speech recognition.

When he graduated from college in 1983, Larry Skutchan eventually found a rudimentary system from a tiny company in Indiana that enabled the user to type the words and the computer to repeat what had been written. "I plugged it in and it talked," Larry remembers. "You can't imagine how easy it was to manipulate what you'd written. Man, I thought I'd gone to heaven."

He got so fascinated with the program, he quit law school and founded a home-based business called MicroTalk, writing software for the blind.

Not only does he make an "excellent income," but Larry is able to work out of his garage, and his software products are opening windows of communication for blind people everywhere. Surrounded by six talking computers, he enjoys a normal, productive life with his wife, who handles his shipping and invoicing, and four kids. "That's the neat part," he says. "When the kids come home from school, I have time to talk to them. We're a really close family."

Abraham Lincoln was a failure at everything he tried, until he was well past the age of forty. He was a Mr. Nobody from Nowhere, until a great experience came into his life, aroused the sleeping genius within his heart and brain, and gave the world one of its truly great men. That "experience" was mixed with the emotions of sorrow and love.

Brent Green joined the ranks of the laid-off one wintry Friday in Denver, Colorado. A middle-aged advertising and direct-mail marketing wizard, he had spent years of twelve-hour days managing accounts billing in excess of $6 million. He'd been given regular raises and frequent praise. But when his boss closed the door and told him he was "regretfully eliminating" Green's job, and even though the boss seasoned his conversation with rhetoric about the company's hard times, there was no doubt in Green's mind that he'd been unceremoniously *fired.* Green told me his story:

''I drove home in bright winter sunlight, absolutely numb,'' Green remembers. ''I fell on the couch in my library and nodded off for maybe ten minutes. I awoke to orange sunlight streaming through sheer window coverings. It was sunset outside, and I could count the number of days on one hand that I had been in this house during the late afternoon on a weekday. 'This isn't real,' I kept telling myself. I felt such an empty, raw feeling. The questions that all newly unemployed people confront bubbled up from my subconsciousness:

Where will I go?
How will I pay my bills?

''Strangely, I felt a certain power during the first few hours following the bomb that had been dropped on my life. Society is cruel when it comes to the unemployed—especially the fired. No matter the circumstances of the split, any job interviewer has to suspect someone who has been fired.''

In this moment Brent Green discovered his true self, an independent individual who would not rush out to reapply to another corporation. He had been in this situation before, when he'd voluntarily resigned from a financially strapped Colorado oil company at the height of the recession in the mid-eighties and resolved to become less accountable to others by creating his home-based marketing communications consultant business. All he had to do was dust off his computer equipment, start up the home-based business full-bore again, and exercise virtual power.

"My clients can be as demanding as any of my former bosses," he says. "Some call me at home late at night, send faxes before the sun comes up, think nothing of asking to meet me on Sunday morning, and have me agreeing to deadlines that allow half the time needed to get the work done. Some are grumpy, whiny, arrogant, insensitive, bellicose, or egocentric. But if anybody gets too far under my skin, I fire his butt. Life is short, and a nasty client can be replaced with a nobler soul. Try that on a corporate boss."

What do all of these stories have in common? They each walked through the firewall of failure to find their "true selves" on the other side.

Ultimately the creative process is an inexplicable thing. Imagine the novice screenwriter sitting in his office in Austin, at work saving a multimillion-dollar movie. The novice is under tremendous pressure, and although his life is a study in self-confidence, he's feeling something akin to terror. He prides himself on his speed and professionalism, but he has been at the keyboard so long that his hands are nearly immobilized from swelling. Instead of quitting, he wraps packaging material around his palms so he can keep typing. His eyes are so fatigued that they no longer focus in unison. He tapes a makeshift patch over his left eye so he can see with his right. It is three in the morning when he finally turns off his computer, but then a woman appears in his mind. She is the wife of the main character's best friend. She will complicate and deepen the friendship between the two men, and at a crucial moment, she will help keep the main character from giving up. And as he writes her lines, it is almost as if he is taking dictation.

"She came to me clean as a whistle, out of my unconscious," Skaaren recalls. "I went and turned the machine back on. When Meg Ryan read for the part, tears came to my eyes."

—*Emily Yoffe,*
Texas Monthly *magazine*

The above story is about a screenwriter, the late Warren Skaaren, whose movies include *Batman, Beetlejuice,* and the subject of the above testimonial, *Top Gun,* whose pivotal character came to the screenwriter-who-wouldn't-quit at three in the morning. I started thinking in terms of the three A.M.'s of my own life, that crucial moment when, facing the wall of physical and mental exhaustion, we either stop or start.

Facing that moment, that crossroads, in my career, when the debt seemed unbearable and the summit of national syndication insurmountable, I vowed to push forward, no matter the obstacles. I really had no other choice. I had cut off all routes of escape the moment I left my JOB. Returning to sell ads for *The Wall Street Journal* was a thought so bad, I couldn't fathom the prospect. The self-esteem issues would have been overwhelming. But if you look around the hallways of almost any conventional corporation, you will see the beaten soldiers of wasted industry, those who tried and "failed," who, in Thoreau's words, are living "lives of quiet desperation." Too timid to hold their course in the storm, they turn back and live the rest of their days in a state of arrested dreams.

Cut off all routes of escape and you'll virtually force yourself to access virtual power. For more proof, I turned again to Napoleon Hill:

An uncle of R.U. Darby was caught by the "gold fever" in the gold-rush days, and went west to dig and grow rich. He had never heard that more gold has been mined from the thoughts of men than has ever been taken from the earth. He staked a claim and went to work with pick and shovel.

After weeks of labor, he was rewarded by the discovery of the shining ore. He needed machinery to bring the ore to the surface. Quietly, he covered up the mine, retraced his footsteps to his home in Williamsburg, Maryland, told his relatives and a few neighbors of the "strike." They got together money for the needed machinery, and had it shipped. The uncle and Darby went back to work the mine.

The first car of ore was mined and shipped to a smelter. The returns proved they had one of the richest mines in Colorado! A few more cars of that ore would clear the debts. Then would come the big killing of profits.

Down went the drills! Up went the hopes of Darby and Uncle! Then something happened. The vein of gold ore disappeared! They had come to the end of the rainbow, and the pot of gold was no longer there. They drilled on, desperately trying to pick up the vein again—all to no avail.

Finally they decided to quit.

They sold the machinery to a junk man for a few hundred dollars, and took the train back home. The junk man called in a mining engineer to look at the mine and do a little calculating. The engineer advised that the project had failed because the owners were not familiar with "the fault lines." His calculations showed that vein would be found just three feet from where the Darbys had stopped drilling! That is exactly where it was found!

The junk man took millions of dollars in ore from the mine because he knew enough to seek expert counsel before giving up.

Think about being five feet from gold! "Failure is a trickster with a keen sense of irony and cunning," writes Hill. "It takes great delight in tripping one when success is almost within reach."

Most people would've sunk into total despair after missing the once-in-a-lifetime chance of striking gold. But not the subject of Hill's testimonial. R. U. Darby used the experience as a gate into another world. Failure had forced him to discover his true self, the person who would never stop at "No" again. He went on to become one of America's leading insurance salesmen, whose expertise at closing a sale was unequaled.

This principle of failure as trickster has perhaps no better twenty-first-century analogy than the man who literally skated his way to fortune and fame. His name is Scott Olson, and for years he was skating on the thin ice of a dream.

Growing up in the snows of Bloomington, Illinois, Scott Olson lived for ice skating. He was a local high school hockey star who went professional with the Winnipeg Jets before finally deciding it was time, at twenty, to go into business for himself. He had no trouble deciding on a field of endeavor. Years of nighttime dreams had already left an indelible road map for him to follow.

The path to his future began on his feet: he knew he had to do something involved with skating.

Since he was twelve, Olson's sleep was haunted by a recurring dream: he'd be skating. Skating, as wild and fast as the wind. But when he'd look down to see exactly what type of skate was giving him such an incredible ride, not only could he not see his skates, he couldn't even tell what surface he was skating upon. Sometimes he would be skating naked, other times fully clothed. But always, despite the cold, he'd be warm, both inside and out—because he'd found his life's passion: a magical apparatus that allowed him literally to skate through life.

After retiring from professional hockey, he sought to discover the magical skates from his dreams, hoping the skates would provide his career path. After years of experiencing the same dream, he knew there could be only one kind of skate that would give him such freedom: an "in-line" skate, whose wheels are lined up as straight as an ice skate's blade. First developed in the 1800s, an in-line skate gives the skater the feeling of skating on ice, even while on pavement.

Olson had seen a magazine advertisement from a small California company that still produced the skates. He ordered a pair and liked them so much, he became the company's midwest distributor, then a distributor throughout the United States. Pretty soon he was modifying the skate and creating his own in-line model, all sleek fiberglass, bright colors, and astonishing speed.

His dream was becoming a reality.

Only now, Scott Olson had no time to skate. He was burdened

with the constraints of traditional business: accounting, marketing, organizing, and, worst of all, the sound of the constantly slamming door. Remembers Olson:

> I went to all the sporting goods stores in Minneapolis, and they basically laughed at my skates. They'd all say the same thing:
>
> ''Those roller skates won't fly!''
>
> ''They're too hard to learn!''
>
> ''They cost too much money!''
>
> Just about anything negative you could think of kept coming up. Mainly, that there was no demand for it. I'd go to the next store, then the next store, and it didn't take long to figure out that I wasn't going to make any sales by going to the dealers. That's why I went direct. Guerrilla marketing, basically.

Scott Olson had reached his "turning point," the gates of failure. But he didn't stop short of the gold. He took his business home, and home became his salvation. He set up his home-based office in his parents' Bloomington home and turned on the computer to jump-start his business.

> I wanted to focus on sales and marketing, because, of course, if you don't get sales going, you don't need anything else. I didn't have a lot of time to figure things out; I was always running out of time. I didn't want to sit around and try to figure out the technical things. So to free myself to go out and sell the skates, I hired someone to help me set up my system at home. I had virtually no experience in any of that. He instructed me to buy an IBM PC, and we set up the accounting spreadsheet and the inventory and my customer database and weekly hit list of marketing contacts. The computer kept track of our whole

system. And that freed me up to go out and start pounding the pavement.

The computer made everything more efficient. Why walk when you can roll? It just made it more efficient and fun. Everything was so easy to access. I mean, with the push of a button, boom! You've got whatever you need, versus running around looking for something in a file cabinet. Instantly, I became much more organized, and I found that the more organized I was, the more work I could get done.

With the power of the computer at his back, Scott Olson was given more of life's most precious resource—time.

Time to sell his skates.

With a Dictaphone in each hand—on which he'd dictate letters, log information about his sales calls, and formulate ideas to be downloaded into his computer once he got home—Scott Olson literally skated to individual potential customers. First he skated to friends and relatives, and they bought his skates. Then it was on to hockey coaches and ski coaches, and they placed orders, too. His confidence building, Olson began skating to television stations, concert halls, and coliseums, and pretty soon most of Bloomington was in-line skating.

Scott Olson was living his dream of perpetual skating! Flying across the city streets, he skated into the dressing rooms of touring superstars like Bruce Springsteen, late night king David Letterman, and ice hockey star Wayne Gretzky, all of whom fell in love with Scott Olson's product. Gretzky even sent Olson home to fill his order immediately, so he could personally take them home to his family. And when John F. Kennedy Jr. received a complimentary pair in the mail, he immediately mailed Olson a rapt thank-you note and was soon photographed sailing on Olson's skates through Central Park with his then girlfriend, actress Daryl Hannah.

On a roll, Olson skated five hundred miles in a typical week, selling his skates one pair at a time. In retrospect, he knows he couldn't have done it without his computer, whose spreadsheet program balanced his books, whose calendar program kept track of his daily sales calls, whose word-processing program handled his communication. Soon he had enough money to hire an assistant, who would take the Dictaphones out of Olson's backpack when he returned from his skating sales days and enter their content into the computer. This became known as the "hit list."

Sales were doubling every quarter. His basement staff grew to ten. Semitrucks regularly streaked down his parents' suburban street, dropping off components for skates. Olson's company grew to $500,000 in sales in its first two years in his parents' basement. The only aspect about the business that remained the same was Olson's computer: the same basic system supported the company from infancy to middle age.

He moved his home office from his parents' basement to his own twenty-acre Minnesota farm, where fifty employees kept pace with mushrooming demand. Fifty roving dealers, young men and women with a passion for skating, sold the skates directly to consumers, and eventually, the dealers who had once laughed off the skates begged to get them in their stores.

In 1986 Olson sold his company for many millions of dollars. It was later sold again, and again, and is now a $350 million giant owned by the Italian clothing giant Benetton.

You might have heard of Olson's product, Rollerblade, or at least seen them whizzing past you on city streets and park sidewalks. Now Olson, thirty-seven, is marketing two new products, a Row Bike and a moving Health Ride, out of his computer-driven Minnesota ranch home office.

Did Scott Olson employ virtual power? You bet he did.

1. He believed in his ideas and dreams and backed them with passion and persistence.
2. He cut off all routes of escape and used failure to propel himself into a success he couldn't have imagined.
3. He admitted computer illiteracy and sought help in setting up his personal computer system, then relied on his computer to handle his administrative duties, thus giving himself more time to go out and market his product.

Never give in. Never! Never! Never!

—*Winston Churchill*

Following Hill's advice to cut off all routes of escape, I stayed my course, kept faith in my idea of a nationally syndicated computer TV show, and tried to keep advertising revenues one step ahead of bills past due. I knew I had another year before I could get my next shot at national syndication at the NATPE convention. But I couldn't afford to wait idly. So I followed a popular late-twentieth-century adage: Networking is everything. To this I would add, "Especially on airplanes."

Naturally outgoing, I looked at every seatmate as a possible advertiser, contact, or lead. Fate had thrown Tom Hoitsma and me together in seats 14A and 14B from Dallas-Fort Worth to Manhattan. I introduced myself and told him a little about my television mission, and he told me about his own.

He was the sales director for the Fox television station in San Antonio.

We stayed in contact with each other. After I'd been on the air in Houston for a few months, Tom had reached a point where he wanted to leave Fox, and I offered him a chance to own a piece of my "company" if he would help me make my dreams of a syndicated *Computer Man* show a reality.

I couldn't believe it when Tom said, "Yes."

Here's a guy who had been making $100,000 a year, who, for whatever personal reasons, decided he'd reached a point in his life where he wanted to do something different. So he moved to Houston to work out of my tiny loft on a three-dollar plastic chair to the audible snickering of his friends and associates, who thought he was an absolute idiot for walking away from his wonderfully secure job to go do some "computer show." His pay plummeted from a monthly $8,000 to $2,000, with no guarantee that we'd even make payroll.

But like the inventor Marconi, Tom had the ability to ignore his critics and stay his course. He'd vowed total commitment. He'd cut off all routes of escape. What more could you ask of a potential partner or employee? We're not talking about the kind of people to whom a salary, a clean office, and a two-week vacation are everything. We're talking about people who thrive on personal growth and a professional mission.

We decided to up the ante on my television career. We suspended production on the Houston-based computer show and moved to Manhattan, first my wife and I, then Tom and I. We lived in a less-than-minuscule apartment on Seventy-first Street and West End, talking to every television concern we could find. CNBC reps had seen my demo tape, thought I would make a good host, and offered me $1,000 a week, which was a lot of money at the time. But $1,000 a week was "employee" money, as opposed to "mission money." I hadn't left a job that paid me many times more than that to go back on someone else's payroll.

"I've got a better idea," I said. "Instead of you paying me $1,000 a week, how about if I just buy the time from you for the half hour and the production?"

CNBC was, of course, delighted to rent me its production facilities and sell me its airtime.

For $25,000 a week.

Tom and I decided to launch the show for thirteen weeks in the first week of October. To accomplish this, I had to make a commitment to CNBC for $25,000 a week. At thirteen weeks that came to $227,500. The payments were due on the first of each week or CNBC wouldn't shoot that week's show.

The contracts were signed. All means of retreat were severed. I'd either strike gold or die trying. I had arrived at what I call the "put up or shut up" moment. Muhammad Ali didn't become the heavyweight champion of the world by sitting in his corner. Bill Gates didn't become a billionaire by keeping his software to himself.

You've got to ante up to get into any game.

I decided to look at the upside: I had time on a national TV series to sell! With our thirty minutes on CNBC, we went out to all of the computer companies—IBM, Microsoft, Intel—and piecemealed the time out, selling three-minute spots for $7,500 each. For the $7,500, I'd interview a representative of the computer company about their product. Once again, the spots would look like regular programming, with the added extra of being shot in a slick, hip, MTV style. Even though the show was basically a series of glorified ads, the show allowed computer companies to virtually go door-to-door to promote their products through the medium of television.

The essence of *The Computer Man* was to force the big boys of the computer industry to talk in layman's terms about their new products. If they got too heavy, I'd tap my "No Nerds" coffee cup and rein them in. For their $7,500 they could reach a national audience that would cost ten times as much to reach through conventional advertising. Because the dollars were small enough, the computer companies were willing to take a chance. We were also the only game in town; computer shows were practically nonexistent at the time. Once IBM signed on, we were home free. After the first thirteen weeks, we had not only covered our $227,000 commitment, we had made $100,000!

In January 1994, determined to get syndicated at the NATPE television programmer's convention, we moved our base of operations back to Dallas and launched *Bunting's Window,* a show designed to give viewers a "window" on the world of computers.

What a difference twelve months of perseverance makes. I spent my first NATPE convention like an outcast. But now people were approaching me! Representatives from United Airlines, who had seen my CNBC show, wanted to buy those shows for their in-flight television network.

Once again I acted from the entrepreneur's, instead of the employee's, mind-set:

"Instead of you buying these shows as they exist today, why don't you do what CNBC does? Sell me time up on your airliner."

I knew I could go back to all of the same computer companies advertising on my CNBC show and sell time to them on the United Airlines show. We struck a deal and started producing a sponsored editorial show on United Airlines called *Bunting's Window.* The lesson? Multiply yourself to the nth degree, and always think like an entrepreneur, never an employee.

Whereas three-minute segments on CNBC cost $7,500, a three-minute segment on United Airlines' in-flight television—seen by millions of passengers—cost the advertiser $35,000. All of a sudden, Tom and I were doing *hundreds of thousands of dollars'* worth of business every month. Our whole company changed rather dramatically. We had to go out and hire a significant staff to keep pace. The United Airlines show was going well. The CNBC show was not only being picked up in practically every market in the country, it was the highest-rated show on the CNBC Sunday lineup. And our syndicated series, *The Computer Man,* was a rising star on one hundred TV stations.

Suddenly, I was thrust into the media spotlight, with appearances on the *Today* show, *First Person with Maria Shriver,* and a host of local and regional news broadcasts. Microsoft asked me to be their spokesman for one of their new product tours. I began to get hired for speaking engagements. I was even offered the host jobs on mainstream television shows like *Hollywood Squares, Talk Soup,* and even *The Gong Show.* But I was too busy with my technology crusade even to think about doing entertainment television.

Talk about the power of a dream! I called myself the Computer Man —and thought of myself as such—and pretty soon everyone else is calling me the Computer Man, too. It became a self-fulfilling prophecy.

By the fall of 1994, a scant three years after I'd quit my JOB, my little home-based, computer-driven company was doing $3 million a year in business. My success was not a miracle. It was not a genie's reward or a lottery windfall. My success was the end result of one good idea backed by faith and coupled with persistence, forces that every person has the ability to access.

Ideas, faith, persistence, and passion—these are the ingredients that form virtual power. They will override skill sets every time. They will override the lack of proper financing. They will override the absence of a detailed business plan. If you've really got the drive to make something happen, and will stick to it and see it through, you will be successful in your missions.

> *Life is either a daring adventure or nothing. Security does not exist in nature, nor do the children or men as a whole experience it. Avoiding danger is no safer in the long run than exposure.*
>
> *—Helen Keller*

That is how I came to glimpse the heart of the Brave New World. Since we were charging computer companies $35,000 for three-minute *Bunting's Window* segments, we thought that we should go into the field and allow our advertisers to speak about their products in their element. Simultaneously I was on the road with my syndicated *Computer Man* series, which was a "location" show.

We came up with an idea, *Fifty States in Fifty Weeks.* Every week we'd broadcast from a different location, showing viewers the latest in cool hardware and software and some of the sights and sounds of that city. At the same time, we'd try to find a home-based business story from the area, making *The Computer Man* a celebration of everything you can do with a personal computer.

My dream of becoming the Bob Vila of computers had come true.

Once again, almost as a reward, a new window opened in my consciousness. I could see the front lines of the home-based business revolution. I went to Phoenix and flew on a motorized hang glider, whose owner founded a hang glider school from his one-computer home office in the back of the hangar. I watched the producer of the Joffrey Ballet in Manhattan design choreography via videoconferencing with a home-based choreographer in Paris through the miracle of a computer modem. I visited a home-based business on the rough side of urban Chicago, where a single mother, sick of the corporate treadmill, created a desktop publishing business and united a network of one hundred other desktop publishers into a vital association. I met home-based car dealers who buy and sell exotic, high-dollar sports cars over the Internet. I witnessed a home-based entrepreneur's computer program that can "morph" the human face and show how you'll look thirty years in the future, technology that can help identify children missing for long periods. I visited a tropical fish farm in the Florida Everglades where three refugees from the nine-to-five are keeping track of an inventory of millions of brightly colored fish on a computer in their spare bedroom. I met one of the world's largest wholesale florists in Maui and walked through the mist of his flower-packed refrigerated storage units, as he told me the improbable tale of how he started his home-based business after becoming dissatisfied with the conventional floral concerns that had once enslaved him.

I stared into the heart of the home-based business revolution, and I was floored. I saw absolutely empowered men and women who had pulled in the reins on their destinies and were living their dreams.

Once again I was knocking on doors, and once again the doors were opening. But now my customers could see more than one computer on a living room floor. Now they could actually grasp the infinite possibilities of the frontier beyond the screen. Now they had visual proof that computer power is not reserved for the top 2 percent of the graduating high school class.

But it was just the beginning. I soon discovered that computer power is not restricted to transforming people's careers, but affects myriad other aspects of their beings. Let me take you now into the lives of men and women who accessed and wielded virtual power to rediscover their own self-worth, take control of their personal lives, and even meet their mates in the amazing window of the personal computer.

CHAPTER SIX

The Human Connection

Tracee Townsend calls it "a miracle by modem," a testament to the power of love on-line. If this sounds a bit like the start of a soap opera, well, go ahead and call it "Ryan's Hope." It all began last spring in a little corner of America Online called the Romance Connection, when a man named Ryan posted a note about his desire for companionship, marriage, and, eventually, a family.

"It got one response. Mine!" says Tracee, a 27-year-old first-grade teacher from Mobile, Alabama. "I had never answered anything like this before, but I'm sure glad I did. We had both given up on ever finding someone to share our lives, but he's the man I've been looking for all my life. It's all still a little unbelievable to me, but we are going to live happily ever after!"

Electronic personal ads are hot, especially on America Online and Prodigy, two of the biggest commercial on-line services. Global, instant, and discreet, cyberspace love notes put a fun new spin on the dating game. The same modem connection that lets you post personal ads works just as well for electronic love letters and even a "virtual first date."

"Ryan and I communicated [by electronic mail] for three weeks or so, then chatted in a private room," says Tracee, referring to electronic conference areas where couples can trade private messages in real time. "During our second chat, Ryan proposed. We continued to chat each evening for a week, and sent each other photos [by regular mail]. Then we began talking on the phone about meeting in person."

Within six weeks, Ryan Townsend, 31, closed his small software business in Carthage, Miss., packed all his belongings, and drove four hours to Mobile to meet Tracee and her family face to face for the very first time. They were married the very next morning in her parents' home.

"It was the ultimate blind date," Tracee quips. She knows many in her family were "still in shock" at the suddenness of her marriage to someone she had known for such a short time. However, Tracee vouches for the intimacy of intense on-line communication by saying that when she and Ryan finally met face to face, "I already knew him and loved him. I just hadn't held his hand yet."

—*Charles Bowen,*
Home PC *magazine*

Let's talk about love. Let's talk about companionship. Let's talk about communication, support, relationships, getting through today, and enjoying a happily-ever-after tomorrow. Let's talk about how we can reach out to others and, in the process, find ourselves through that box that's forever waiting patiently upon our desks, a box of bits and bytes that can become your most important window to the outside world.

"Okay, Mark, enough!" the skeptical among you are undoubtedly saying. "A computer is not a nurse, a psychologist, a matchmaker, a dating agency, a shoulder to cry on, a friend in need!"

But the computer can become all of this and much, much more. The only thing that holds back its power is your own reticence. So cleanse your mind of negativity! Erase from your thoughts the idea of being absolutely alone! Forget about the scary, solitary specter of seeking fellowship in a bar full of strangers. The age of computer relationships has arrived, and it runs the spectrum from casual conversations to vital information networks to finding the love of your life. Extreme caution must be exercised. But wonders can—and do—happen.

Whether you're seeking advice, counseling, or companionship, entering this new cybercommunity requires four ingredients: a computer, a modem, a service provider, and a willingness to explore. I believe that one of the main reasons the on-line communication services like America Online, Prodigy, and CompuServe have flourished has been because, or as a result, of opening the floodgates for interpersonal communications. This is done in several ways: on-line personal ads, which resemble newspaper personal ads, except that the respondent answers the ad by e-mail; discussion forums, where you can find people interested in a vast variety of subjects merely by entering forums about those subjects; and, the most popular, "chat" rooms, where two or more users exchange ideas via lines of written text, creating a virtual conversation.

Getting started is as simple as connecting to America Online's Romance Connection (which offers options on meeting people by age, geographic location, and common interests) or Prodigy's Online Personals (where you can browse seekers' ads by area code, read their eighty-word ad, then click on a box that dials a 900-number where you can hear the advertiser's voice before responding). You won't have any trouble finding prospects; America Online's Romance Connection routinely lists thirty-five thousand messages. Once you've met someone you'd like to get to know better, you can join that person in a private chat room, where things begin to get deeper.

Chat rooms are a great place where you can meet other people and talk about common subjects and ideas and actually find the community of people who have similar profiles, or at least similar interests. Romance is probably at the top of these interests, and the romance-based chat rooms are, of course, infamous, attracting everyone from millions of lonely-hearts to the famous conservative broadcaster Rush Limbaugh, who met his current wife on CompuServe.

Romance is perhaps the fastest-growing on-line marketplace. But it's not the only communications avenue available. The computer is also becoming a vital hot line of communication among people who are dealing with the ill, injured, and disabled.

Let's say you're caring for a relative with Alzheimer's or a friend with AIDS or some other illness. In days past, you'd likely be stuck alone at home with your loved ones, sometimes with only their doctor and far-flung relatives for commiseration. Enter the age of the computer networks: hot lines where you can seek out help and advice, lifelines where you can pour out your emotions to people in similar circumstances.

In the area of Alzheimer's, the two hundred-member Alzheimer's hot line is a place caregivers congregate to share ideas, seek help, and generally commiserate.

The May 1996 issue of *Wired* magazine illustrated how emotional first aid is traded on these hot lines through a computer-illiterate woman named Sally. She had been loaned a computer terminal by a social worker after awakening one midnight to find her Alzheimer's-suffering, two hundred-pound husband towering over her, holding a knife. The husband was, of course, oblivious and couldn't even remember the incident the next morning. Absolutely alone and terrified, Sally was *desperate* for help. The social worker had told her that all she had to do was press the F1 key on the keyboard and the computer would log on to Cleveland Free-Net and the Alzheimer's hot line. "Within seconds, she was connected to a whole world of people just like her, wives and husbands and daughters who were caring for relatives with Alzheimer's disease," reported Michelle Slatalla.

Late one night Sally punched the F1 key and began typing words that came straight from her heart to a fellow caregiver named Linus.

The e-mail correspondence is reprinted in the *Wired* magazine story:

> Ed is getting harder and harder to handle physically and emotionally as the temper tantrums are getting worse, and I could do without all the name-calling. . . . I know the time is coming when I will have to have him in a nursing facility but I dread thinking about it. . . . Linus—HELP ME.[1]

At the other end of the country, Linus Gottas, seventy-three, who had put his wife, Ruth, in a nursing home in 1989, read Sally's message and immediately responded:

> Reading your various messages two things stand out real strong to me—your sense of humor

[1] *Wired,* May 1996, both this quote and the one following from Linus.

> and your LOVE for Ed. . . . With me I didn't have the luxury of the hospital making the decision for me. She went from our home to the NH [nursing home]. This was positively the most difficult and heartwrenching decision I ever made. . . . I went ''to pieces''—fell apart at the seams. As I look back . . . I am more and more convinced that the decision I made was the best for Ruth and me. . . . She's getting more care than I was able to give her at home. Linus.

Who among us isn't going to come to this crossroads in our lives? The decision of whether or not to put a parent or spouse in a nursing home is one of the most wrenching we'll ever make. Having someone to turn to makes a tremendous difference.

But it became a decision Sally never had to face. One morning she sat down at her computer, alerting the loved ones of other Alzheimer's sufferers words that showed how important their association had become:

> ''Ed died at 3:00 this morning, and you are the first people I'm notifying.''

Sally's computer had transcended its conventional role as a business tool and become an integral part of her life. For Sally and hundreds of people just like her, the Alzheimer's hot line became such a powerful source of strength and support that it won the 1995 National Infrastructure Award, exemplifying "what it means to live in a network society," said one of the judges. Some users endure two hours of busy signals just to log on. That's how important this network has become.

Imagine the potential of similar computer networks. Whatever struggle you're facing, there is power in connecting with others in similar straits. These networks provide emotional first aid, a clothesline of camaraderie, and support that users can ferry back and forth, from house to house, from life to life.

That is the essence of the burgeoning cybercommunity: a world where nobody ever has to be alone. It's the same technological power, with just a slightly different application, that we discussed earlier in my father-in-law's Internet search to find information about opening a driving range. How would he have found that information in days past? It's awfully specialized, but we found a wealth of resources at our fingertips.

Where else can you turn these days for support? Do you stand out on the street corner and start shouting, "Does anybody who is driving by here happen to know anything about opening driving ranges?"

Of course not. It's the same for more grievous situations, when the day arrives that you'll be caring for a terminally ill relative. Where can you find a support group? Where do you find other people who have the same sorts of problems and issues to deal with? Before, you'd have to drive back and forth to support group meetings, piling more work onto your already heavy daily burden and leaving your loved one at home alone. Computer support groups afford you twenty-four-hour access from the comfort of your own home. They allow you to erase the boundaries of time and place and to commune with others.

We have become a world of isolated citizens who don't even know our next-door neighbors. The computer can bring us together. Whether you're dealing with Alzheimer's, AIDS, or a host of other afflictions, the potential of having a lifeline with others suffering the same trials is, to me, the essence of virtual power.

It's nice to know that help will be waiting at the other end of the modem if we ever find ourselves in the trying situations described above. But the miracles of the computer aren't reserved for those caring for the sick.

The computer also serves those who seek to help themselves.

Consider an e-mail message I received from a man who calls himself Shock:

> I was in the midst of a nasty divorce. I had way too much time on my hands and I needed to fill every minute, lest I get all self-pitying. The divorce was on my mind. I needed to occupy myself, so I didn't dwell on it. I was falling into the ''poor little me'' sit-at-home-dwelling-on-my-problems kind of fool.

He was a Las Vegas paramedic with a broken heart. When his wife left him, his world ended. With too much idle time on his hands, he retreated inward: stressing out and surrendering to loneliness. He was absolutely unsure of his future, when, for a diversion, he sat at the keyboard of a computer at work, and a new world opened before him.

He was a computer illiterate, but that didn't stop the young man whose on-line name is Shock. He taught himself to use that computer and, through that teaching, took a giant leap into the Brave New World.

> I knew that I had to get over being computer illiterate. I learned the computer myself. No manual, no classes. I had a *lot* of time on my hands, so I sat down at the computer at work and learned it, from the bottom to the top. The rewards came slowly, not like magic, no ''Poof!'' But, one day, it was just there.

"It" was Shock's new life. The magic was his change of focus. One day, after months of self-lessons at the computer, he looked up and his emotional clouds had lifted. His focus had shifted, from his internal sorrow to the computer screen, and that simple switch meant the difference between misery and salvation.

> It began with a recognition that every song on the radio didn't hurt any more. It came with the recognition that each car that looked like hers didn't jog painful memories. It was like a stampede that ended.

How many millions have been in this stage of their lives: heartbroken, time on their hands, going nowhere? Once, you turned to family, friends, a psychiatrist.

Now, you turn to the box.

> The computer became the vehicle for change. I wish I could say it was by design. But it wasn't. It just happened. I chose to learn the computer, true. But the choice was solely to fill my time. What the computer did for me,

however, was to become a dot on the horizon, my new focus, my new destiny. I picked up some marketable skills along the way. But the trip was the journey. The trip was the focus.

The computer allowed him to "get out of my own head," Shock says. It provided him with something to look forward to, instead of constantly looking back on his broken marriage. It gave him a place to heal.

Shock not only healed; he was reborn. His computer experience won him two promotions at work. Now, as a middle manager, he handles practically every aspect of his job by computer. He is developing cutting-edge computer programs for his employer. His pay has doubled since his divorce. At home, he communicates around the globe through his modem. Best of all, he got remarried. For his honeymoon, he connected with America Online, chatting with locals in the places he wanted to visit and discovering the inside scoop on sightseeing, museums, special events, and most astonishing sunrises.

Ain't life grand?

Life can be whatever we make it.

In the same way that the computer can hook you up to worlds of information for reference, entertainment, news, and emotional help in trying times, it can also be the vehicle to transport you into your new personal life.

I'm talking about love here, about romance, about the burgeoning, frequently crazy world of "chat" rooms, where, it seems, the world is on-line. Every computer user knows that many of these chat rooms are sexual in nature, and I'll leave that for your own exploration. But we cannot dismiss the entire medium as a stadium of blue banter. There is gold on those chat lines, merely because they offer a chance to meet others.

This is a power that should not be ignored, because when you look at people's number one need, outside of food and shelter, it's communion with others, fellowship with others, the attraction and the love of other people.

Let me show you where all of this is happening on-line through the love story of Carole and Bill.

```
  [Carole:] This is a short story about how two
people who lived three thousand miles apart
from each other met and fell in love. There
were two ingredients that were needed to
complete this task. One was a computer and a
modem, and the other was Prodigy, the first
computer networking service.
  This is the way Bill and I met.
```

This is no country club dance. The romance-based on-line chat rooms are cabins of craziness and absurdity, a world where you frequently must conversationally kiss a lot of frogs before you can meet a prince or princess. But for the multitudes who have struggled through cocktail hours and late nights in bars, it's not such a bad alternative.

I know a smart, successful, perfectly attractive woman who is a marketing director for a major company in New York City. She's thirty-five years old, and she's single. She travels twenty days a month. She has been on the fast track for quite some time, and like many people, she's reached the point in her life where she would like to find a potential spouse. The problem is finding the time to go through the arcane world of dating to find that person. She hates bars! She dreads singles groups! She cannot fathom blind dates!

So she turned to the Internet. As she travels around the country, she camps out in chat rooms whose members live in the cities where she's headed. Initially she did this just out of curiosity, to find restaurants and interesting places to visit. Then she turned her efforts to actually trying to meet people for the purpose of dates.

My friend has a very strict criteria. She wants a man in his mid- to late thirties who is, like herself, an extremely driven professional. She wants someone who's interested in having a family immediately. Although she isn't obsessed with physical features, there are certain aspects that she would ideally like to find.

Try advertising these specifications in a bar. You would be laughed out of the saloon! But in the chat rooms you can state your expectations explicitly. So when my friend travels to, say, Seattle, she'll jump on the romance connections on either America Online, Prodigy, or CompuServe a couple of weeks in advance and have an opportunity to find gentlemen who meet her criteria—or get close to meeting that criteria—and chat back and forth. When she finds someone particularly interesting, she'll up the ante with a telephone conversation. At this point, things get *very* detailed. If she's still interested, they'll meet for coffee or a dinner date, always meeting in a public place, always taking separate cars, always using caution.

My friend's been on this search now for a little over a year, and while she hasn't found Mr. Right, she has developed some long-term relationships with several nice gentlemen with whom she can pass an evening when she returns to those cities. This is a woman who doesn't have the time or the desire to be floating around a Seattle bar as an out-of-town businesswoman, trying to meet people. Most of the people she would meet in that setting certainly would not meet her strict criteria anyway.

But here is a way for her to accomplish her goals.

Men are much more aggressive when it comes to finding mates and relationships and encounters on the computer. I've found that the bulk of people on the chat services are men, but they do not own the medium. My friend is a great example of someone who can really use the power of technology to help fill a void in her life.

Still have doubts? Well, let's return to the story of Bill and Carole, proof that computer chat rooms can become more than a night of blue banter or a one-night stand for two people at opposite ends of America. Let me show you how the computer can become a place where people find their soul mates and live happily ever after.

[Carole:] I was employed part-time with the Department of Motor Vehicles and also worked as a substitute teacher in Southern California. A close friend of mine moved out of town and suggested that I sign up with Prodigy to keep in touch through e-mail.

I had been on Prodigy for four days—just generally looking around—when I noticed a posting about video poker on one of the bulletin boards, where people post messages about their interests, inviting others to send them e-mails back or post a reply on the electronic bulletin board. I love video poker. I'd spent literally hundreds of hours researching and playing it, so I thought, Why not respond?

My response ended up being a six-page note describing how I play the game. Bill, who identified himself as a chef in the Northeast, was one of many people who wrote me back. The date of our first e-mail was December 2.

We started writing back and forth until Christmas, when Bill left on a two-week vacation. I had some e-mail waiting for him when he returned home. Bill immediately wrote back. Somehow, from his writing I just felt he was an honest, sincere person. From that point on, every night we wrote back and forth to each other. As we discussed things, we realized how much we had in common, how much we liked one another. He just seemed so sincere in the beginning. Later, I began to notice an incredibly romantic side. We spoke about so many things! A trust began to grow between us. Both of us had experienced bad relationships in the past. It was a common thread that drew us together.

If you want to draw close to someone over a computer, you have to rid yourself of a lot of excess baggage, then start from scratch. No game playing; sincerity is a must, plus honesty and trust. The words written by the other person must be truthful or it's a disaster from the word ''go.'' You know nothing about each other except what they spell out to you.

Living on opposite coasts, they were two ships in the night. But out of the several million Prodigy users, they collided through their common interest in video poker. They came to the table with nothing but their minds. They didn't have to dress up for a date, to play the games and corny come-ons of cocktail conversation, to engage in the mating dance of twenty-first-century romance. Their hearts were full of possibilities; their words, black type on a white screen, had taken on a life of their own.

What a difference it was from the conventional singles marketplace, where you frequently endure months of superficiality before you get even a clue of what's really inside.

On the computer you start with what counts the most—the other person's mind. As Bill and Carole's cyber-romance shows us, it's a person's words that matter most over the computer. If Bill and Carole had met in a crowded bar or restaurant, perhaps they wouldn't have given each other a second glance. The physical would have meant everything, perhaps preventing a perfect match of minds.

On the computer, however, the exact opposite occurs. You discover what's happening on the *inside* first. When you do that, one of two things happen: first, what's on the outside doesn't matter, and it really shouldn't anyway; second, the other person's physical appearance might be what you've been searching for as well. When both things click—and, believe me, I've heard of countless cases where they do —then you can skip haunting smoky bars and restaurants and singles groups. You'll have discovered your soul mate on-line.

Within a few days on-line, Bill and Carole had acquired a voice, a voice as strong as if they were in the same room. By typing out their beliefs, desires, thoughts, and dreams, they got to the "core" of each other, faster and easier than they ever could have if they'd met in person. They created an intimacy level, without the pressure of face-to-face, without the first-date butterflies, without the superficial mating dance that modern-day romance has become. They knew each other's *minds* before they met face-to-face—instead of the other way around.

They had become best friends.

[Bill:] After you talk to someone for a period of time, you really get to know their character. Over the first three months, Carole and I spoke on-line about just about everything. Thousands of pages were e-mailed back and forth. Funny, when you're sitting next to someone, you're not always talking to them. But when you're in a computer relationship, you *have* to talk to the other person. We learned about how we dealt with our emotions, with money, with families, everything. I learned very quickly that Carole had almost all of the same ideas and values as I did.

Whenever we wrote, Carole and I were totally honest with each other. I think that's the most important part of any kind of relationship. You can find love over the computer; you just have to be patient about it. You have to wait for someone decent to come along.

Then, one night, the conversation turned serious. Carole started telling Bill one of her personal fantasies, and Bill started getting intimate back. They won't divulge the exact fantasy, but it must've been a pretty good one. Next thing they knew, they had exchanged phone numbers and were stacking up $400 monthly phone bills. "On the few short months that we had our long-distance romance, I learned more about Carole than I knew about a woman I went out with for *ten* years," says Bill.

They knew they had something special together—so special that when they finally arranged to meet for a weekend in Las Vegas, it was something magical, something straight out of the movies.

[Carole:] March 12, 1992, was the date we met. Our planes were scheduled to arrive in Las Vegas ten minutes apart. We were both more than a little scared meeting for the first time. Bill was a candidate for a heart attack, and I wasn't much better.

After we landed, we couldn't find each other for the first forty minutes. We paged each other back and forth, and finally, there we stood, eye to eye, across the concourse. Bill looked just like he did in his pictures. But there in the airport, staring at someone you've spent hundreds of hours with, we were both suddenly tongue-tied.

I think I mumbled a weak, ''Hello,'' further proof that an in-person introduction is inferior to the depth and power of meeting first via the computer.

I walked over to Bill and gave him a quick kiss.

He got his luggage and we walked out the door toward the best four days of our lives. After we got over some initial anxiety, everything was perfect. We were both on cloud 9. Not only did we find out that we were crazy about one another, we also came home winners at the gambling tables. It was very sad when we had to say good-bye. We were both crying. But, by then, we had already exchanged friendship rings.

It's no surprise that this powerful tool of information technology is being put to work to solve man's most basic fundamental need outside of food and shelter. The wonder is why it's taken so long to be accepted. Does it really matter that people like Bill and Carole met in somewhat unusual circumstances, as long they found that measure of happiness together? I think we would all agree the answer is no.

But marriage by modem? That may seem like a major leap. Still, it's not really so revolutionary. Turn on the midafternoon talk shows and you'll see infinite couples who got married after meeting on-line. It's gone from being an oddball phenomena to a common occurrence. While most people aren't actually walking down the aisles together, they're at least bonding in cyberspace, where people can meet each other in the security of their own homes.

Now, many of you will immediately think that's a weird way to meet people. But what's so sane about the archaic mating dance of seeking out strangers in a smoke-filled bar or restaurant, where physical presentation means life or death? We all are not graced with physical perfection. So where is the logic of turning the most important meeting of your life into a beauty contest?

On the computer, you're a personality *first.* Everything depends on the way you communicate. The fear of rejection eases. I'm not saying that meeting others on the Internet is a perfect system. There are predators—liars, impostors, con artists, one-night-stand shysters, and worse—on-line, just as there are in that smoke-filled bar. The difference here is you can get to know someone on-line first—sometimes for months, sometimes for years, sometimes even for decades—before you meet them face-to-face. It just makes it that much easier to weed out pros from cons. You can ask intimate questions over the computer in a way you never could in a bar or at a party, where serendipity is key.

I'm not suggesting that all romance should be cyber-based, no matter the technological advances. This is simply a tool to find people with the same interests you have, someone with whom you might want to hold a conversation and, perhaps, even get to know better. Here is a much easier, faster, safer way for you to make initial contact with people.

Bill and Carole were married within three months after their trip to Las Vegas. Carole packed her bags and moved across the country to Bill's home in Connecticut and discovered that their on-line synchronization was no fluke: they complemented each other perfectly. They were such a model of harmony, and so dedicated to the potential of meeting on-line, that they took over the Prodigy's Singles Bulletin Board and Personal Connection interest groups, overseeing the big, sprawling world of matchmaking in cyberspace.

> We've had close to seventy success stories of people who met [on-line] and either got engaged or got married. This is proof that this is a vital way to meet people. Bill and I think it's the best way. If you don't believe it, try it or contact us via e-mail at Personal_Connection@Prodigy.com, and we'll tell you more about it.

Their story is only a hint of things to come. In the not-too-distant future, meeting on-line will become routine. When videoconferencing becomes a standard feature in most households—and that day is just around the corner—then an explosion is going to occur. Chat rooms are going to go from being text-based to video-based, and your cybercommunity will become as familiar as the characters on your favorite TV shows.

Only now *you'll* be playing the major role.

Your computer screen will be carved up into windowpanes, and there might be sixteen boxes on your screen, with sixteen different video feeds. You'll actually be talking to fifteen other people on-line, with both video and sound. Everyone will see each other's faces, gestures, and expressions.

The day of the "cyberbar" will have arrived.

From the convenience and safety of your own home, you'll be able to enter one of many local interest groups. Maybe you'll drop in to find vital information. Maybe you'll be seeking camaraderie. Maybe you'll be searching for the love of your life. Whatever you seek, the computer will help you find it.

We have used technology to solve many of mankind's basic needs. Now we're on the brink of using technology to solve what I would argue would be next in that food chain of basic human need: human companionship.

> [Carole:] Since I've gotten on-line, I've discovered a world of very lonely people who want to find their soul mate—or just friend, companion, or pen pal—so badly they can taste it.

Now celebrating their fourth anniversary, Bill and Carole are testament to the power of love blooming on-line. But they add one note of warning: Use caution.

Do not walk into this garden blindly.

"Before you even *think* of meeting someone face-to-face, ask for their real name, address, telephone number, their place of employment, even their driver's license number," says Carole. "It may seem extreme, but you can't be too careful. There are lots of crazy people out there. Make sure you know the person is real before you agree to meet them. And when you meet them, do it at a public place. Drive your own car and insist that they do the same."

Then, buckle up your seat belts. It's a Brave New World out there. Love can, and does, bloom on-line—because a computer offers people not only a place to find potential mates, but also a place to rediscover their souls.

If you have any doubts, just listen to the amazing story of Marietta, which she related to me via e-mail:

> In my real life, the loneliness seeped in at every turn. I'd been married for all of these years, but never really had a partner. The sleeping alone got to me. Not just sleeping alone, but walking alone. Everywhere I went, I went alone. I saw others holding hands, being close. My husband traveled in his job, so when he was home he refused to go anywhere. So year after year, I went everywhere alone. After my divorce, I couldn't go to movies. I didn't go to dances. I just hurt to see people holding each other and kissing. The computer was another way of escaping from that.

She was a middle-aged woman with every conceivable problem: angry, divorced, depressed, rural, isolated, with a trio of fast-growing children, her mother and a few close friends as her only support group. Clamping a locked jaw on her emotions, she walked around in a state of constant rage. The "before" picture is horrendous. The prescription? Computer and Internet. Result? A cyber-renaissance.

Let's examine Marietta's amazing reawakening, the saga of a woman who dramatically awakened her life on-line. Now she takes daily journeys of the imagination and spirit. Her computer is her time machine, transporting her across continents, across fears, across endless plains of loneliness and pain.

Her rebirth began in late 1995.

> I always used computers in my work as a bookkeeper and as an accountant. But it wasn't until I got the first Macintosh that came out that I discovered it was more than a tool. The Mac had a personality. It was an extension of me.

She got on-line in 1995 and followed her curiosity into one of the chat rooms on an on-line communications service called eWorld. She had come to the right place at the right time. She was getting a divorce. Her husband had sought solace from their friends from high school, including several women Marietta thought were her best girlfriends. The Christmas holidays were approaching, and it was going to be rock-candy hard; there was no joy in either Marietta's home or her heart.

> I wouldn't fight him for my friends. I just walked away from it to save them from having to choose. My mother gave up on her last attempt to reconcile our family differences, and together we had our first holidays with nobody. My ex-husband went to our friends' party. It was shattering. . . . The divorce was over, my family was gone, my friends had deserted me.

On one cold, lonely September Sunday, with her kids away for the weekend and her house quiet, Marietta sat at her computer and entered a chat room. One name kept popping up, asking her questions, leading her into increasingly lively correspondence. His name was Bobby and he was a Los Angeles screenwriter. He couldn't see the woman at the other end of the computer screen; all he knew was a line of her words, words that became a lifeline leading to Marietta's rebirth.

> We had the best times acting out sitcom silliness. I came on so strong. I didn't tolerate any abuse against myself or anybody else. My anger was let out. Bobby was so funny! I laughed until I cried. On-line is just minds connecting. No interference, no body language to affect the impression. It allows the imagination to create much more. Wonderful, funny, tragic things. Bobby and I compared our feelings about ourselves. I'm very intelligent. I have a great brain. But I don't express it well in real life. Maybe it's the people I

```
associate with, or the depression I had
suffered, or the hurt. With Bobby, I let loose.
It was a wonderful boost to me.
```

How many people are imprisoned in similar situations? Here's a bright, intellectually stimulating, absolutely incredible woman who never felt comfortable showing the best parts of herself to others. So for half her life her obviously very vibrant, radiant side was kept hidden away. All because she was trapped in a severely oppressing, dysfunctional relationship.

Where did she have to turn?

It's not easy to leave your abusive spouse on the ranch and run into town and strike up relationships at the feed store, the diner, or the saloon. How could she interact with others without fear of embarrassment or retribution?

Going to town, when the town is tiny, is just not a viable alternative.

On the computer, the town is the world. You are immediately interacting with people you would never meet in the constraints of Small Town, U.S.A. These people know you only by what you choose to reveal to them on the computer screen. There is a comfort level that comes with that, especially for someone just emerging from the shell, like Marietta. You can connect with people who don't judge you by your appearance, people who simply enjoy the communication and the communion of being on-line and sharing ideas, jokes, craziness, *everything*. . . . It gives individuals a chance to flourish, to take their lives to a higher level.

Marietta's story is testament to this power. She had a tremendous amount of pent-up energy, many gifts and much to share, things that had become bottled up inside of her. Certainly her abusive spouse played a large role in that. With the touch of a keyboard, she became connected to the Brave New World.

Marietta and Bobby became something of a legend on-line. They acted out sitcom scenarios, line by line—scenarios so funny that they became legend. Their respective families would pull up chairs to watch their chats. The correspondence was so hilarious that nobody dared to leave, even to go to the rest room, afraid they'd miss something crucial to the on-line scenario.

Marietta's on-screen persona began to spill over into her real life.

Her mood of supressed anger was soon replaced with a lighter, funnier, far more energetic soul.

> Sometimes I'd be driving down the street and think of some silliness from on-line and burst out in laughter. I started seeing all of this nonsense in my real life as total nonsense. The thing with my ex and my girlfriends, well, I finally thought how stupid it was. Both that he would pull that and that they would fall for it!

Things came to a head one day when Marietta's big, burly, three hundred-pound, six-foot-two-inch "ex" came over to visit the kids and found his ex-wife—what?—happy, laughing, having a wonderful time! He was shocked to find her staring into a computer screen; he couldn't understand what was going on—except he didn't like it. His ex was supposed to be miserable, a plain Jane. *He* was the one destined for fun and laughs!

Enraged, he began screaming at her, waving his hands wildly as if he were going to explode. Five-foot-four-inch Marietta always froze at the sound of her husband's voice. But that voice couldn't get to her now. Now something "clicked" within her and that voice suddenly sounded like a character out of one of her own on-line comedy sitcoms.

> He told me I had no friends, that nobody liked me. But instead of getting upset, I broke into laughter. The more he screamed and yelled, the more I rolled in laughter, tears streaming down my face, holding my sides. He was suddenly a character out of a sitcom! He told me I had no friends, that nobody liked me, that I was useless as a human being. But I had opened my own chat room on-line. I had about 150 people on my room list. I knew he was describing himself. We on-liners say that we know when our lives have changed: when we laugh at seemingly

inappropriate times, when we see the silliness in serious situations.

At this instance, something incredible happened. Marietta knew that she had broken free, escaped her past, and embarked upon a brave new future.

I found my voice. I discovered intelligent, wonderful people on-line and that I'm as intelligent as they are. In real life, I quit tolerating rudeness, quit worrying that what I said would make people dislike me. So just as I popped off uninhibited on-line, I popped off uninhibited in real life. And people respected me for it. I just felt release, both from the anger and from the laughter that had been held up inside of me.

Within the incredibly short span of six months, she became an on-line celebrity, the star of her own chat room, which eventually attracted hundreds of participants. She created "events" on-line: a wedding, a pregnancy, a baby shower, a birth. Her fame grew. She started an e-mail "newspaper" to which she and her friends contribute, chronicling their escapades and their personal growth on-line.

Her real life grew apace with her on-line persona. Finally she held a face-to-face party on her ranch for all of her cyberfriends. They talked and laughed and partied. There was an art professor, a doctor/scientist/psychologist, two teachers—from all over Texas. Then, in later events, celebrants came from such far-flung locales as California, Oklahoma, Nebraska, Florida and Maryland. Now, with a laptop computer to send reports from the road and a camera to take pictures to send to her network along the way, Marietta's hosting retreats and parties with her cyberfriends across the U.S.

Now that she's healed her personal life, Marietta's ready to move forward, and has totally opened herself to love again.

The computer can change your life, extend your horizons, expand your knowledge, take your creativity and imagination into new realms. It can give you your voice, if you didn't have it before. It can improve your real-life relationships, bring your sense of humor back if you've lost it, give you a forum upon which to express your feelings and thoughts, and help you ''delete'' those who have harmed you. It's as easy as pushing the delete key on your computer. You just say, ''You hurt me. I believe that you will hurt me again. So you are now deleted from my life.''

On the other hand, I have met some incredible men with whom I have shared some wonderment and a bit of myself. They've each touched a different part of me or taught me something new about myself, or together we found something new in them. With each one I've learned a little more of who I am, where I want to go and what I have to offer. They've given me new dreams to dream. They've let me know I'm special just by wanting to be in my life. They are incredible and I have been truly blessed by their love, their passion and their continuing friendship.

For the still skeptical among you, I have a simple question: Which is better, to be cynical about the possibilities of meeting others in cyberspace or to at least get the chance? What have you really got to lose? Your loneliness? Your pain?

Every one of us has some imperfection that magnifies in our minds. On the computer you're completely free to express yourself, to be yourself, to really show who you are as an individual, without any of your exterior wrappings getting in the way. If you're a 225-pounder, your exterior isn't going to open any doors for you; it's going to close doors. Here's a chance to really show who you are as a person.

Dear Ann Landers: You have said that the Internet has disrupted relationships between couples and destroyed marriages. That is not the fault of the Internet. Those relationships were already in trouble. We still use the telephone, even though some people make obscene calls. Newspapers have a "personals" section, and people who post those ads are usually living just as much a fantasy life as are the Internet flirts. They're just as disappointed when Prince Charming turns out to be a frog, or the "girl of his dreams" is indisputably an idiot. But we still buy the paper. The Internet offers an opportunity to exchange ideas with people around the globe. . . . I find that most people are simply interested in being part of a larger community and nothing more. Please don't ascribe sinister motives to something that is basically human nature—K.G. in Birmingham, Alabama

Dear K.G.: You have made some valid points. . . . In fact, I just received this letter from the American Self-Help Clearinghouse, an excellent resource that provides listings of self-help groups of all kinds. Read on:

Dear Ann Landers: We wanted you and your readers to know that there are many supportive communities of people helping each other on the Internet. Now, over 1,000 different self-help groups are available online. There is support and information for abused women, alcoholics, those dealing with mental illness, parents of children with disabilities, smokers, diabetics, overeaters and those who have had lung transplants or those suffering from cardiac disease, spinal injury, stroke or deafness—the list is endless. The emotional support given by individuals who share the same kind of problem can be incalculable. . . .

I'm not suggesting that computer communication alone will break down all the barriers that block you from your dreams. But if it can become a first step, then that's valuable enough. Whether you're holding yourself back because of a weight problem or low self-esteem or unempowering relationships, this is your chance to break free, an equal opportunity forum to express your ideas, dreams, and fantasies.

Most important, it's a place where others will answer back.

CHAPTER SEVEN

The Five Secrets of Virtual Power

I've decided it all comes down to this basic thing. It used to be [that] work sucked, but there was an OK trade-off: You worked hard, but you got to go home sometimes. You got raises, promotions and a pension. But now businesses have taken away all those things and [have begun] playing this kind of confidence game. "Yeah, we want your loyalty and your best work, and by the way, we'd like you to work mandatory overtime. And what are you getting in return? Ummmm . . . T-shirts for everybody!" [Corporations no longer] have anything to trade for any of those things they're asking for. But people are creatures of habit, so they're playing along until they're actually downsized.

—*Scott Adams,*
Home Office Computing,
July 1996

It starts with a whisper and builds into a scream. It's something itching in the back of your brain, a general uneasiness that becomes a full-time preoccupation. If you analyze the feeling long enough, you will eventually focus upon the forces that have the ability to whisk you up in their whims and put everything you thought secure in your life into freefall. You think you're safe and, then, one day, you know you're not. Whether you're caught in a minor corporate reshuffling or a full-blown layoff, whenever you put your destiny into the hands of others you're never going to be in complete control of your destiny.

One day you'll look up and see some domineering he or she with the power to turn your dreams to dust.

I'm talking about bosses, bureaucracy, and the boredom of nine-to-five.

As we've discussed in previous chapters, an anticorporate revolution is spreading across America in this era of downsizing, inspiring legions of the dissatisfied, as well as the soon-to-be, to reexamine their belief in one stable job for life and one boss over all. When examined logically, the whole idea just doesn't make sense: to spend your life slaving for some monolithic corporation, represented by some ogre of a boss who has frequently risen to his or her position more by naked aggression or corporate attrition than by ability or knowledge.

In his best-selling book *The Dilbert Principle,* cartoonist-turned-author Scott Adams lambastes the traditional corporate promotion process as "the Evolution of Idiots" and describes the traditional Western world corporation as a house of horrors, full of "sadistic talking animals, troll-like accountants and employees turning into dishrags after the life force has been drained from their bodies. And yet the comment I hear most often is: That's just like my company."

You've come to a crucial part of this book. You've heard the story of my own computer-generated renaissance, as well as manifestos of home-based business revolutionaries. You've delved into the software of your brain to determine your goals and learned how to build a personal computer system to drive you toward your destiny. You've jumped on board the Internet and learned how to find human companionship on-line. Now the time has come for radical reinvention. How do you break free? How do you embark upon a new path when you can barely afford to continue on the path you're treading? You do it gradually, then suddenly. I wish I could sit down at your keyboard and show you personally. But until books are invented with modems—and I'm certain that day is coming—I can only show you through examples.

Just as a computer must have power before it can operate, virtual power is nothing until it is exercised. By employing the five secrets of virtual power, you can transform every aspect of your life.

Here are five secrets that can set you free.

1. Use Your Aggravation!

The Boss had spent a life in private schools, while the Employee had always attended public. The Boss was from the East Coast; the Employee was from the Southwest. The Boss knew fine wines and favored classical music; the Employee's drink of choice came from a can, his favorite music from a jukebox. He was a hardworking, fiercely dedicated Employee, eager to do whatever it took to exceed his sales quota and please that increasingly hard-to-please Boss. But the Boss was set more on personal career advancement than nurturing employee growth. No matter how well the Employee did, the Boss could always find something wrong, and that something was usually in the Employee's expense report.

Then, one day, the Employee raised the white flag of surrender. He had endured enough! He saw the ceiling and knew he'd never break through. Security be damned! The end was coming soon enough; why wait for the guillotine? So he walked into the Boss's office and delivered the news in two words:

"I quit."

He could say these words rationally, calmly, pleasantly, because he had already released his aggravation on a lunch with a favorite client the day before. After picking up that client, he'd driven him out to an airport, telling him the lunches were in brown paper bags in the backseat. Then the Employee and his client, an adventurous Aussie who'd always dreamed of flying in a helicopter, climbed into a $750-an-hour chopper and took a lunch-hour ride high above the Silicon Valley, a perch from which the Employee issued his Emancipation Proclamation:

No more corporate constraints on his future!

No more taking whatever is given in his life!

No more bosses, bureaucracy, or boredom!

Now, love is a wonderful force, inspiring incredible poetry, art, and music. But aggravation, disgust, and angst, when effectively employed, can be as empowering as rocket fuel. I know. Because that hellion in the helicopter was me.

The next day, after I'd formerly resigned from my JOB, calmly giving my reasons to my Boss, I left behind a final expense report almost as a manifesto, a $750 lunch on my expense report to show a client his dream and to launch myself formally from the corporate culture that had reined me in for so long.

That done, I used my aggravation—at the constraints of corporate culture, at the glass ceiling, at bosses more concerned with their own destinies than those of their employees—as fuel. I wanted never to return to another corporation again, and that kept me leaping obstacles that would have otherwise seemed insurmountable.

Everybody deserves a "take this job and shove it" moment at least once in their lives, a moment of Zen-like clarity when you can see your road stretching forward, leaving behind that Grinch of a boss who expected nothing less than your soul for a warm fuzzy lapel pin or a raise with pennies attached to the end.

But while the "take this job and shove it" moment is sweet, it's not the sweetest. That comes later, when you make your own technological transformation, harnessing the power of the computer to blaze a trail that makes that conventional boss-dictated office seem like a dot on some long-departed horizon.

Do not waste your angst! Let it fester unheeded and it will turn into cynicism, the poison of many a life and career. Recognize it, harness it, and use it to your advantage.

2. Never Say No to the Force!

He was the original Jedi knight, the young, blond, swashbuckling Luke Skywalker, who saved a galaxy far, far away. But in 1991 Mark Hamill was approaching forty, and at times it seemed that the Force had left him. Since completing *Return of the Jedi,* the third installment of the *Star Wars* trilogy, he had done mostly off-Broadway stage and TV work, a strong and steady career for an actor but nothing approaching the explosive trajectory he'd experienced as Luke Skywalker.

Then, in 1991 he entered the Brave New World of personal computing, a realm as astounding as the galaxy he'd conquered in *Star Wars.* By never saying "no" to the equally awesome "Force" of new technology, even though he had no idea how to use a computer himself, he became, according to *Entertainment Weekly* magazine, "a multimedia missionary."

Hamill had originally become introduced to computers firsthand in *Star Wars,* one of whose themes was the growing alliance between technology and humans. By showing that robots had become as ubiquitous as "used furniture," the movie correctly predicted that computers would become as commonplace as the couch or the easy chair. But while many of Mark Hamill's costars were robots, when his day on the set was done he returned to a totally nontechnological environment.

Hamill recently told me about his adventures in cyberspace:

> I guess it wasn't something that was part of my life. I don't know that I consciously thought about whether or not computers would become part of our future. I mean, you're acting in a scenario, which is a whole other universe. It's not even supposed to be related to ours. At the beginning of the first *Star Wars,* it said, ''A LONG TIME AGO . . .'' I had always been a fan of science fiction and fantasy. I'm a big stop-frame animation fan, and I read *Famous Monsters* and loved all of those things. I didn't consciously decide in my mind whether or not [computer technology] was going to be part of our future.

But he never said "No" to the Force of computer technology. After *Star Wars,* he did eight off-Broadway plays, where he discovered that even the theater had become computerized, that computers were running everything from the lights to the revolving stage. Still, Hamill didn't have a computer of his own at home, even though his three kids had been clicking away on *their* keyboards for years. Hamill was so computer illiterate, he was almost cyberphobic.

> There was a part of me that had doubts. It was like a fear of the unknown. I learned that once you investigate and explore and learn what you're talking about, your understanding becomes greater and your fear becomes less.

The personal computer eventually transformed his life, all because when the revolution began banging on his door, he didn't say "No." That willingness to explore eventually provided him with an amazing new avenue in his career, just as it can do for you. Like Hamill, you don't have to be a whiz on-line to become part of the burgeoning world of computer technology. Hidden worlds await you! New marketplaces are at your feet! All you have to do is say "Yes" to the Force of new technology.

If you need future proof, look how far the medium took Mark Hamill.

Through his agent, he was offered something called a CD-ROM game, entitled *Gabriel Knight. What?* Knowing nothing about the explosively growing CD-ROM industry, Hamill had to ask his kids to show him how a CD-ROM game worked. They had, of course, a vast library of games and were glad to oblige Dad. They slipped a CD in their computer slot and the screen came alive with the vivid images, music, and motion that have made CD-ROM games the fastest-growing segment of the video games market.

Hamill took the meeting. He was told the plot: his character, Christopher Blair, was battling toward the end of a twenty-year war with an alien race; the CD-ROM player joins Blair in battling the aliens to a win, loss, or draw in the war.

Hamill had already been doing more than a hundred voices on TV cartoons: the Joker on *The Adventures of Batman and Robin,* Dr. Jack on *Saturn 20/40,* Gargoyle on *The Hulk.* But he quickly realized that this job required more than a voice-over for computer-generated characters.

> Here you have this medium where you're asking the players themselves to become part screenwriter and part cast member, because they're inhabiting your character. That was totally unique. I felt, in a way, as actors must have felt when sound first came in.
>
> I thought the script was very sophisticated, very adult, in its tone. I did it, then promptly forgot about it. The first reaction I had was from someone who sent me a letter of

congratulations because the CD won an award at Best Games.

Then, another call came through his agent, an offer to "act" in a CD-ROM game produced by Chris Roberts, the creator of the phenomenally successful *Wing Commander* series. For the series' third installment, Roberts planned to use live actors for the first time.

As he'd been in *Star Wars,* Hamill was once again about to find himself on the cusp of a new entertainment revolution.

I went in and met with Chris Roberts. I remember coming away *thinking* it reminded me of working with [*Star Wars'* creator] George Lucas. Both guys were considered ''boy wonders,'' who created these fantasy or science-fiction universes with more than one installment. Chris was going to do this thing [*Wing Commander III*] virtually all in front of giant green screens, which would later be computer-generated backgrounds. I was sort of in awe. I remember driving home and thinking, When this thing gets better and better and better, it will get to the point where computers can generate background elements that can withstand scrutiny on thirty-five- and seventy-millimeter projection. In others words, it really will revolutionize the movie industry, because projects that were previously prohibitively expensive will be within the realm of possibility.

I knew what had been happening, where they're able to use computers to print multiple images for extras, so that you can turn forty extras into four thousand. I was looking at things from the standpoint of someone who wants to produce and direct films of my own. There are no limitations on your imagination when you write a screenplay. You can draw and paint anything. But getting it on film is another story. Computers are going to help us do that. The possibilities are endless.

So Hamill said "Yes" to Chris Roberts. He took a ten-week leave from his TV cartoon voice-over jobs.

"Are you doing a movie?" the producers asked.

"Well, kinda," said Hamill.

He made *Wing Commander III,* which, because the player ends up at one of three endings, meant three times the work for the actors. It would turn out to be more than worth the trouble. Upon its release, *Wing Commander III* would become the best-selling CD-ROM game of its day.

I thought the *Star Wars* movies were great when we were making them, but who knew what kind of response the public might have. You can never anticipate. Shooting *Wing Commander,* I had a sense of déjà vu because I'm back in a drama set in space, which is something I hadn't done since *Star Wars.* I was riddled with déjà vu.

Hamill's sense of déjà vu only intensified once *Wing Commander III* was released. He flew to London to meet the computer press, and the reaction was similar to what he'd experienced as a *Star Wars* star: absolute bedlam, magnified each day since the CD-ROM's release. Hamill and producer Chris Roberts went on to do on-line press conferences, sending real-time pictures over the Internet, talking on-line to users from New York to New Zealand.

They had a videocamera, and every so often they would hit a button that would take a still shot of Chris and me. It was like being on a talk show set and the pictures were sent out around the world. What a great toy!

Well, the reaction was astonishing. I mean, who knew? *Wing Commander III* had an enormous opening day. It's gone on to do nearly $100 million in sales. I had asked for participation. I wanted a royalty, and I offered to lower my up-front fee if they would do that, and they kindly did. I wound up making more from royalties than I did on salary.

I don't think I realized the impact it would have until the public responded. I mean, if *Wing Commander III* had been a movie, it would have been one of the highest-grossing movies of the year.

Hamill's performance was so sterling that he was nominated for a Gemini Award, the Oscars of the CD industry. He thought it would be a small-time operation. He was wrong.

I didn't know who I was up against. It wasn't until I got to the awards ceremony that I found out two other nominees were Sting and the Rolling Stones. Much to my surprise, Oliver Stone comes out, and after a long plug for his *Nixon* movie's CD, he pulls out the envelope and . . . I won.

But perhaps the best sign that he was on to something big came when his middle son, Griffin, began playing the game at one P.M. and didn't emerge from his room until dinnertime. His only complaint? "Well, the game is really awesome and I love it," said Griffin. "But I go off on a mission and I battle and it's really cool, but then I come back to home base and my dad shows up."

Hamill went on to make *Wing Commander IV: The Price of Freedom.*

Again, the enormity of the market reveals itself to me over and over. . . . We're on the threshold of what it can and will become.

This has sort of created a pocket of my career that I never could have anticipated back when I just did whatever I was doing: movies, television, plays. It really is a whole new kind of entertainment, and I think that anything that creates jobs for actors is a good thing. Most of my colleagues are unemployed. I mean, actors have a ridiculously high percent of unemployment—like in the eightieth percentile—on any given day.

There's just no downside to this . . . It's like potato chips. You can't eat only one. As soon as you get a taste of what it is, you want more.

Recently Hamill purchased his own computer, to work on screenplays with his cousin. They are already well into their first project, *Black Pearl,* which they're turning into a graphic novel. Now Hamill's ready to upgrade to a more sophisticated computer system.

I think it's part of the human existence to explore and conquer new technology and integrate it into our everyday lives. It's here to stay. And for every old convention that it renders obsolete, it creates a huge new set of possibilities. The moral of my story is ''Get over your techno-fear,'' because knowledge brings enlightenment.

What can we learn from Mark Hamill's adventures in the galaxy of the CD-ROM? That a new world awaits beyond your skepticism and cynicism, a world without limits, without ceilings, a world of incredible growth and limitless potential. All you have to do is recognize this new world, say "Yes!" to it, and you're halfway there.

Hamill's story of computer empowerment reminds me of the deep themes within the movie that made him famous as Luke Skywalker in *Star Wars.*

Let's take a moment to remember.

Star Wars is a classic of the "coming of age" film genre. Throughout the movie Obi Wan Kenobe is trying to teach Luke Skywalker that the Force is within him, a Force that, if recognized and employed, can accomplish the impossible.

If you have the Force, Obi Wan tells Luke, you can do anything.

In the final scene of *Star Wars,* Luke Skywalker faces an impossible task: to destroy the Death Star before it destroys the planet. There's one major problem—the only way to stop the Death Star is to drop a bomb or shoot a laser through a very small opening. This opening is Luke's only window of opportunity, and it's a near impossible hit. All around the hole, a dozen fighter pilots are flying, each with bad guys hot on their tails. Everybody's pulling down their radar and aiming and shooting at the opening and missing the little hole every time.

Finally Luke flies over with Darth Vader shooting at him. The movie makes it clear that it's Luke's last shot. If he misses, the Death Star will obliterate the universe. He pulls down his radar. He's aiming and preparing to fire, and just before he pulls the trigger, he hears a voice in his head, the voice of Obi Wan, saying, "Luke, remember, the Force is within you."

Luke finally understands the power within him.

At that moment, with the whole world hanging in the balance, Luke lifts his radar screen out of the way and, going strictly by intuition, aims, shoots, and hits, and the Death Star blows up.

Star Wars isn't merely a movie; it's a lesson by which to live your life. You also possess an awesome Force that can empower you to obliterate the Death Stars of your own life—the dead-end jobs, the demeaning corporate bureaucracies, the retirement Timex, the unfulfilled existence. You can escape all of this and achieve victory in your life with the same power and magnitude that Luke Skywalker achieved in *Star Wars.*

All you have to do is remember that the Force is *within* you and that the computer is the key to unleashing that Force upon the world.

Look at anything great in the world. You've got the Wright brothers, and there were two of them. You've got Einstein, and there was one of him. Apple Computer—basically two of them. . . . So the law of numbers is number one."

—Scott Adams,
Dilbert *creator*

3. Affirm Your Way to Success!

What do the following have in common?, aside from being excerpted from the book *The New Doublespeak* by William Lutz:

Force management program
Release of resources
Involuntary separation from payroll
Career change opportunity
Involuntary severance
Career transition program
Rightsizing the bank
Reshaping
Reduction in force
Elimination of employment security policy
Strengthening global effectiveness
Repositioning
Schedule adjustments
Reducing duplication or focused reduction
Normal payroll adjustments

They all mean the same thing:
You're fired!

Each of the listed mouthfuls of verbiage were given by companies, ranging from AT&T to Tandem Computers, as reasons for layoffs, downsizing, unemployment scenarios. Millions of people have remained silent in the middle of this undeclared workplace war. But one man among them has stood up and screamed the loudest: "Enough!"

His name is Scott Adams, now the creator of the phenomenally successful *Dilbert* cartoon and books. But before his rebirth as a best-selling cartoonist and author, Adams was just another middle manager in cubicle 4S700R in the Northern California headquarters of Pacific Bell. He'd majored in economics as a backup for his dream: becoming a professional cartoonist. He was racking up $70,000 a year but, faced with out-of-touch bosses (so devilish, one sports hair-as-horns in the *Dilbert* comic strip), emotionally decimated colleagues, and the constant specter of a layoff, he knew there had to be more: "I figured that if you worked hard and you were smart, you could get promoted," Adams told *Newsweek.* "It wasn't until I was well into it that I realized you also had to be tall and have good hair."

Adams is five feet eight and balding.

"In my seventeen-year career, I never once did anything to help a customer," he said.

All that changed when he created *Dilbert,* which lampooned the corporate culture with dead-on aim. Almost overnight, Adams's book, *The Dilbert Principle,* hit number one. His cartoon strip became syndicated in 1,100 newspapers. His Web site began receiving hundreds of e-mails each day.

How did Scott Adams go from a frustrated cubicle worker to a best-selling chronicler of the American corporation, and how can you use his method to get out of your own rut?

By *affirming.*

"The basic idea is that fifteen times a day, you just write down whatever it is your goal is," Adams explained to *Newsweek.* "Then you'll observe things happening that will make that objective more likely to happen. It's actually a process of forcing your environment to change."

Let's see how Adams put his theory to work. First, he tried affirming the ultimate GMAT test score he could make to get into business school. He began writing down his goal—ninety-four—fifteen times a day. He took the test. Adams's score? Ninety-four. Even though he made the lowest grade in his college drawing class, he began affirming about a future career as a cartoonist, writing, "I will become a syndicated cartoonist," fifteen times a day. That goal realized, he began writing, "I will be the best cartoonist on the planet," fifteen times a day. Two cartoonists, however, stood in Adams's way: *The Far Side*'s legendary Gary Larson and *Calvin and Hobbes's* Bill Watterson.

"I actually consciously thought, I need those two guys to leave," he explained. "I started thinking very consciously, and probably every day, that I just really wanted them to retire. And they did."

When Adams put his e-mail address on his comic strip and switched its focus to stronger business and technology emphasis, he realized his dreams with a greater ferocity than he could have imagined in his cubicle days. Now he's affirming a new line fifteen times a day: "I will win a Pulitzer Prize."[3]

Let's study how another individual affirmed his way to success in a far different field:

To create a revolutionary system in call management.

This could have been the one-sentence affirmation of Sohail Sattar of Dallas, who was toiling as a $40,000 computer systems developer for GTE. After years of designing and developing computer systems for banks and credit unions, Sattar stared into his computer screen and had a brainstorm, an "a-ha moment." He hit upon an idea for a computer system that would allow its users to sort and respond to phone calls via their personal computers. He called the system Personal Secretary because that's exactly what it was: a call response system that could be personalized for different users. Whether handling voice mail, connecting to a bank via modem, or allowing taxpayers to check on the status of their tax refunds, the Personal Secretary's potential was unlimited.

Excitedly Sohail went to his bosses and laid out his dream. The answer that came back was as forceful as his enthusiastic presentation: *"No!"*

"GTE was trying to do something similar to this. I was trying to get them to take some of my ideas and adjust what they were doing. But they had been doing it for a while and they had too much pride. It was very political. They were too busy doing their own products to listen to what I had to say. The large company bureaucracy basically kicked in."

Sohail Sattar didn't give up on his dream. Instead he exercised virtual power. He used his aggravation as a force for momentum, not as an excuse to surrender. He began affirming his dream through his thoughts and actions.

> One day I just said, "I've got to go." I was stagnating. It was frustrating, but my frustration was my motivation to get out of there. If everybody had been very nice, I wouldn't have done anything by now. I would

[3] *Newsweek,* August 12, 1996.

still be working over there. So, in a way, I'm glad that nobody listened to me.

Sattar withdrew $30,000—his entire life savings—from the bank and bought two personal computers and assorted equipment and office furniture. He turned his living room into an office/laboratory and himself created the system that would become the Personal Secretary.

He almost went broke. But pretty soon potential clients—small companies—began to see the potential uses for his system, and things began to take off. From Australia to Venezuela, Sattar's Personal Secretary has become a staple for connecting businesses with their clients via the personal computer. It was such a success that GTE—too busy to listen when the company could have had Sattar's entire project for the cost of his $40,000-a-year salary—called. The company was interested in buying his Personal Secretary company. But by then half a dozen other firms were competing to purchase Sattar's home-based start-up.

GTE became a Personal Secretary customer. But Sattar sold his company to another suitor, called Intervoice, for . . . $13 million!

We won because we were innovative. We were creative and we didn't have any shackles or rules to hold us back.

The key to Sattar's success, as well as that of thousands others just like him, is not merely the act of *doing,* but one of *knowing.* He knew who he was and what he wanted to do in life. He could state his objective in a single sentence, which, like Scott Adams's affirmations, could be easily stated or written, like a mantra, fifteen times a day. He knew that he was not cut out to be some corporate bureaucrat; he was an entrepreneur. With that knowledge he was able to unleash the power of the personal computer to drive him to a destination that he never could have imagined as a $40,000-a-year, nine-to-five middle manager.

You have to know who you are and where you are going. I love the way political operative Ed Rollins describes his onetime boss, Ronald Reagan, in his new book, *Bare Knuckles and Back Rooms:* "He might have forgotten your name, but he never forgot who he was or what he believed in, and that was his magic."

In these days of infinite TV channels and people whose personalities change with their audience, knowing who you are and where you want to go is the key that can unlock the doors to your future.

Once you know, you're ready to "do" . . . to move on to the fourth secret of virtual power.

4. Find the New Way to Do the Old Thing!

Consider this e-mail message I received from a woman whose on-line address is Lucy@The Buzz.com:

> I separated a year ago, after four years of marriage. I had no real hobbies. For Christmas this year, I bought myself a computer. It sat in the box for a month. In February I plugged it in. Please realize that I knew *nothing* about computers. I was the chick with the blinking (12 Noon) VCR. Soooo, I start talking about my computer on my Houston radio show. I mentioned that it came with this AOL (American Online) disk and I thought AOL was state-of-the-art. I was soon contacted by an Internet company that offered me a home page. I took it and started to write things that came to mind: things I thought were humorous, cynical, etc. I put in photos and appearance dates and all of the celebrity gossip I encountered. Well, the home page took off! I started getting a lot of national press and the page was growing at a rate of 250 percent a month! Well, the first month I got 650 hits and this month (nine months later) I will get close to 650,000! This has truly taken over my life. Now, I am this computer *nerd!*

As the above scenario illustrates, finding the new way (Internet home page) to do the old thing (communications) can lead to a radical rebirth. These days the power of technology is being applied to virtually every field imaginable. The personal computer is providing new ways to do everything from finding a job (World Wide Web employment home pages like the Monster Board, on which employers have posted more than fifty-five thousand jobs in fifty states for which prospects send their résumés on-line) to stock trading (investors buy and sell directly via the Internet) to virtual vineyards.

Wine making is the most ancient of professions. But in the increasingly crowded market of modern-day wine, a wine maker has to find a way to get his product marketed, sold, tasted, and, most of all, identified among the crowd.

In a bedroom community called Saratoga in the Silicon Valley, Bill and Brenda Murphy were ready to begin the second act of their lives. Bill was the director of global accounts for Hewlett Packard. Brenda, having raised three children, was seeking a home-based business career. They didn't have to look far for their future. It was growing around them. "If you're familiar with this part of California, well, it begs to be a vineyard," says Bill. "The soil, the climate, everything is perfect."

Their backyard, like hundreds around them, was overflowing with high-quality Northern California grapes.

At first they saw the vines merely from the landscaping beauty they imparted. But when they sought a second business, with an eye toward retirement, all they had to do was follow their bliss. Pretty soon they were talking about starting their own vineyard, a business that, considering the enormous costs of conventional start-ups, would stop most entrepreneurs cold.

But the Murphys found a new way to do the old thing.

They didn't seek out a majestic winery with vast acreage—and an even vaster overhead. They created a home-based business office, installing a computer, modem, fax, and other essentials in a spare bedroom of their home, and began following the "outsourcing" revolution of their high-tech neighbors, computer giants like IBM, Intel, Apple, and Hewlett Packard.

Bill Murphy explains:

> Outsourcing is basically using the assets of other organizations that already exist, leveraging as much as possible: vineyard,

wineries, physical distribution facilities. That's our strategy. The wine business is notoriously capital-intensive. But we do it on other people's land with other people's money. . . . So it's kind of like having a virtual vineyard.

Bill and Brenda Murphy don't own a conventional winery; they lease space in one.

They don't grow their own grapes. They buy them from fourteen "backyard" vineyard owners—"people who don't want to be in the wine business but nonetheless produce high-quality grapes," says Bill.

They don't own the massive storage space it takes to age wine in barrels; they rent the space in a San Jose warehouse.

They don't invest the millions it would take to create their own bottling plant; they merely farm it out to a mobile bottling operation.

They don't distribute their product; they rely on five freelance distributors around the United States.

They don't write or type every report, tax statement, and check by hand. They turn over those duties, which would have sapped their energies in the prehistoric pre–personal computer days, to the computer.

Without the proper use of a computer, getting into business would have been impossible. We would have just been completely bogged down with detailed paperwork. From the various tax reporting to other transactions, I shudder at the thought of doing it manually. When it's set up right on the computer, a couple of points and clicks and keystrokes and bingo! You know exactly what you want to do. There is no magic to it. We use Quicken. We use Word for Windows. We use Microsoft Access. And we built some data applications on top of that, which allows us to do inventory management and things like that. The computer basically allows you to get into a small business without a huge investment and significantly improve productivity from the way things used to be done. If we had to manually log all these transactions, two things would happen: we would need a whole lot of clerks, and it wouldn't be a lot of fun. The computer takes the drudgery out of the business. It automates all of that. The key is setting it up right on the front end. Once you've done that, you can take a lot of the mundane tasks out of running a business and you can concentrate on the things that matter.

By computerizing the mechanics of their business, Bill and Brenda Murphy were able to go out and do what they do best: marketing. Not merely marketing their product in the conventional arena of trade shows and advertising, but marketing by finding the new way to do the old thing.

They turned to the Internet.

In 1993 the company was the first vintner with its own home page on the World Wide Web. Thus the Web became the connection between the virtual Clos la Chance vineyard and the Web's audience of between fifteen and thirty million people.

This gives the Murphys more of life's most precious natural resource —time—to concentrate on what they do best: marketing. They keep more than 1,500 customers up to date via a computerized mailing list, ranging from individual customers to restaurateurs.

The old-fashioned way to do it is by calling them all the time. Using WinFax, a neat piece of software to do faxes, I built a distribution list, and when we have a new release—our new Pinot Noir, for example—I'll just draft a short fax and send it to our entire distribution list.

In days past, that simple keystroke—mass faxing—would've required days of work and mail and toil. With programs like WinFax, one person can have the look of a conglomerate. No matter what you're selling, there is magic in keeping in touch with your customers! With one keystroke you can turn a customer base into a constituency, an audience for your dreams.

Bill and Brenda Murphy took it one step further: having led the way with wine on the Web, they now want to continue to stay ahead of the curve.

The analogy in my mind was kind of like the Internet as a shopping mall. When it was first built, there weren't too many stores. So a lot of traffic passed by your store and a lot of people popped in. Now, the shopping mall is huge. So people aren't just going to ''pop in'' because there are so many places to go on the Web. The key now is to become proactive. One way to do this—which many of the big companies are doing—is to advertise on the Web search pages, which costs a lot of money. The way we do it is on our home page: we have a guest book. Over time I'm going to proactively acquire e-mail addresses. When we do wine tastings, we have people write their name, address, and e-mail address in a guest book. The idea is to build a list of interested people, not just mass e-mail to a bunch of people who aren't interested. We'll periodically send out e-mails: about a new release, about a gift program, about awards. And if the recipient wants details, they can go to the home page.

How has this strategy worked?

We get orders for our wine over the Net every day. But what I'm anxious to do is be more in front of our customers a little more often, and not just rely on somebody stumbling onto my page. I want to go after them, to say, ''Hey, we just released this Pinot Noir and it won the gold medal at the Sonoma County Fair last week. It's really good stuff. But it's not going to last. If you're interested, act quickly.''

The world is responding to the Clos la Chance call. A scant three years after releasing its own commercial vintage, Clos la Chance wines were served at the White House. Gold and silver medals began raining down on the wine, and the esteemed *Wine Spectator* magazine gave the Clos la Chance Chardonnay and Cabernet eighty-nine and eighty-eight points, respectively.

A conventional wine maker would have kept these achievements mounted on their wall or released them to the public via written press releases and well-paid public relations specialists.

All Bill and Brenda Murphy had to do was post the news on their World Wide Web home page and mass e-mail it to the winery's constituency.

Oh, you better believe it. I'm not going to keep that stuff a secret. Two months after our wine was served at the White House, we got a nice letter from Mrs. Clinton and a copy of the menu card. You can see that on our home page. That's great stuff. That helps put you on the map. Technology levels the playing field between the small and large businesses by potentially allowing you to get to a vast market that would have previously been unavailable to you.

Whatever career you're pursuing, find the new way to do the old thing. Unleash the power of the computer. Employ technology, not physical staff and high overhead, to handle the mechanics: the accounting, filing, scheduling, and organizational duties that can drain time and energy. Then concentrate on the things that really matter, the things that can build your business and enrich your life.

5. Employ Software, Not Staff!

If you're still stuck in that conventional job, with no earthly idea of how to break out, then look to your passion. If you're not sure of what you're truly passionate about, take a long look at your hobbies. Try to imagine what business you could make of those hobbies, those passions, with the help of a personal computer. Then seek out a corresponding software program. Chances are one has been already written for your specific line of endeavor.

Maybe your passion is wine, as it is for Bill and Brenda Murphy, and you can apply a spectrum of conventional software programs to ease the burdens of your home-based business. Or maybe it's something even more specific, as in the case of Ann and Tom Dooling, who, in the wilds of Montana, built an incredible home-based business, using an amazingly specific software program, around their passion for . . . fiber.

Fiber? That's not an everyday passion. But Ann Dooling, married for fifteen years to a Harvard-educated country lawyer in Dillon, Montana, is a self-confessed "fiberholic," someone who, like an alcoholic or a chocoholic, just can't get enough of the substance of her obsession. From fur to wool to cashmere, she's always been a spinner, a knitter, a garment designer, and an animal raiser. But when the alarm clock struck at dawn, she didn't go to work in the field of her dreams; she headed off to work in conventional jobs, first as a registered nurse and then, after marrying Tom, as a one-woman replacement for two legal secretaries, using the personal computer to easily handle the workload that it once took two women to accomplish manually.

> [Ann:] I'd spent almost twenty years working as a registered nurse. One day Tom says to me, ''Guess what? You have a new job, and what's more, you get to use a word processor.'' I said, ''Is that like a food processor?''

But Ann learned fast. The Dooling's law practice became the first in Dillon to become computerized, and the results showed. They became more efficient and able to use the time they saved on conventional process to better serve their clients. But in back of their minds, the Doolings dreamed of breaking free, Tom as a writer, Ann working with her passion, fiber.

They lived on a 106-acre ranch, raising chickens, turkeys, geese, cattle, horses, sheep, and even worms. They canned their own fruit and made their own butter, ground their own flour for their own homemade bread, made their own soap, and butchered their own meat. But every morning they were forced to leave their idyllic existence for the town of Dillon, where their office was the doorway to a world of trouble: divorce, bankruptcy, criminal defense, probate, contracts, and wills.

> [Tom:] When I first started practicing, I thought of law as a very noble and honorable profession. But now the legal profession has become somewhat akin to selling used cars, except there are more lawyers than there are used-car salesmen. Litigious society has turned lawyers into people who go out and do dirty work for whoever will pay the most money. I think very poorly of it.

Redemption was required. It came via the personal computer, when Ann Dooling led her husband in following her passion for fiber. Seeking to find a home-based business based on fiber, they considered a slew of possibilities, from leasing their land to farming it themselves. Then they stumbled across something unique: one of the world's most precious fibers was grown on one of the most common staples of the international barnyard, the goat.

Cashmere!

The word lit a fire in their minds. They began doing research and discovered that cashmere doesn't grow on just any billy goat; arguably the finest goats on Australian goats. Eventually shuttering their law office, the Doolings flew to Australia and returned with not only two hundred cashmere goats, but, perhaps more important, a computer software program called Cash Stud. Developed by the goat herders who sold the Doolings their flock, the program tracks herd, breeding performance, and ancestral data of every goat in a herd.

> [Ann:] The program was built particularly and specifically for cashmere goats, for tracking all the genetics and fleece information. It sets up breeding groups. Each goat has an eight- or nine-digit computer number, which translates into a certain set of colors and numbers on their ear tags. When I enter the kid through the mother's number, it automatically builds that kid's pedigree, and that pedigree stays in the computer forever. This gives us a breeding performance and life history not only of every animal we've ever had on the farm, but on some of their Australian ancestors, going back several generations. We now have three or four thousand goats in our archive program alone. The program gives us seventy-nine parameters on each goat, everything from fleece information to mane fiber diameter. . . . It's an incredible program, and I couldn't manage this herd without it.

Any doubts about how specific a computer software program can be? I wouldn't have believed that a program existed on cashmere goat herd management. But here it is. What program already exists that can radically revolutionize your home-based business? Don't reinvent the wheel. Research software! Consult others about what programs are being using in your field. Check out new software in the current issues of the many computer magazines. Access the software indexes at computer stores.

Through a computer software program, you can revolutionize your life as radically as Ann and Tom Dooling did theirs. Their herd of eight hundred goats grazing along the banks of Montana's Beaverhead River has now become the largest producer of cashmere in the United States, accounting for more than half of the cashmere produced annually in America. In their first year of business they sold their cashmere yarn for approximately $22 per pound. The next year they got $145. When they discovered that their yarn was retailing for $500 a pound, they decided to eliminate the middleman. They bought five computerized knitting machines and began producing their own yarn, and using a computer to design everything from sweater patterns to the number of stitches per inch, they began producing their own Great American Cashmere line of sweaters. Their goods are sold on their own World Wide Web home page as well as at fine stores like Neiman Marcus.

Ann and Tom Dooling's world has expanded dramatically. They travel frequently from Australia to New Zealand to China, where they addressed the sixth annual Conference on Goats. Their ranch has become a fiber empire, their lives the personification of virtual power.

> [Tom:] It's the realization of the nineties of computer software, communication on the Internet, chat groups, the World Wide Web, telefacsimile, and all the other ingredients that allow Ann and me to live on a little ranch in the High Rockies and do business in the world at large. It's the realization of a dream. The immense advantage to living in the nineties is, for us, that we can live in the country and still work with the world at large without having it in our lap. We believe that there aren't, as yet, many farm families in Montana who receive faxes and e-mail in Chinese or who concern themselves on a daily basis about the time differential between Dillon, Montana, and Melbourne and Paris and Beijing.

What is your dream? Look to your hobbies and you'll find some clues. Chances are there's already a computer software program that can help you manage your dreams by computer, leaving you more of that incredible resource that is the essence of virtual power: Time.

Then, with your technological systems in place, you can leave behind the four walls of your office and take your show on the road. Let's now study the scenarios of some individuals who have stripped the tethers from their existence and learn how the computer can truly set you free.

CHAPTER EIGHT

Going Portable, Getting Free

Every man dies. Not every man really lives.

—*Mel Gibson as William Wallace in* Braveheart

Freedom.

That's the quest, isn't it? Freedom is a calling as strong as hunger —maybe even stronger. It's the quest that rules both the kingdoms of animals and mankind, a hunger for which many a man and almost all beasts will stake their lives.

In the old days, wars were waged for the sake of freedom. These days, a new war is raging, a war against the bondage that blocks us from our dreams: dead-end jobs, glass ceilings, tyrannical systems of employment.

Now, a computer is not a cannon. By itself it cannot blast down the walls that imprison you. But the computer can become a lever with which you can gradually wrest control over your own destiny and find the time to do the things you want to do most in life.

How? By gearing up, getting out, and breaking free.

By going portable.

I trace the chief agents of personal freedom as follows: wheel, buggy, train, car, plane, and battery-powered notebook computer. The "notebook" is, of course, the chief agent of the new portability. With the advent of the modem, which connects the computer to the world through the telephone, notebooks have become ubiquitous, an accessory in every briefcase, airline seat, and mountaintop. Suddenly the salesman doesn't have to be chained to the telephone! The stockbroker doesn't have to be stuck on Wall Street or the brokerage house to buy and sell stocks! The writer can escape the rolltop desk and write his works on notebooks in the middle of nature or the sidewalk cafés of the city! Entrepreneurs can run their offices anywhere, anytime, with the click of a mouse!

Freedom, however, isn't usually easily won. Why? Because it is anathema to conventional businesses, which are ruled by the clock and the theory that each employee butt must be in its designated chair, a world whose first commandment is "Thou must show up."

But there is a new form of corporation emerging: once traditional companies like AT&T, which outfitted a major percentage of its staff with notebook computers and linked them through a wireless data system, allowing them to work from home-based offices. Chiatt-Day Advertising, which disbanded its conventional offices, gave employees lockers and notebooks and set them free to work wherever and whenever they can be most productive. "We're trying to structure things more like a university than an elementary school," CEO Jay Chiatt told *Wired* magazine. "Most businesses run like elementary schools. You go to work and you only leave your office to go to the bathroom. That sort of thing breeds insularity and fear, and it's nonproductive. The important thing is to focus on what kind of work you do."

The executives at these companies are proving that "showing up" isn't everything, especially when the employee who shows up hasn't got his or her heart—much less butt—in the tasks at hand. Portability, the ability to work wherever the employee feels they can do the best work, breaks the bonds of the conventional workplace and makes every employee an entrepreneur, responsible for his or her own time and productivity.

What is your dream? I'll bet it doesn't include sitting eight hours a day in an office. I'm no psychologist, but most dreams are set in environments without fluorescent lighting. Dreams are cast in places like islands, mountain towns, and sidewalk cafés. If you're stuck in a cubicle, can you ever truly be living your dreams?

Going portable takes commitment. You can't make the leap by "thinking" about it. I know people who for years have "thought" about taking their act on the road. But whenever I speak with them, they always seem to be impossibly backlogged, too busy to talk, much less to meet, breathlessly exclaiming, "Can't make it! Too busy! Gotta gooooooo!"

How can you unleash yourselves from chains that perhaps you haven't even taken the time to see? First, open your eyes to the new ways of doing the old things. Then and only then can you begin to appreciate the technology at hand. Freedom is an emancipation proclamation that you must declare for yourself. Nobody else can unleash you from drudgery. The power is, as always, at your fingertips.

To access the power, all you have to do is turn that power on. But access alone cannot create miracles. The computer cannot free you from work, only the confines of work. Miracles happen slowly. The computer is a tool, an instrument able to effect change only when employed over time. Gear up. Get out. Then, one day, you'll look up and find yourself . . . *free.*

> *Imagine if everybody had a computer for $9,000 and you were stuck by a table every time you have to learn anything or read anything. . . . And all of a sudden somebody invented a whole new thing—a newspaper! You know what would happen? Everybody would say, "What an invention! A newspaper!" For half a dollar you got the same thing [as a computer]! Not only that, you can take it wherever you want to go. You can't take a computer to the toilet. . . . You can take this wherever you want—wherever you want! The dog: he's about to go—do you put a computer underneath?*
>
> —*Jackie Mason, in his one-man Broadway show* Love Thy Neighbor

Sorry, Jackie, but you *can* take a computer anywhere you want to go. I wouldn't recommend putting one beneath a dog. But you can take a computer to the toilet or on a train, even to Tibet. Wherever a newspaper can go, a computer can go, too, with the added dimension that the computer is not obsolete by the end of the day.

Don't believe me? Consider this experiment conducted by *Condé Nast Traveler* magazine, which sent acclaimed travel writer Paul Theroux to "a tropical, terminally remote uninhabited speck of an island. We outfitted him: the latest in electronics communications gear. His mission: to go away—but stay in touch."

Theroux's desert island was a tiny, nameless spit of land in the Ngemelis group of islands at the western edge of the reef of the Rock Islands, a group of several hundred islands that even Robinson Crusoe would find too isolated to survive. Theroux carried five heavy bags, one with his clothes, one with snorkeling equipment, and the other three with electronic gear: a tiny handheld Apple computer called a MessagePad, satellite telephone, camcorder, shortwave radio, satellite, and more.

How did Paul Theroux fare? He watched *Top Gun* on his Sony camcorder. He listened to the BBC and Voice of America on his shortwave radio. He checked his tent for vermin with his ITT Night Mariner night-vision binoculars. He located the position of his tiny island on his Trimble Global Positioning System. Beneath a palm tree, he phoned his brother and his mother and his office back in New York. And he could have sent e-mail and accessed on-line news with his tiny handheld computer—if he'd only brought along a stronger model and stocked up on enough batteries.

Okay, so the medium's not perfect. But it's getting there. The technology Paul Theroux brought into the wild allowed him to keep in contact with the world at large, proving that there is no place on earth where you can't take a computer. "I had the strong impression of the physical world as a peaceful room," concluded Theroux.

If you can take a computer to a desert island, what reasons could there be for not being able to take a computer into every corner of civilized society?

WILLIAM WALLACE: You've come to fight as free men . . . and free men you are. What will you do without freedom? Will you fight?

SCOT (considering the specter of fighting an army many times larger and more powerful than his own): Against them? No! We will run and we will live!

WALLACE: Aye. Fight and you may die. Run and you will live—at least a while. And dying in your beds, many years from now, would you be willing to trade all of this—from this day to that—

for one chance, just one chance, to come back here and tell our enemies that they may take our lives, but they'll never take our freedom!

—*From the movie* Braveheart

Consider your own battles in life. If you're in a dead-end job, you can remain where you are and you will survive. But there will come a time in your life when you'll look back and wonder, "What if . . . ?"

Like the army of Scots in the movie *Braveheart,* you face enemies much greater than yourself. But the computer levels the battlefield. To win, you've got to access the full force of the revolution at your fingertips.

To understand how powerful that force can become, let's study the testimonials of a few people who found freedom through virtual power.

Breaking free of the constraints of geography.

The book you are currently reading is historic: the first book written by two collaborators who, in the course of a year of writing, never sat in the same room. Even though we live and work in Dallas, Texas, writer Mark Seal and I made a vow not to be together physically until the book's publication party. Then we would *really* have something to celebrate: the first book written entirely in cyberspace.

Only a few short years ago this would have been impossible. Collaborators on a book were forced to meet together constantly, sharing thoughts, comparing notes, reading and rereading endless drafts—all to the craziness of ricocheting automobiles, snarled schedules, cold coffee, and congealed pizza. But Mark and I had something to prove: to show from personal experience that it's possible to collaborate on a book through virtual power.

We never had to climb in our cars, meet at odd hours, or wad up forests of paper to meet our publisher's deadlines. We met all right; we met almost daily. But not in confining cages called offices. We met in the comfort of our own separate homes or offices, and all we had to do to hold a face-to-face meeting was turn on our computers. Within seconds we could see and hear each other in living color on our screens. We met via the Intel ProShare Personal Conferencing Video System, a $1,500 computer program that allowed us simultaneously to see each other and to work on pages of this book on our computer screen—creating a virtual meeting that is nothing less than a glimpse into tomorrow.

Videoconferencing works like this: An ISDN line, which transmits video signals and is presently available in almost every city in America, is installed at each of our home bases. A tiny Intel videocamera is installed atop both of our computer screens. The Intel ProShare Personal Conferencing Video System software is loaded into our computers. Switch on the program and two windows appear on our screens: one with Mark Seal's face, the other with mine. Our voices are projected via a tiny microphone installed on the side of our computers; we hear each other through our computer's normal speakers.

The ProShare System allows us to work on any document merely by accessing it through our computer's standard word-processing program. By providing us one shared "slate" to work on together, Mark and I became a better writing team than we ever could have been sharing two unconnected computers, typewriters, or tablets. It wasn't "as good as" being in the same room. It was better. I could work on this book in the comfort of my home or office or even while on the StairMaster in my gym, beside which I've installed a ProShare System.

Can you begin to imagine the possibilities? What if you could meet face-to-face with the collaborators in your life? What if you could meet with your creative partners in your business and personal life? What if you could meet with your creative partners, consult with your accountant, visit your parents, talk to friends—without jumping in a car or plane, without schlepping across town, country, or continent?

Well, you can. Videoconferencing is not some Jetsonesque test project. It's available now! Already revolutionizing conventional meetings, videoconferencing is enabling people to hold face-to-face conversations without ever leaving home, giving them more of that most precious natural resource—*time.* Additionally, we had the luxury of interviewing most of the testimonial subjects in this book via e-mail, allowing our interviewees to answer our questions at their convenience in their homes or offices.

Videoconferencing and e-mail set Mark Seal and me free from the cage of geography, giving us more time for what matters most: concentrating on producing a book that can show you how, through the personal computer, you too can break free from bondage and become all that you can be.

Breaking free from the cage of convention.

"It was a dark and stormy night," says trucker Philip Pickering.

It was always a dark and stormy night when Pickering was on the road. For thirty-five years he had repeated the same grueling cycle: twenty-one days trucking, then home for three days before going out again for twenty-one days.

It was always dark and stormy in the prehistoric pre–CB radio days when Pickering's truck broke down and he would have to walk or hitchhike to the nearest phone, then frequently be forced to stand in line when he finally found a phone. It was dark and stormy when an accident snarled traffic and Pickering, not knowing of the accident in time to take an alternate route, would be stuck at a standstill for hours. It was dark and stormy when he crawled into his cab at night, bone cold and lonely, with no way to communicate with his family except through truck stop pay phones, amid the cacophony of other dark and stormy souls like himself.

Then one day the stormclouds cleared for Pickering and hundreds of thousands of truckers just like him. The age of computer trucking arrived, freeing the driver from the cages of mechanical breakdowns, accidents, and on-the-road isolation. A satellite went up on the truck's roof and hooked up to a notebook computer in the cab, allowing the trucker to be tracked by his or her family and client. The notebook allowed the trucker to access software programs that provide detailed road maps for any street in the world, to click on a red panic button to summon emergency help, and to use an on-line trucker's information bureau to be forewarned of problem clients before accepting their load. Connected to the Internet, the computer enables truckers to correspond with their families and to access hundreds of trucking-related World Wide Web pages, advising on everything from available loads—why head home empty when there's a lucrative load waiting up the road? —to practical advice on long-distance driving.

> [Pickering:] Basically, the computer has saved me many lost miles and I don't know how much on my phone bills. It enabled me to keep

> up with my financial records and my trip sheets on the road. It's like a lightweight bookkeeping system, an entire office, a one-by-two-foot secretary. The computer gave me freedom. I didn't have to be chained to the telephone all the time.

Corresponding with his wife and family through e-mail, Pickering figures he saves more than $200 a month on correspondence that once had to be done exclusively by phone calls. No more idle vigils by truck stop jukeboxes. Now Pickering could use his café time to read and answer e-mail and handle what used to be called "paperwork" without ever having to touch a piece of paper. Back in his truck, he can plug his computer into the portable phone line, activate the modem, and send out his mail in seconds instead of languishing on a telephone for hours.

To employ the old CB radio phrase: Are you copying all of this, good buddy?

Best of all, the computer has allowed Pickering to move up in his world; he was recently promoted to a management position. What did the computer have to do with that promotion? Plenty, says Pickering:

> It let the company know that I wasn't just going to be one of these sit-back, potbellied truck drivers, just out there to drive. It showed them that I have initiative, that I have other skills than just jamming gears and blabbing on the radio.

Breaking free from the heartbreak of loss.

For years his computer had been connected to the Internet's medical pages: CancerNet, medical libraries, and journals, as Gene Senyak conducted an exhaustive search to find hope for a cure for his wife's cancer. His work as a Santa Rosa, California, marketing entrepreneur suffered, but even the faintest glimmer of hope was worth the search.

But when his wife died, Gene Senyak had to embark upon a new search, a search to restore his own soul.

Writes Senyak's son, Isaiah, in the November 1995 issue of *Home*

Office Computing: "The year my mother died, my father rented out our house, packed everything in an old van and trailer, and drove us around America for three months."

Added Senyak: "Camus said, 'Whatever keeps you from your work becomes your work.' After we lost a brutal war with leiomyosarcoma, it soon became obvious that for [his son] twelve-year-old Isaiah and me, neither school nor business could keep us from our real work of recovery. My solution was to use the interstate highways to change our scenery and visit friends and associates and the information highway to maintain client relations and then build my consulting business."

Eight months after his wife's death, Senyak and his son, Isaiah, packed up their computer equipment, business files, two dogs, and a parrot and set out on a three-month, coast-to-coast journey across America to reclaim their life.

Along the way, Senyak planned to keep his business running through computer technology. On board the van he called the Blue Lagoon, pulling a vintage Shasta trailer dubbed the Electronic Scow, were three notebook computers, a cellular phone for wireless access to the Internet, a pager, and a portable fax. "Our destination isn't clear, but our objective is: we need a fresh start," wrote Senyak in his diary.

You, too, must embark upon a "healing quest," a journey to reclaim your soul. You must trust, as Gene Senyak did, in the power of computer technology to communicate with the world. Then, with those systems in place, you must set yourself free. From their home in Santa Rosa, California, Senyak and his son would drive through Oregon, Utah, Washington, Idaho, Colorado, Oklahoma, Florida, South Carolina, and New York City and back again.

The trip did not turn out to be professionally perfect: Senyak's computers broke down temporarily, as did his van. But the trip succeeded in ways he and his son couldn't have imagined. Let's study some entries in Senyak's log reprinted in *Home Office Computing* magazine to see how a van full of computer equipment and three months of freedom can dramatically jump-start the emotionally ravaged life of a father and son.

As a healing quest—as a way of understanding what the world has so rapidly become—it's no small thing to be among the Anasazi Indians this dark, warm, early morning, high above Cortez and Durango. From this vantage point, the precise blocks of the Norwell Building under the snow-streaked mountains of Orem are cliff dwellings, pit houses, and kivas of a century that streaks to an uncertain close.

He is hitting on something important here. As one is traveling across America, unfettered by bosses or bureaucracy, the office buildings that house conventional industry seem as ancient as cliff dwellings, remnants of some long-vanished culture. Gene and Isaiah Senyak, on the road but still in close contact with the world, could be prototypes of tomorrow, a country of people who dedicate their lives to expanding their horizons, not shrinking them by boxing them into cubicles. When Senyak was halfway through his journey, the trip's significance suddenly became apparent.

The trip has been about recovery, not business. It took more than ten thousand miles to realize it. Emerging from this trip means a fresh start. And isn't that why we left in the first place? Life rewrites the scripts we overlay on it. Last September I had a meeting with the president of a biotech company scheduled weeks in advance. It turned out to be the day my wife died. Going out into America the way we did may not have been good for business, but it was good for the soul.

The three cyberscenarios detailed here illustrate one of the most potentially powerful aspects of the personal computer revolution: its power to set you free.

I got my first notebook computer in 1993, and immediately it radically redefined my life. Being able to take your work with you, instead of constantly going to your work, is quite a revolution. I call the notebook computer a "lifestyle extender," enabling me to go anywhere on earth and still stay in touch with my world. The notebook gives you the ability to take everything you have at your office with you, even the ability to do videoconferencing—wherever and whenever you travel.

At first I used my notebook computer primarily for sending and receiving e-mail. Through e-mail I could stay completely wired to my office in Dallas. Considering that one-half of my company's fifty employees are equipped with notebook computers, I can keep in contact with them via e-mail as they travel—closer contact than I could if we were all cooped up constantly in the same building.

I have two e-mail addresses: one at my office and another for viewer mail from my television shows. I probably get three to four hundred e-mail messages each day. What if I had to physically talk to each of these three or four hundred people? I wouldn't have time left over for anything else! In the old world, meeting face-to-face or phone to phone took an incredible amount of time and effort, especially when you consider how much time is spent on phone tag and dealing with people who are terminally late. Once you get on e-mail, you'll see the incredible inefficiency of that old system. For me, sending e-mail from the road has become such a major part of my life, I don't see how I lived without it.

It can become an equally powerful revolution in your life, as well. I believe that what voice mail brought to telephone calls—the power to leave messages for people, instead of physically speaking to them—has been multiplied many times over with the advent of e-mail. Just imagine: you can send ten e-mails in the time it takes you to make one conventional telephone call. The ability to communicate with someone without having to be "live" is such a tremendous resource that you cannot afford to ignore it in today's world.

But e-mail is just one reason for the tremendous growth in notebook computers. The second reason is the ability to accomplish considerable work, whenever or wherever you are. Consider the airplane, where the notebook computer has become ubiquitous. Once considered dead time for busy travelers, flights are now among the best places to get work done.

Here's how I spend a typical transcontinental flight, say, from New York to Los Angeles: I'll get on board, catch my breath, unwind, have the meal, then pull out the notebook. I'll first plug my computer modem into the telephone that's now a fixture of almost every airline seat back and I'll download my e-mail. The in-flight phone call costs me about $5—$2.50 per minute on-line. I can usually download all of my e-mail messages in two or three minutes, retrieving as many as thirty, forty, or fifty messages. Once I've downloaded the incoming messages, I'll disconnect from the telephone so I'm no longer paying phone charges.Then I'll read the e-mail and type answers to each one, then plug back into the phone to send my responses.

Mail answered, I can then turn to my administrative duties: letters to be written, spreadsheets to run, notes to my assistant. Once that's done, I can send these letters, spreadsheets, and notes back to my company immediately, instead of waiting until I'm scrambling on the ground. So with the flip of a few computer switches, I've turned a four-hour plane trip into four extremely productive hours.

Look at the amount of time this process saves me! No phone calls, no meetings, no lengthy discussions with employees, no assistant typing letters and then waiting for me to read them before they're sent—the notebook cuts out a dozen steps and frees up hours of time. Just as the standard desktop computer set us free from drudgery of the conventional ways of doing business, the notebook computer cuts the tethers of our geography by allowing us to work whenever and wherever we choose to be.

The notebook computer allows you to bring your professional and personal lives in closer sync with each other, while the traditional workplace always seems to pit the professional against the personal. Imagine you're in a conflict because you want to go away for the weekend with your family, but late on a Friday afternoon your boss drops a major project in your lap, a project that, come hell or high water, must be on that boss's desk first thing Monday morning. When the flight schedules won't allow you to get back early enough Sunday to get your work done, how many times have you postponed or canceled a trip to accommodate that demanding boss? I can hear you now: "I just can't get away this weekend, honey. I've got a tremendous amount of work to do! We'll have another weekend, honey."

And I can also hear the epithets of your spouse—who's been planning this particular weekend for months—and see the dark clouds circling over his or her hairline.

With the notebook computer, you can handle that work on the three-hour flight to your sunny destination or in the beach house or beside the swimming pool once you arrive. With the notebook computer, you can polish off that work without ever even considering canceling a trip —and you can e-mail or print it out long before that boss even rises Monday morning. All you've got to do is take your notebook computer, plug it into a modem or printer, and hit the "print" or "send" key—and the mission is accomplished.

Now, all of the sudden, this idea of the notebook computer "setting you free" has some genuine value. Who couldn't use this kind of portable power? A sales professional who's on the run? An administrative assistant who has a lot of correspondence to handle and would rather do it in the sun than beneath the fluorescent lights of some office? I'm not just talking about executives. I'm talking about everybody.

When it's a beautiful June day and you're yearning to sit out in the sun, but there's work to do and you dread getting dressed and schlepping downtown to your desktop computer at work, the notebook can really set you free. The notebook allows you a secondary computer, on which you can load all of your files from work and then work beside the swimming pool. Now can you see the lifestyle benefits that mobile office concept can afford?

Let's study the stories of a few individuals who used it to spark a real revolution in their lives.

> *Someday your descendants will look back and be amazed that people of our generation worked in things called "cubicles." They will view our lives much the way we now view the workers from the Industrial Revolution who (I've heard) worked twenty-three hours a day making steel products using nothing but their foreheads.*
>
> *Imagine our descendants' disbelief when they read stories about how we were forced to sit in big boxes all day, enduring a stream of annoying noises, odors, and interruptions. They might think it was the product of some cruel experiment.*
>
> —*Scott Adams,*
> The Dilbert Principle

The big, bearded man on the menacing black Harley-Davidson motorcycle is not a Hell's Angel. But you'd never know it by looking at him. Wind in his hair, leather on his back, gears at his boot heels, he is living his dream: barreling free across America on a hog, scenes from God's country constantly flashing across his windshield, then heading home not to some congested city, but to a thirty-one-acre Kansas farm near the place where he was born.

This is a portrait of virtual entrepreneur Dick Grove, fifty-one.

Open up his saddlebags and you will see that he is no ordinary cyclist. Packed into the Harley is everything Grove needs to run his burgeoning thirty-person international public relations company, Prime Time Publicity and Media, from the road: laptop computer, modem, cellular telephone, and a business philosophy that says it all:

> I don't care where my employees work—out of an office, a garage, or a bedroom. I just care whether, at the end of the day, the week, the month, we've been productive.

All of his life, Dick Grove had loved the wide-open spaces. He was a Hutchison, Kansas, boy, and Kansans are men and women of the earth, most at home among the endless acres of corn, wheat, and soybeans. His dream was to ride those endless ribbons of Kansas road on his Harley.

But Dick Grove had spent most of his professional life in cities. In early 1991 he found himself cooped up in a conventional California skyscraper in Sausalito, California, where the company he had just been recruited to take over, Prime Time Media, was hurting, on the brink of both financial and spiritual ruin. Strangled by high overhead, Prime Time recruited Grove as CEO to turn the firm around. With a background in both journalism and computers, working for most of the brand names in Silicon Valley, Grove had all of the qualifications for the job.

Except computer literacy.

Although he had worked in Silicon Valley for twenty years, responsible for introducing several revolutionary personal computers, he had never even turned on the computer that sat on his desk! He had used the computers he had been responsible for marketing "for sticking up Post-it notes. I just never got around to figuring out how to use one.

Fear isn't the right word. It just seemed all more complex than it was worth."

But at Prime Time, Dick Grove proved that you don't have to be a master of the computer medium to use it to turn your life around. The company he was recruited to run was already revolutionary, a public relations firm whose staff consisted of former reporters, editors, and television producers, living in the cities of their expertise. They worked from home-based offices across America, and in an even more unconventional practice, the company was paid only for the stories that it placed for clients in the media, not in the usual fee-based way public relations companies earn their keep.

It didn't take a computer nerd to know that one major component was missing to make the unconventional company work.

> The one thing they didn't seem to have anywhere was computers. The employees out in their home offices didn't seem to be into computers at all. I thought, As soon as we can afford it, we need to get these people computers.

Grove couldn't afford not to buy the computers! How else could he communicate with his employees without conducting constant meetings and having endless phone calls? Knowing that freedom without connection leads to isolation, Grove decided he had to link up the members of his firm. He invested $50,000, buying each employee a notebook computer and a modem and connecting them through an electronic mail system called QuickMail. Each employee could easily communicate with each other and the CEO—from wherever they happened to be in the world. Of course, some employees were skeptical at first.

> One of the guys in our company who had said at first, ''I'll never understand how to use a computer,'' is now the greatest propeller head in the company. I mean, he can't function without the computer. I tell [my employees], ''Think about if you had to hand-write

everything you've written as a journalist over the years on a legal pad.'' I mean, my God, think of what typing has done for us. Think back when we didn't have fax machines. It doesn't take much to convince people of the power of technology.

Almost overnight, Prime Time was a virtual corporation; every employee was on-line with the company as a whole through the power of their computers. Grove went on-line with a vengeance. Becoming computer literate so quickly it astonished him, he sparked a series of revelations that dramatically changed every aspect of his life.

Pretty soon, I was discovering something else. That Dick Grove, CEO of the company, didn't have to sit in that office anymore.

That was quite a revelation—because Dick Grove had been the quintessential eighties businessman, working his way up the corporate ladder in New York City and the Silicon Valley, always looking up to where he was supposed to be headed instead of down from the place where he had come.

Suddenly he discovered he had been headed in the wrong direction. It happened when he returned home to Hutchison, Kansas, to attend his twenty-fifth high school reunion, driving twenty-two hours straight with a friend from California, prepared to snicker at the home folks, to show everyone how far he'd come in corporate America.

Instead the home folks had the last laugh on him. Nobody in Hutchison cared how far Dick Grove had climbed, a reaction that made him wonder about what he had really become as a person. He had everything—a good job, a loving wife, a happy family—except peace of mind and, even more important, freedom. Without freedom, he asked himself, what did he and his family really have?

An idea began percolating: If his employees could work from their home-based offices across America, why couldn't he? And why did that office have to be in Northern California? If the computer really had the power to enjoin the far-flung members of his company into one room, why couldn't his office be in the place he felt most at home? Why couldn't he base his life out of Hutchison, Kansas?

Grove called his idea "reverse migration." It was precipitated on his conviction that man wasn't born to live in cities and work in skyscrapers.

> I wanted to reverse migrate from California, where I had spent the last twenty-something years, back to Kansas, where I could buy a little farm with some horses, ride my motorcycles, and have a different quality of life than I had in the crowded, overpriced San Francisco Bay area. I describe it as ''not riding elevators anymore.'' I made the decision several years ago that I didn't want to ride an elevator to work every day. There are just better ways to function. Maybe it's midlife, maybe it's part of the aging boomer generation. But the same thing that makes me enjoy jumping on a Harley and heading off into the sunset is the same thing that makes me love having the ability to communicate from afar. It gives me that freedom.

There's that key word again. Freedom. For Grove and millions of people like him, finding freedom begins with analyzing the past and questioning the present. Grove discovered that change begins by asking yourself the most rudimentary question: "Why?" Why ride an elevator when you can ride a Harley?

> Your quality of life must become far more important than simply adapting to the way things have been done in the past. A lot of people are saying, ''Hey, wait a minute. Why?''
>
> That's the key: to ask the question ''Why?''
>
> When somebody answers, ''Well, it's always been done that way,'' ask, ''Well, why?''
>
> There are technological tools that can enable

us to have a better quality of life. Doesn't it make sense to put those tools to use?

Asking himself "Why," Grove discovered that he had no reasons to keep holed up in that skyscraper. His computer allowed him to keep in close touch with his administrative staff while making sales calls across the country. Interacting with all of his employees via e-mail, he had, like the author Paul Theroux on his "wired" deserted island, the feeling of the world as one big, peaceful room. As Grove told *Success* magazine: "A CEO gets many messages just walking down the hall or standing in the men's room. But it's impossible to keep track. In a virtual environment, you have a record of everything people say."

Grove was quickly receiving and answering one hundred e-mails a day. He was running his business from the road with his laptop, using his office only as a place to meet clients and handle routine administrative duties. Expenses were cut to the bone. Productivity was rising. Morale was skyrocketing. Prime Time Media was on a roll.

Why did Grove need the high-priced office? Why did that office have to be in a crowded city? Why did he have to ride an elevator? If Grove had a boss, he would have certainly heard many vague answers to his questions. But Grove was the boss! As such, he could see no reason for his imprisonment.

So Dick Grove set himself free.

On a trip back to Kansas, Grove and his wife, Teresa, stayed at the Eldridge Hotel in Lawrence. Grove wasn't sure his wife would love the country as much as he did. But sitting in a hotel window, Teresa Grove saw something happening in the street that cemented their future. "Maybe it was a Mother's Day parade," Teresa Grove told *Forbes ASAP* magazine. "Something so pure and corny that you couldn't help but smile."

The parcel of farmland they found in the cedars beside the Kansas River was a steal: thirty acres for $225,000, the cost of a run-down, one-bedroom Northern California condo. Across from his farmhouse, Grove built a home-based office. He works there a couple of days a week, heading into a small leased space in a Lawrence, Kansas, office building only when it's necessary to meet clients face-to-face.

With his technological systems in place, Grove loaded his computer gear into his Harley saddlebags and hit the road: the canyons of Utah, the Grand Canyon, the western slope of the Rockies. Dick Grove has become at peace with his existence and, through the connection of a computer modem, in constant contact with his company.

This freedom sparked a revolution in both his personal and private life.

> Within two months I noticed a dramatic increase in everyone's productivity. After the first year of being "on electronic mail," and connected with each other through computers, we had an almost 40 percent increase in revenues, and that growth has continued. . . . The computer is a tremendous tool. Milliseconds don't mean a thing to the average person. But hours make a difference. Computers save hours.

What can we learn from Dick Grove's example?

1. Ask yourself, "Why?" Every revolution begins with questioning the prevailing way of doing things. Question your own existence. Break down the things that bother you and ask yourself why they have to be that way. Discover the difference. Then go out and make the difference the reality. If there's not a reason for you to be cooped up in a cubicle, get out.
2. Practice reverse migration. Base your life in a location precipitated by lifestyle desires, not dictated by your job.
3. Move slowly. As Grove says, computer literacy is "an evolution, not a revolution." Gear up, get out, and set yourself free one step at a time. You'll be amazed at how far you can travel.

Don't wait for extraordinary opportunities. Seize common occasions and make them great. . . . Weak men wait for opportunities; strong men make them.

—Orison Swett Marden,
American author

His job was a perfect metaphor for the way he felt: he was stuck in the dark. A photographer in the U.S. Geological Survey Department in Reston, Virginia, he was stuck in the dark for most of his existence.

> When I went to work it was dark, at work it was dark, and when I got off it was dark, too. It's a nine-to-five job in the public relations department, and I was in a darkroom most of the day. I grew up in Southern California. I'd been skiing and fishing in the Rockies. I just knew that I didn't need to spend the rest of my life in a darkroom. I didn't see any future in it. I needed to get outside.

The man, whose nickname is Wigs, was twenty-two years old in his darkroom days—and that was the good part. He was young enough to take a gamble, to follow his heart. He didn't have to think too long to know where his dreams lay: the farther west the better, and if he could land a job in the fields of his passions—fishing and skiing—even better still. So when an old friend he'd dated in college called from Aspen, Colorado, and, hearing the desperation in Wigs's voice, said, "Why don't you come out here?" Wigs packed up his bags and headed west.

He became a ski instructor in winter and a fishing guide in summer, supplementing his income with restaurant work—dishwasher, prep cook, and, finally, waiter—until he could afford to ski and fish full-time.

As the years passed, he found himself enjoying an ideal lifestyle with only one drawback. He had absolutely no financial savings or security. Then, one day, he found the answer—and it was in the hands of a four-year-old boy!

> I was out in Los Angeles visiting a friend. He had an office in his house with a fold-out couch that I'd sleep on. On his desk, my friend has a computer. One day, I came off the beach and saw my friend's four-year-old son sitting at the computer, playing an educational game called *The Oregon Trail*, which lets a kid

travel the Oregon Trail by answering questions to travel farther along the trail.

I couldn't believe it! A four-year-old sitting at the keyboard typing! Reading at that age. He probably never would have read that early without that computer. And I'd never even touched one. I was pretty humbled. I felt like, ''Whoa, look what these kids are doing! What's going to happen in twenty years? I better get with the program.''

I asked the boy about the computer, how he learned it, asking finally, ''What other games are there to play?'' He pointed on the shelf and said there was a flight simulator game up there. He said, ''I don't know how to play it, but you can ask my dad.'' When my friend came home from work, I asked him about the flight simulator game. He said I could play it—if I could read the manual. It was about four hundred pages, extremely technical, but I read it. My friend showed me how to load the game onto the computer and work the joystick. I sat there for a week, learning how to fly this plane. I literally sat there for eight hours a day for the rest of the week, playing that computer game. I got completely addicted; I just had to have a computer after that.

He had experienced his "a-ha moment," the blinding flash of realization that computers can provide an answer to something essential, something deep inside. He didn't know the questions, much less the answers, only that he *had* to have a computer of his own. After saving "pennies and dimes," he ordered his first system and software programs, first using the computer mostly for games and personal accounting. Then he stumbled across CompuServe. He bought a modem and was amazed at the world he encountered on-line.

I discovered I could use a computer to get out, instead of just keeping me in.

About that time, a gift dropped from the heavens: his grandmother had to give away some of her savings to her grandchildren for tax purposes. Wigs's share? Ten thousand dollars—more money than he had ever had before. He deposited the check in a savings account, planning to use it "as something to fall back on." But when he discovered that the money wasn't earning significant interest, he began looking at the myriad investment avenues exploding on the Internet, everything from the ability to read financial news and watch stock quotes to actually buying and selling stocks on-line. Soon his attention was glued to something called E*TRADE, one of the many on-line trading services through which individuals can buy and sell stocks on their computer for an inexpensive fee, without brokers or other middlemen.

Wigs quickly became proficient at stock research. He was amazed at the extent of the information he could access via E*TRADE and other on-line networks with names like WealthWEB, PC Financial Network, and Silicon Investor. He could download a company's tax records and annual reports. He could study a company's financial records, look at their profits and losses for the quarter, peruse their price-earnings ratios. He could tell how much money they spent on research and development and evaluate the expertise of their financial officers by where they'd worked and what they'd done in the past. He could see if the company had any new products coming out and what impact those products would have on the market. He could access every report the company is required to submit to the government. Soon he was starting his investment day at six every morning, downloading quotes and checking stocks.

He didn't dare gamble his $10,000, not at first. So he devised a "trial run," creating a dummy account and keeping track of what $5,000 in investments would make if he really did invest real money in the stocks he picked. Before long he'd doubled his phantom $5,000.

He decided to play with real money, and, doubling his $10,000 many times over, he hasn't stopped since. Wigs has revolutionized his life in ways that no amount of conventional work could have ever done. Now, at forty-seven, tracking twenty-two different securities, he's on his way to building solid financial security in his life.

I'm saving for the future. Before, when I'd do my taxes I'd wonder, ''Where did all the money go?'' The computer allowed me to teach myself about finances. Without that, I never would have learned. I wouldn't have had the interest. I would probably have taken the money like my father and stuck it in the money-market account and made pennies and dimes like those poor guys have made. The Internet gave me a window on the world. It never ceases to amaze me.

When the stock market is closed, Wigs uses his computer to access information about his skiing and fishing trips. He can study water levels in the Frying Pan River, see which mountains are blessed with the most snow and interact with other skiers and fisherfolk from around the world.

The computer gave him financial security, allowing Wigs to pursue his passions—skiing and fishing—without the age-old specter of growing old with nothing in the bank. That's the essence of freedom: to not only live, but thrive in the fields of your dreams.

Freedom via the notebook computer comes with a caveat, however, a warning label. Being constantly wired to your world is an incredible benefit, but being wired constantly can make your life all work and no play.

You've got to know when it's time to turn off the computer.

I've been guilty of falling into the workaholic mentality of the perpetually wired. Consider a recent "vacation" I took with my wife to Aspen, Colorado. There we were amid the beautiful mountains, the incredible trees, and the rushing water. I had committed myself to taking a break from work. But there in that wonderful country, that notebook computer called me, beckoned me, seduced me with its many charms! It offered me the opportunity of doing what I like to do most: work. And I succumbed. Oh, Lord, did I succumb. I actually spent my entire Aspen weekend wired to work: receiving and sending e-mail, handling administrative chores, surfing the Internet.

We all have to learn when it's time to hit the "off" button!

I learned a lot from that Aspen vacation. I learned that being mobile carries a responsibility of restraint. Since that experience in the mountains, I've set up a few guidelines to which I've sworn to adhere:

1. Discipline yourself. You have to set parameters in advance on when you're going to work and when you're not. Once these parameters are set, do not deviate from them. Know when you're going to turn that computer on and, most important, know when you're going to turn that computer off. If you're in that dizzying workaholic tailspin, you've defeated the real purpose of virtual power: to find time in your life for the things that matter most.
2. Designate days off. On the seventh day, even God rested. At least one day each week declare a moratorium from technology. Designate this day to be "personal." Spend it with the people you love. I have a rule that I do not work on Sundays. That's the day for me to spend with my family, in church, at leisure.
3. Set specific hours. I always caution would-be home-based business entrepreneurs to avoid the "sleep in late" trap. It's easy to think, Well, now I've got my own business, I can work my own hours. These people typically work later to compensate for the extra shut-eye they stole. In the mobile world, the ability to set your own hours increases even more—and the traps multiply considerably. Set hours that allow you time off, both in the morning and at night.

Freedom always comes with a price. Pay that price by working smart. For that is the only way you can become truly free.

CHAPTER NINE

Ten Ways to Keep Pace with the Revolution

Let's take a step into tomorrow.

It sprawls across 250 acres of rolling green land outside of Toronto, Canada, then pops up again in the Blue Ridge Mountains of Virginia, then again in the Sangre de Cristo Mountains of Taos, New Mexico. It's traveling westward to California and zipping east to New York City, before eventually spreading wild like kudzu into every city, town and rural hamlet in America and then to the world at large, ubiquitous as McDonald's, billions and billions served.

The completely wired community is headed your way.

Today the computer is still considered part of a growing culture. Tomorrow it will be as ubiquitous as the television or the telephone. You won't be able to avoid the new computer technology when you're sitting in the middle of it. By staying one step ahead of the revolution, you can not only survive, but thrive in a totally wired world.

Blacksburg, Virginia (pop. 35,000), is a perfect example of what's headed our way. The community is so computer-literate, it was proclaimed "the Most Wired Town in America" by *USA Weekend* magazine. On-line via the Internet, residents can confer with their children's teachers, consult a doctor, gossip with neighbors, apply for a credit card, check out prices at the grocery, visit the current exhibit at the local art gallery, access the police department, and complain to or compliment the local politicians—without ever leaving their computers. A prototype community of Bell Atlantic, which actively enlisted citizens to go on-line, almost half of Blacksburg is on the Internet, and 62 percent have electronic mail, far above the national average.

Signing up at the Blacksburg Electronic Village (BEV) office, two hundred businesses have launched themselves on the Electronic Village Mall Web page. In one month 3,996 electronic visits were paid to one vendor's Web site, Raine's Real Estate, according to *USA Weekend* —more than the number of visitors who walked into the real estate office in the entire year.

Computers are embraced by every sector of Blacksburg's community, from students at the local Virginia Polytechnic Institute to senior citizens, who have embraced the new medium with particular passion. Locals say on-line communication has introduced them to neighbors they'd ordinarily never known. Parents say the computer has brought them closer to their kids, providing a way to both work and play together. Teachers say getting e-mail from parents and students has enabled them to know and serve their students more effectively.

As retired law enforcement and intelligence officer Carter Elliott told *USA Weekend:* "The way the Net has opened up the outside world has been like a fairy tale. We've started visiting the BEV business page before buying. I found a piano tuner through BEV, chatted with him via e-mail, and worked out a deal that would have been put off indefinitely without the electronic village."

Added Andrew Cohill, the Virginia Tech architecture professor who spearheads the local Web page: "People in rural communities see the Internet as a way of overcoming geographical isolation. We're giving people a new way to communicate with friends, family, neighbors, and local businesses. We're providing the modern equivalent of the old general store front porch."

That front porch concept has become a reality fifty miles north of Toronto in Montgomery Village, Canada's first truly wired community. Here, 160 pioneering families have moved into homes built specifically for the home-based business owner. With prices ranging from $100,000 to $200,000, the houses feature home offices with built-in computer desks and separate entrances for client traffic—set amid a woodland atmosphere of trees, wetlands, and streams. The zoning not only allows, but encourages, home-based businesses. You can post your business sign in your front yard, and a Mainstreet, U.S.A.–style downtown, in easy walking distance from the residences, will feature low-rise buildings whose ground floors can switch from living room to storefront merely by opening the front door.

Through a strategic alliance among Bell Canada, Shaw Cable TV, and an Internet service provider, every house, business, and school in Montgomery Village can be immediately wired, both via the Internet and through ISDN lines for videoconferencing, offering instant computer access to the library, schools, town hall, and local businesses. Each resident can be connected to the community via the Montgomery Village home page (www.headwaters.com). Anticipating future technological developments, the streets are wired with conduit able to accommodate any new type of wiring without ripping up the streets.

Futuristic? You bet. It's a picture of tomorrow in every way but its appearance. Because Montgomery Village does not look like something from a sci-fi film. It looks like the small towns of yesterday. Now, everyone knows that most North American subdivision houses are geared for the automobile. From the street you can see home after home with their monstrous two-, three-, or four-car garage doors, with only a tiny front door for the homeowner. Don't the architectural priorities seem skewed? Who's living in these houses, cars or people?

Montgomery Village's residents work from tree-shaded houses with their front porches pushed to the street and their garages exiled to the rear, accessible through a back alley. This creates a neighborhood whose emphasis is on what matters most: time with friends and family, instead of the daily commute. Says the village's developer, Marvin Green:

> Companies are sending people home. The equipment is available for people to work from home: faxes, copiers, computers, telephone. All we're doing is listening and trying to help make home office work possible. To promote the health and quality of the community simply by the fact that its citizens are there, instead of being away all the time. . . .
>
> We're trying to create a situation for people to not necessarily drive, and maybe not necessarily own, a second car. There's a

recognition that people spend approximately $700 a month to acquire, maintain, fuel, and insure a car. Most people do the same for two vehicles. By placing one of your jobs in the house and eliminating the need for that second car, you could pocket that $700 a month. That would cover most of the mortgage of your house. So you can have a car to go to work or a house with a job in it. You'd also get back all the time you'd spend in a car if you had to commute back and forth to work two and a half hours each day. If you figure it up—two and a half hours a day times five days per week for fifty weeks a year—you end up spending sixty workdays in the car each year. The idea is that if you can get that time and money back, you can have a pretty good life.

Who couldn't use an extra *sixty days* a year? Who wouldn't want to invest that time with their families? Who wouldn't relish the thought of a life without being addicted to a car, gas, parking fees, and business suits?

Peter Howard is among the citizens of Montgomery Village. For him, it's always been home. He grew up in Orangeville, the nearest town to the development; his wife worked fifteen minutes away from the residential development. But Howard, thirty-one, a former cyberphobe, was stuck in a Toronto skyscraper. His job as a public affairs consultant, handling everything from writing speeches to preparing issues management reviews, meant that he had to be available, reachable, headquartered, by phone and in person to his clients in a major metropolitan skyscraper.

He had to ride elevators.

With the advent of Montgomery Village, Howard could have the best of both worlds: life in his hometown with constant connection to the world at large. Through instant access via his modem, Howard can use his computer to trade files, letters, financial records, reports, audio correspondence, even books, to colleagues and clients anywhere in the world.

> Montgomery Village provides me with an environment where I don't feel like I'm off in some half-acre lot in the middle of nowhere; yet it's quite rural. Because all of the houses have an ISDN line to the front door, I'm presently sharing a project with consultants based in Atlanta, San Francisco, Washington, and Ottawa. We're doing everything on the computer, from sharing two hundred- to three-hundred-page documents to on-line edits of papers in progress. The computer has really stripped away all of the geography that once separated us. Has it eliminated the need to meet face-to-face? No. Has it reduced that need? Absolutely.

"Stripped away all of the geography." That really says it all. Peter Howard has brought the once pie-in-the-sky concept of a global village literally to his doorstep. If your community isn't wired, you can get it wired yourself. Whether you're talking about a community of ten or a hundred thousand, you can launch yourself, friends, families, and associates on-line via a community Web page. A 1996 issue of *Inc. Technology* offered five tips for launching a community in cyberspace: organize a group of individuals interested in getting Internet access and training; reach out to people and community organizations and show them how the Internet can help their business; educate people who aren't already familiar with the Internet; target specific business groups to demonstrate the benefits of going on-line; and offer free public access to the library or community center to "let people get their feet wet gradually."

You don't have to live in a wired community to join the wired world, however. Merely by becoming wired yourself, you can join the world on-line, wherever you are.

Says Howard:

> The technology has become so user-friendly that the only thing missing is the willingness for people to buy a modem, stick it into their

```
computer, and go. Get on with it! Don't wait
around. Don't think you have to work in a
particular space. With the new technology, you
can work anywhere. Who benefits? Everybody. If
you're working in an environment you like, it
adds value to your community and to your work.
It benefits everybody all around.
```

Montgomery Village and Blacksburg, Va., are just a glimpse, a preview, of what our world is rapidly becoming. It's up to all of us to do our best to step into that new world, to move, to change, to grow, to evolve.

In my own company we're stepping into that new world in a very aggressive way. We've launched WorldWide TV.com, the Internet's first superstation on the Web (www.worldwidetv.com). We're beginning with the Computer Broadcast Network, which offers Internet users live-action video segments, using the latest Internet video technology known as "streaming." The content comes from my four television shows about the new technology, as well as news about the computer industry. The site is updated daily. Already we have more than 120 hours' worth of content. Click on our site and our Web page features both text, video, audio, and graphics from my shows *Bunting's Window* (as seen on United Airlines in-flight programming), *Bunting's Window to the Net* (as seen on CNBC), *The Computer Man* (as seen on the Learning Channel as well as syndicated nationally on television), and *Computer City Television* (as seen in Computer City stores everywhere). There's a morning newscast, an afternoon newscast, and Web reviews of interesting sites, updated weekly. Eventually we'd like to run movie previews, travel segments, golf course previews, and other features on the site. And while the idea of a Web network might be new as I write this, by the time this book is published it could already be routine. That's how fast the wired world is evolving. The important thing is keeping pace, not standing still; entering the game instead of watching it from the sidelines.

Now that you have joined the community of computers, your enemy is no longer cyberphobia; it's complacency. "The greatest danger is in standing still," writes Intel CEO Andy Grove in his new book, *Only the Paranoid Survive.* Grove discusses the concept of a "10 Times

Force," something so powerful that it renders everything that came before it obsolete, forces like electricity, the printing press, the automobile, and, most recently, the personal computer.

Talk about a 10 Times Force! We are dealing with a power that would have been considered a miracle only a couple of decades ago. Leapfrogging technology enclosed in a lightweight box that can send your mail, balance your books, organize your days, research your papers, book your vacation, and allow you to virtually visit everything from your local grocer to the White House. If you'd told your friends and neighbors about something with this kind of power in, say, 1979, they would have called 911 or the local Loco Patrol. Today it's *not* having a PC that's considered crazy: an estimated 57 percent of American households are expected to be equipped with PCs by the year 2003, according to a spring 1995 issue of *Time;* 42.5 percent of the 153 million TV-equipped households in Europe are expected to have PCs by 2003.

The personal computer is more than a 10 Times Force; it's a tsunami of 10 Times Forces, each wave—from the PC to the Internet to the World Wide Web—unleashing a 10 Times Force of its own. If you're not already surfing, you haven't a second to spare. Because by the time you reach the end of this paragraph, more waves will be headed your way.

In the age of the personal computer, to stand still is to pedal backward. To access the full power at your fingertips, you have to constantly keep pace with the perpetually changing curve. How? Here are ten ways to keep pace in a world of 10 Times Forces.

1. Constantly Reinvent Yourself!

A personal computer is not a television. It does not work for the couch potato. Sit before it, turn it on, and do nothing—and you'll get absolutely nothing back. Halfway won't work here. To access the computer's power, you have to fully dedicate yourself to the technological revolution. You have to get off the sidelines and into the game. Remember: You have the potential to be one of two different people, one who lives up to his or her ultimate potential, another who forever languishes unfulfilled. As one of President Clinton's aides told author David Maraniss in his book, *First in His Class,* "[Clinton needs to be engaged in] some important, valiant fight to lend coherence and structure to his life. When he didn't have those fights, he would eat away at himself. He would become depressed, paranoid, surly, and, one suspects, escapist."

Determine the switch that jump-starts your own passions—and switch it *on!* Then you can reinvent yourself according to a plan designed by your dreams and not dictated by bare necessities.

Follow the lead of unlikely computer pioneers like Richard "Zap" Zoppo of East Orange, New Jersey, who used the personal computer to reinvent himself, not once but twice: first as a pest extermination company entrepreneur; second as a home-based record producer.

Says Zap:

> I never thought I would be involved in computers. Computers were something I read about as a kid in Isaac Asimov science-fiction stories. I never thought I would touch one.

But Zap did more than touch a computer; he used its power to radically redesign his life.

> I was a jack-of-all-trades: warehouseman, burger joints, chemical plants, inventory controls, counting cans on grocery store shelves . . . Finally I found a home in pest control.

First he worked for a salary for another exterminator. Then, with the help of a personal computer, he set out on his own, launching his home-based business out of his parents' garage. His truck logo: two knives crossing over a skull wearing a Green Beret cap over the words "LICENSED TO KILL." While Zap scoured his world of bugs, his PC could easily handle his administrative duties back home: filings, scheduling, correspondence, printing.

> The computer helped me to grow my business from $25,000 to $125,000. I couldn't have done it without it.

But his real dream wasn't extermination, it was entertainment. Zap's passion had always been to become a rock music producer. He was so devoted to the music, he endured a backbreaking schedule: running his company from eight to five, pest-fogging restaurants after hours, then playing rhythm guitar with a band from midnight until three A.M.

His computer eventually helped him find the light at the end of the tunnel: facing his forties, he decided he could produce and record music in a home-based recording studio. All he had to do to reinvent himself was to dedicate himself *totally* to the computer revolution.

> A friend of mine was a janitor in a company that made computer components for the military; now he's a computer consultant. [How's that for reinvention through technology?] He told me how the computer could create whatever kind of music I wanted, from an entire orchestra to basic rock 'n' roll. Not only would the computer help me create the music, it would also print out a notated score.

Zap called his garage-based production company the Digital Dungeon, and it was the epitome of the home-based world: totally run by computer, a ten-by-twenty-foot space where Zap could create the music it would've required a symphony orchestra to create conventionally. By dedicating himself totally to the computer revolution, one man made the step from dreams to action.

That, to me, is the essence of beautiful music.

For others, beautiful music comes from a bubbling stream, a wide-open sky, a mountain vista. Stacey Williams is one of these people. But she had spent her professional life cooped up inside Silicon Valley skyscrapers, working as a public relations director for high-tech companies. After years of working on salary, she found herself under the iron rule of a former Green Beret who used interrogation techniques on his employees. That pushed her to become a freelance public relations manager. Business was booming. But no amount of money could compensate for the way she felt when she was stuck in traffic, riding elevators, and dealing with impossible bosses.

I was freelancing, working out of my home, and I just decided, ''I can do this anywhere!'' Why am I doing it out of a thousand-dollar-a-month apartment?

So she reinvented herself—as a fishing guide on the Green River, living atop a mountain near Dutch John, Utah.

You won't find Dutch John on a map. It's a tiny hamlet with no more than one hundred citizens. Stacey Williams rode into the mountains with her PC, her modem, her fax machine, and fishing gear. Were there problems connecting her phone, modem, and fax to the tiny municipal phone system? You bet there were. Big problems. When she called the phone company to complain that her fax wasn't working properly, the operator replied, "Sorry, ma'am, we ain't got nothin' to do with the fax system."

Oh, my God, thought Stacey. I'm in big trouble!

But even in this remote location, where elk graze daily on her lawn, Stacey Williams is as wired into the world of technology as if she were still in Silicon Valley. The local phone company reoriented some of their microwave relays to accommodate Stacey's technology. Now she fishes half a week and works on public relations materials the rest. Her income is still at a solid six figures. But now she's not merely surviving. She's living her dreams. She fell in love and married a fishing guide on the Green River and has no intention, or reason, to ever live in a big city again.

I probably work as many hours as I used to, but now I don't feel the pressure and don't waste time in traffic. I feel like I'm a lot more productive for my clients without having to do lunches and sit in traffic jams.

2. Surrender the Superfluous!

In the old world, process always stood as a roadblock to high achievement. Process—all of the necessary functions of running a business or a life—blocked us from our real dreams. Like hamsters on a treadmill, we ran in our cages in a circular, instead of a straightforward, motion, wasting so much *time* on the process that we never arrived at our imagined destinies.

The testimonials in this book have run the gamut of professions, income levels, and personality types. But the people all have one thing in common: they plugged in and discovered new ways to tame the beast of time. As we've discussed, the computer's greatest gift to humanity is its ability to give us more time, life's greatest natural resource. The best way to access more time is to surrender to the computer anything that it can handle more easily than you can manually: correspondence, accounting, research, scheduling, and the myriad other processes that the computer can accomplish in seconds, compared to our hours. Then, freed of process, you can dedicate 100 percent of your time to your dreams.

Searching for a job over the computer is a prime example of how computer technology enables its users to rid themselves of conventional process. Just as e-mail revolutionized the process of communication—obliterating the daily need for fancy stationery, expensive staffs, endless phone calls, and reams of message slips—on-line employment bureaus like the Monster Board on the Internet have revolutionized the process of getting jobs. Talk about surrendering the superfluous! Through the Monster Board, which advertises fifty-five thousand jobs across the United States in a wide variety of positions, applicants can skip a dozen steps: from résumé printing and mailing (you type your qualifications directly into the Monster Board) to endless meetings with employers who may or may not have a job (why beat on dozens of doors that may not open when you can apply electronically to jobs that anxiously await applicants?).

Conversely, the Monster Board offers employers a place to post their job openings, allowing both employers and employees a place to surrender the superfluous, the drudgery of flying blind when it comes to seeking employment or employees.

As Jeff Taylor, CEO of TMP Interactive and the Monster Board's founder, says on his company's Web page: "In the job search process, traditionally you have to kiss a lot of frogs to find a prince. You have the ability to reduce the number of frogs in the electronic process."

Reduce, eliminate, obliterate—these are the verbs of downsizing, the language of job reduction. But they are also the verbs of personal freedom, of home-based salvation, of surrendering the superfluous. As we've discussed earlier, what pushes you out of the old world can set you free in the new one. How do you begin? First determine the processes in your life that slow you down, then assess how the computer might help you surrender those actions. Make a list; go through it one action at a time.

If you're seeking a job, surrender the superfluous by conducting your search on-line.

If you're running a company, surrender the superfluous by getting the necessary software to handle communications, accounting, tax filing, scheduling, and phone call management.

If you're researching a paper, surrender the superfluous, the hours and days in the library, by conducting your search over the Internet or via one of the on-line research firms like Lexis-Nexis, which provides everything from annual reports of companies to back issues of practically every newspaper and magazine ever published.

If you're trading stocks, surrender the superfluous by trading online, avoiding the high overhead of brokers, offices, and paperwork.

Whatever you're doing, surrender the superfluous and invest the time saved in what really matters: actively achieving your dreams!

3. Make Your Home a Technological Tabernacle!

You cannot weather a revolution without a place to stand. But a computer-driven, home-based office must have as many, if not more, boundaries than a conventional office. To this end, the first rule of the home-based business entrepreneur can be boiled down to two very simple words:

Get dressed!

This may sound obvious, but it's imperative for high-tech success. Carve it in stone and mount it on your wall. While the home-based business revolution may conjure up visions of people sitting around in jeans and T-shirts, lounging lazily before their computers, cappuccino in hand, this picture is a lie. Not getting dressed—and its accompanying mind-set of not being mentally groomed as a professional at work—can be absolutely suicidal to a fledgling home-based entrepreneur.

You have to be structured to succeed in, much less stay ahead of, the burgeoning technological revolution.

Here's how one successful home-based entrepreneur does it. Her name is Susan Sharp, and she survived a layoff, a divorce, the death of her father, and the bankruptcy of a client who owed her $20,000 and found eventual salvation as the proprietor of a $1 million–a-year home-based, computer-driven graphic arts business, by sticking to her own version of the "Get dressed" rule.

> I used to be called functionally unemployable, but now they call me an entrepreneur. I think if you have a certain spirit about you, which leads you to become an entrepreneur, a lot of times that's counter to success in an organization. I always felt if I had an idea on how something could be done better, I should talk about that. I usually tell people I've been fired from some of the best ad agencies in Washington, D.C. I got tired of being fired, so I set up my own home-based business. Now, of course, I can't fire myself.

Her last layoff came in 1985, when a small Washington ad agency laid her off just before it went belly-up. So Susan, then thirty-three, took her computer and her graphic arts equipment home to her wooded neighborhood in Rockville, Maryland. She, her then husband, and her young son moved into the two upstairs bedrooms, and she devoted her entire downstairs level to her home-based business. The layoff happened on a Friday; she was up and running first thing the following Monday morning.

She built her home-based business on a simple premise: Structure rules. Her home has a separate entrance for clients, and while the office atmosphere is relaxed, the boundaries are strictly enforced.

> When you don't have that external structure, when you don't have somebody like a boss breathing down your neck, it can be easier to

slack off. That's definitely been a problem. People say to me, ''If I had your business, I would be sitting upstairs or sitting out on the deck, drinking coffee all day.'' And I say, ''Sure you would, until your first MasterCard bill comes in.'' The reality is this: If you've got to work, you've got to work. You have to be disciplined.

Once she had her physical office set up—her computers and other equipment—Susan set up the even more important office, the office of physical and mental boundaries.

I've always paid myself rent. I've set my business up as a corporation, and everything is done as a very arm's-length transaction. I'm an employee of my company. I still take a paycheck. I always have. I take a salary, what I need to live on, and, toward the end of the year, I bonus myself out. It would never occur to me to say, ''Oh, I want a new dress. I'll go dip in here and take another twenty or seventy dollars.'' I have to manage on a salary, just like everybody else. I don't think of myself as working at home. It's more like I have a business that just happens to be in a home.

Most important, Susan Sharp gets dressed to go to work every day before she even takes one step downstairs into her home-based office. We're not talking about cutoffs and a T-shirt. Susan Sharp's dress is a reflection of her mind-set, and this woman's mind is totally devoted to her business. Once she's at work, she doesn't return home until the business day is done.

Most days, I'm here in a suit. But that's also because I'm in meetings a lot. I'm sometimes out of the office as much as I'm here. You have to make that distinction. People say to me, ''God, you have your business at home, so I guess you can bake cakes during the day, right?'' I sort of look at them squirrelly. It would never occur to me to go upstairs and cook. A friend was over the other day and she started laughing, saying, ''It's so funny that you have your purse down in the office with you. It's like you're at work.'' I said, ''Well, I am at work!'' I don't leave things upstairs. I get so busy that if I haven't organized myself in the morning before my day starts, it ain't gonna happen.

Susan Sharp's home-based business, built from scratch, now grosses $1 million a year and has two full-time employees. She is able to stay ahead of the technological curve because she has created an organized space, a place to stand, grow, and thrive with technology. Best of all, her sense of organization has given her confidence, inspiring a resolve to never discount herself or her talents.

I'm the kind of person who is going to put 110 percent into whatever I do. I needed to find clients who would pay for someone to do 110 percent. When I made that decision, my business really turned around. It all comes down to believing in yourself, to constantly upgrading. Amazingly, we do very few competitive bids. I'll sit down with somebody on the front end and I'll say, ''Is price what you're looking for?'' If they say, ''Yes,'' I say, ''Well, I can give you the names of five companies that are less expensive than we are.'' That attitude has made a huge difference. I stopped trying to be everything to everyone, and we ended up with a much higher grade client.

4. Constantly Seek out Enlightenment!

Literacy is a never-ending process. However, books and the computer are vastly different mediums. Books don't change. But what you learn today about computers will likely be different tomorrow. You have to keep current on what's happening by constantly reading, studying, and interacting with others. Whether you're seeking information to grow your home-based business or enlightenment on a more personal level, look for it first on-line.

On the computer, you reap what you sow. If you spend your time on-line in noble pursuits, enlightening Web sites, and intelligent on-line conversations, then you will get enlightening information back. If you dawdle away your days on trivia—vapid chats, dumb and dumber Web sites, slick business hustles, and the Web's vast array of porno—then you're most likely going to eventually walk away disillusioned and disappointed.

The World Wide Web can be the most enlightening place on earth, merely because it is a convergence of the greatest simultaneous congregation of voices in history. These voices discuss everything from auto repair to medical help to their love life to politics to spiritual enlightenment.

You're probably thinking, Jeez, Mark, now you're telling us that the computer can give us religion?

Yes, you can get religion over the computer. To see the wide variety of enlightenment available over the Internet, try conducting a search on religion. Just connect to the Internet and type the name of any religion into your search engine. Here's what I got in about five minutes of searching.

I'll list the search word I typed into the search engine first, followed by what came up on the screen. I'll start with the Yahoo search engine, a company whose acronym is the essence of the endless capacity of the Web: You Always Have Other Options.

Spiritual: A list of 22,197 documents containing the word "spiritual" popped up on the Yahoo search engine. One Web site entitled "Enlightenment On-Line—The Spiritual Search in Cyberspace" (www.holistic.com/lonny/enlight.htm) was particularly intriguing, a virtual cafeteria of spiritual enlightenment, with pages and pages devoted to inspiration, transformation, wellness, wisdom, and many other subjects, with this promising introductory greeting:

> Welcome, Fellow On-Line Wisdom Seekers! Is There Spirituality in Cyberspace? If so, ''where''? If not, can we ''make it so''?

This introduction led to many pages of spiritual discussions, including, my favorite, "Prayer of a Cybernaut":

> Are You out there, Lord? . . . Is your cosmic energy behind the millions of hooked-up hackers, bleary-eyed Internet addicts, students viewing cyber-porn, working single mothers getting email support, buzz-cut cyberpunks publishing outrageous electronic anti-zines from their basements? . . . Teach me, Lord, to see Your All-Dimensional Interface behind this flat-screen display, to hear your multi-media message of Truth, to plug in to your divine program . . .

Catholicism: A list of 9,810 documents on Catholicism came up on my Magellan search engine, offering everything from the "Catholic Information Center on Internet" to the "Harvard-Radcliffe Catholic Student Association."

Judaism: A total of 1,870 documents came up on Magellan. I called up one, "Judaism.com . . . the Internet's most comprehensive source for Jewish-related products," and was soon staring into "A Jewish Global Village," including a shopping mall, classified listings, and a host of religious insights.

Episcopal: A list of 137 documents turned up on Magellan, ranging from "Anglican Kids Association, devoted to resources for Anglican and Episcopalian children" to something called "Uncle Jimbo Gets Religion and It Gets Him."

Zen: I found an astonishing 1,057,830 documents in the Lycos search engine [which, I've found, usually has far more entries on most subjects than other search engines], running the gamut from Zen writings to Zen monasteries to Zen magazines.

If you can access this much information about religion, what could you access about computers or politics or any other subject? The options are endless—and I was searching only for about five minutes! Extrapolate this power by many millions—and apply it to whatever subject you can conceive—and you can begin to understand the computer's power to enlighten.

The Internet is reaching out to help you. There is a glut of help lines and search engines and Web sites. Use this power for constant enlightenment, not merely entertainment.

5. Keep Ahead of the Computer Software Curve!

With the amazingly wide spectrum of computer software programs constantly being developed, you have to make a conscious effort to stay current. By itself, the computer is just a vehicle that can go nowhere and do nothing; software is the fuel that transforms it into a rocket ship. Like the food you put into your body, the software that runs your computer determines how much you can learn and how fast you can grow. Your software dictates the quantity and quality of your accomplishments.

The story of Judy Slomovic Gunter, who is deaf, is a perfect example of the importance of finding the right programming to accomplish a particular task. Her journey from silence into the world of a zillion electronic voices serves as a metaphor for everyone who's traveled from the relative quiet of the conventional world into the dizzy new rooms of cyberspace. Judy learned the importance of proper computer programming when she bought her first PC in 1985.

As she wrote me via e-mail:

At the time there was only MS-DOS 3.3, and I had a real hard time understanding the computer. I simply used it for word processing and games.

As an administrative assistant in a Los Angeles nursing home, Judy longed to take the leap from employee to entrepreneur. After reading press reports about growth in the field of computer technicians, she took vocational courses and soon graduated with a certificate as a computer technician. But she couldn't get a job. Employers required two years' experience. Worse, the computer world was changing so fast, technicians were already becoming obsolete.

> Computers were becoming more reliable and getting easier for people to upgrade on their own.

That's when Judy discovered that computer power is dependent not upon hardware alone—but also upon the programming she put into her PC. She began learning about new computer programs and software after meeting with a deaf woman who introduced her to the burgeoning world of BBS (electronic bulletin board systems that allow the computer user to retrieve files, enter chat rooms, and seek support via computer and modem).

On-line, Judy's deafness didn't matter. She got software from America Online and CompuServe, connected a modem from her computer to the telephone line, and became a citizen of the Internet. This software dramatically expanded the horizons of her computer, which had previously been used exclusively for typing letters and playing games. Through software, Judy became an *active,* not passive, participant in her own renaissance.

> I decided I must make a paradigm shift if I was to accomplish anything in my life. Today I have to be on my toes to see the constant technology advances and how they can benefit deaf people.

She kept abreast of new software through the computer press. She got a job at Egghead Software and began putting the world of new software at her feet into action. She met a woman who ran an on-line service called DeafNet, which connects people with organizations for the deaf. Once she discovered the GEN (the Global Entrepreneurs Network) on the Internet, Judy knew she'd found a home. She posted her own Web page, started a home-based business handling collections for small businesses, and began living her lifelong dream of being her own boss.

If connecting her computer with the right software allowed a deaf woman to hurdle over her handicap, what could the new software do for you? Explore new software programs like a prospector seeking gold. This is the true treasure of the technological world, and it can enrich every area of your life.

6. Go Portable!

To leave a cubicle in an office to be chained to an equally oppressive office in your home is merely to trade one form of slavery for another. The Brave New World of computing isn't limited to what you can see through your computer screen. The Brave New World is about *doing.* It's about what you can accomplish once you release your life from conventional drudgery. The magic of the computer is its power to set you free, not lock you indoors! First step? Buy a notebook computer and a modem. Second step? Walk out of your house and use the equipment to keep in touch with your world.

Learn from mobile entrepreneurs like Bill Tobin, who founded twelve different successful businesses over the past thirty years, everything from plastic cup dispensers to airline travel kits. Through it all, Tobin was always seeking to fulfill a singular passion: to live on his boat and cruise the Caribbean.

As he wrote in a 1995 issue of *INC.* magazine:

> Today I have an office on my fifty-five-foot yacht, *Breeze*. It houses a Compaq Presario 850 PC that I keep belowdeck, an IBM ThinkPad with video capabilities—it's great for presentations—that I can use anywhere, a modem, a cellular phone, and a cellular fax machine. . . . With

> *Breeze*, I spend about three months a year sailing—and working—in the Caribbean. The yacht serves as one of four offices I use to run my current venture, PC Gifts and Flowers, a shopping service on the Internet I built with IBM. Through it, people can order a couple hundred products—from cameras to balloons to video games and watches—using their computers.

Where would you rather conduct your business and personal life, in a cramped cubicle or sailing around the Caribbean?

I know what you're thinking. Sure, Mark, it sounds great. But how does the guy actually run his company from a yacht?

Tobin answered the question in his *INC.* article by listing his daily routine:

> When I'm on board I get up around five A.M. From six to ten, I dictate my business correspondence—about twenty-five letters a day. . . .
>
> To prepare the letters, I use a handheld Dictaphone voice processor and my cellular phone or, if I'm docked, a dedicated line to connect directly with a Dictaphone recorder that sits on my secretary's desk at company headquarters in Oakton, Va. When she gets to work, she types up the letters and sends them back to my desktop computer via a software program called PC Anywhere. . . .
>
> I make and return phone calls, up to fifty a day. Most of them are in response to messages left on my voice mail—only a few people have my yacht number—and delivered to me by my secretary, whom I talk to ten or more times daily . . .
>
> When the letters arrive, I print them out, make corrections, and fax them back to my secretary to ''sign''—she has a little stamp

> that says ''Bill.'' Then, if I'm not already at sea, I let loose from my slip at Sapphire Beach, in St. Thomas, Virgin Islands, and set sail for the afternoon.
>
> My ThinkPad runs the yacht's navigational system, though I bring a captain and a first mate when clients are on board. The computer is tied to a ground positioning system, which feeds the necessary latitudes and longitudes to the yacht's autopilot. It has a CD-ROM drive, too, so I can slide in a series of CDs and call up the world's nautical charts. . . .
>
> Communication—whether by phone, fax, or teleconferencing—is key to my management philosophy. That's how I tie together the operations of my four offices. . . . And unlike a big corporation, I don't have to waste time in planning meetings and strategy sessions.

You don't have to have a yacht to find the same freedom in your life that Bill Tobin has found in his. Whether your vehicle is a yacht, a car, or a Winnebago, get out of the house and stay in touch with your world via technology. Then, and only then, will you be exercising virtual power.

7. Establish Yourself On-line!

Don't be a hermit in the Brave New World. Immediately enlist one or more of the growing number of on-line service providers—from Prodigy to CompuServe to America Online to a host of Internet chat lines and specific issues forums. They're very inexpensive to join; some of them are even free. Communicate with others via e-mail and the Internet. After all, what's a Brave New World if we don't take the time to discover it?

Barry Diller, the first president of Fox Broadcasting and later the QVC shopping network, gave a speech to America's leading magazine editors, in which he urged them to experience the world on-line instead of just automatically publishing their printed magazines on Web pages:

> *The question I'd like to ask everyone here is: How much time do you spend on-line? Have you gone into a chat box for six mind-destroying (and expanding) hours? Have you played around in different parts of the Internet? If not, before you push your publication on-line, go on-line yourself, play with it, let it and its possibilities seep into you.*
>
> *You cannot begin to understand the nexus of all these new technologies until you jump in and experiment. Open your mind to new ways of perceiving and processing. Learn the unique properties of this new universe. That takes patience, the patience to pursue the possibilities of unintended consequences. Knowing that should not be inhibiting, but liberating.*

Whom might you meet on-line? Anybody and everybody. Listen to this description from the December 1994 *Esquire:*

> *All of a sudden, it seems that everyone is online. Rosie O'Donnell tests out punchlines under dozens of names on America Online, and Madonna "reads bedtime stories" to promote her new single on the Underground Music Archive. ("You can interact with me," she begins, "but you can't touch me.") Rush Limbaugh and Billy Idol, NBC and* Scientific American, *are on-line. There are downy-cheeked B-1 pilots and grizzled B-35 vets, gay square-dance clubs and bagpipe players. For all the high-minded, high-tech visions, a lot of the Net is soft-core porn on ThrobNet, discussions of Spam and* Star Trek *on Prodigy, sad-sack stories in "discussion rooms," and lounge-lizard come-ons in Teen Chat on AOL's People Connection. The Net is the Lubavitchers and the Russians—Relcom and GlasNet helped turn back the coup of 1991. It is a report on the National Information Infrastructure from Al Gore's office and bits of gossip about Amy Fisher.*
>
> *Once, the vision of cyberspace was a shimmering city in the sky. But what we've got on screen so far is mostly words—words of SEC filings and NASA shuttle maintenance schedules, of conspiracy theories and alt.sex stories.*

Whew! Is there anything that's *not* on-line? If your answer is, "Me!" you haven't a moment to waste.

The best way to network with others is to put your life on-line. If you're a member of America Online or CompuServe, you can receive and send e-mail with the click of a mouse, instantaneously communicating with either one person or, through mass e-mail, thousands. But the most permanent and valuable way to put your life on-line is by creating and maintaining your own Web page. As we've discussed in previous chapters, a variety of software companies offer programs to easily create your own Web page. Once you've created yours, you'll be one of the 250,000 Webmasters out of the 2 million people using the World Wide Web.

Why establish a Web page? If you're in business, your own page offers you an on-line market presence. Potential customers have a way to find you via the many search engines that will list your Web page. You can direct customers to your Web page through conventional advertising or via e-mail, then post ads to promote your product. You can update your page without incurring printing costs. And customers in different time zones can access your page twenty-four hours a day.

You'll be in good company. Everyone from TV networks to magazines to government agencies to major corporations to schools have their own Web pages. But for me it's the individual pages that seem to offer the most enlightenment. Listen to the testimony of the comedian Sinbad, who uses a PC to create and organize his work, doing everything from keeping his budget to editing his jokes on-line. His Web page (www.Soulmusicfestival.com) advertises his activities and allows Sinbad to pass along his own particular style of wisdom.

As Sinbad told *Computer Life* magazine in its August 1996 issue:

> The Web's like the Wild, Wild West. It's the only place that's left where you can be creative without any money and compete with the big-money boys. . . . I didn't want to put a site together just to have one. Everybody's jumping on the Web, trying to find a way to sell T-shirts. I like people like Thomas Dolby and Todd Rundgren, who actually enjoy the computing side of it. I feel I have something

to say and I've got some content, so now I've come up with something funky . . . like a soul food restaurant of the mind.

Your own Web page opens an exciting new avenue of communication between you and the world. It announces to your customers and colleagues that you're in the revolution, not sitting on the sidelines. By establishing my own Web site (www.guytv.com), I've been astounded by the multitude of visitors we've had, recorded as "hits" on a computerized counter on the page. We've enjoyed some new business we wouldn't have otherwise had and gained some insights from viewers that were well worth heeding.

Do you have some soul food you'd like to market or merely pass along? If you're a fledgling entrepreneur, it's going to be hard to advertise your new company, much less your company's aspirations. Your own Web page allows you to advertise easily and cheaply in both your community and in the world at large.

8. Forever Upgrade!

The one given of the computer industry is that faster, cheaper, and better computer hardware is constantly being developed. Once developed, the next technology immediately renders the old out-of-date and, eventually, obsolete. Being stuck with last decade's PC is akin to reading last decade's newspaper. You do it more for nostalgia than news.

Michael Koss, president and CEO of Koss Corp., the pioneering developer of stereo headphones and speakers, is a survivor of most of the stages of personal computer development, epochs of amazing advancement. Michael has been at it so long, he can break down his life into computer model cycles, each cycle eclipsing the other by the escalating power of the computer at his fingertips.

Before Michael tells you the story of his computer journey, let me tell you a bit of his amazing rise to the presidency of Koss Corp. He definitely wasn't given the presidency of the company on a silver platter. His father, John Koss, was a Chicago TV repairman who dreamed of becoming an entrepreneur. When he got married in 1953, he took the $200 he and his bride received as gifts, bought some old TV sets, and mounted them on rolling carts to rent out to local hospitals. A home-based business was born! One day in 1958, in the garage he used for his company's office, Koss mounted two tiny hi-fi speakers in plastic cups and attached them to opposite ends of a wire hanger, creating the first stereo headphones. Neither rock 'n' roll, nor stereo equipment, nor John Koss would ever be the same.

What his father did in that garage, Michael Koss has done in his own life: created a personal revolution through electronic technology. It's easy to see the crucial importance of constantly upgrading your computer equipment: Michael's evolution (one computer leapfrogging over the other in size, weight, and, most importantly, power) is the perfect example. Just as his ascension to the presidency of Koss Corp. has been a slow and steady climb—from passing out business cards with his own name handwritten over his father's in grammar school to pushing a broom to working his way up to soldering and then on through a variety of jobs before eventually reaching the presidency—Michael's progress in computers has been a step-by-step process.

Koss told me his story through a series of e-mail messages:

The man we had running our company from 1979 to 1984 did not believe in personal computers. He finally broke down in 1984 and let us buy an Apple IIe with Visicalc or whatever the stupid thing was called, to run some forecast and sales reports. It was unreal! We had to sign in to use it so they could keep track of how many man-hours were being wasted on the machine.

I was driven to look at PCs because I had read about two new software packages coming to market. One was called Context MBA, and the other was called Lotus 1-2-3. Running either product was not possible on an Apple. The Lisa or the Mac caught my eye . . . but it was so darned expensive and restrictive—small hard drives, proprietary peripherals—it was a joke. So I thought a PC would do the trick.

I bought two books, one on the IBM PC and the

other on Lotus 1-2-3. I digested them at night, often in bed to the complaints of my wife. ''Wow,'' she would say. ''I've married a computer nerd.'' (The term ''geek'' hadn't been applied to the techies yet.)

Did you ever try to learn how to run a program from a book? Without a machine? It is madness, but when the time came to sit down at the computer I had it made.

We bought two machines, one desktop 8086 mono monitor IBM and the second an IBM portable. What a joke. It was the size of a sewing machine! It weighed a ton, and had a tiny monitor. I learned how to run the programs DOS, MultiMate, and Lotus 1-2-3 on that beast at night and left it here at the office by day. Wow. What agony carrying that thing around . . . and no hard disk! It had two floppies!

Upgrading his PC equipment as soon as new models were introduced, Michael Koss entered the world of dual floppy disk drives, which required endless disk shuffling and wasn't really worth the effort. The introduction of the first hard drive was a revolution. But the drive was so weak and the machine so cumbersome, Michael keeps it displayed in his office as a reminder of how far we've come. Looking at it now—so big! so heavy! so anemic!—he is amazed at how quickly the computer hardware world has changed.

But even though the first machines were unwieldy, they offered capabilities light-years ahead of the alternative: doing things manually. PCs changed Koss's life overnight.

It was as though a light bulb went on! Soon I graduated to faster machines. We went through a bunch of 286s and then 386s. Windows drove us into Microsoft Word and Excel. I bought another portable, a Toshiba monochrome unit that weighed a ton, and before you knew it, I'd pass it off to someone and get the next model. The key was to get as much personal freedom as possible for an open systems approach. . . .

Now I use an IBM 760cd between the office and home every day. I am on-line in the office with an ethernet PCMCIA card (which enhances a computer's memory and serves as a modem connection). I am on-line at home via modem. Not an ISDN yet, but soon. The products we will buy tomorrow will be smart products. Computers on board will adapt to the way you use the item: everything from car seats to cameras, from VCRs to your microwave to your exercise bike. Is it a PC? Yes. Not a laptop; it's a *personal* computer. PDA [handheld personal digital assistant] products are already rocking, and they are infants. In less than two years what I am doing tonight [writing e-mail on a laptop computer] will be antiquated. A PDA in my hand, not my lap, will do it all!

Michael Koss's passion for computers isn't restricted to his work. His home is as wired as his office, not just for himself, but for his children.

The house is a mass of techno stuff. My kids have Apples (thanks to the local school system). Three of my four children have personal computers. The fourth, who just turned seven, has access to an old 486 that I have at the house, and my wife is using an old IBM 720 laptop. I am looking at putting in a LAN at home and running an ISDN line to the house.

Why so many computers in one house? Well, I went overboard. While I believe that kids must learn to share and not be spoiled, I thought that when it came time to do homework, worlds would collide. So I made a big decision and got them all set up so that they'd be ready for the real world of computers. I really did not want to deny them this key advantage, and I feel bad for parents who can't afford to do the same thing.

9. Become Bionic!

Once you revolutionize your life through technology, something amazing begins to happen. You actually become *one* with your machine. I'm not talking about some Frankenstein's monster with a computer chip for a brain, incapable of human emotion and unconcerned about human contact. I'm talking about creating a more orderly, productive, and satisfying life.

As his computer skills began to keep pace with the rocketing technology, Michael Koss began to feel that the computer was becoming more than a machine. It was becoming an integral part of his life. Finally, he couldn't separate the two.

I began to structure my thinking better, more focused. I began to understand that the computer was a tool that I could use as a weapon or as a research ally. I subscribed to CompuServe, AOL, and Prodigy. Jumped into the Internet through Delphi and later through an Internet service provider and [the program] Internet in a Box. Suddenly the world was open. The World Wide Web made it all so available.

Pretty soon Koss was doing what he calls "time shifting," the ability to work on anything, anytime.

I can read my mail when I want to, in my bed or at my desk. I can work with people from other parts of the world. Different time zones became easy thanks to Lotus Notes. Within the next few years I will be on-line at all times via a wireless digital cellular modem. The computer has made me more free. Before, there were things I could do only in my office, at my desk, with other people, during work hours. Today I can time shift to right now, ten P.M., Thursday, in my bedroom, in front of my big TV, watching CNN and tracking Hurricane Fran in my slippers. I can log on to the Internet, read the news, read my mail, contribute to a database discussion on a new product or a problem, check the weather in a city I am soon to visit, send e-mail or a fax, read a report, check sales against forecast, or read the mail we received at our Internet site—all in my PJs, in my jeans, on a plane or sitting on the end of my bed, the way I am right now.

I am attached. I can answer my mail quickly . . . I move in synchronization with others . . . I am informed . . . I am in tune . . . I am quicker . . . smarter . . . better prepared. . . . *I am the Bionic Man!*

He isn't joking. He *is* bionic, and you can become bionic, too. Once you get to this state of absolute ease with your machine, when using the computer is second nature, something close to magic happens. It's as if the computer becomes part of your brain. Become bionic! Isn't that better than becoming lethargic?

Look at what becoming bionic did for Michael Koss.

I track activity better. It isn't a chore. I can keep tabs on more things with less searching. I can extrapolate by playing "what if?" games. I can spell-check words like "extrapolate." The key thing that I realized was that I needed to be a player-coach vs. a coach. The computer emphasizes personal productivity because it makes informed personal output more possible than ever. I have friends running solid companies who no longer have their own assistants. They do it all themselves on-line. Pagers, cell phones, modems, PDAs, and laptop computers make it all work.

Consider the concept for a moment: a player-coach vs. a coach. The conventional corporation exiles the executive to the executive suite, allowing the executive to serve only as a coach. But the computer-savvy executive can move his or her base of operations into the trenches, where real life is happening, without losing touch with the executive suite. Thus, the executive can become a player as well as a coach.

Best of all, I know that I am more transportable. I can conduct my business from a rock in Australia or a cab in Switzerland. The skills I have for managing change, products, and people's activities is now totally transportable. It is as though I have a toolkit that works anywhere and everywhere. This means big change for middle management in the future. Loyalty will now be [computer] chip deep, and serving a company will have more to do with where you want to live, how flexible your organization is, and how plugged in they will allow you to be.

Believe it or not, I actually think differently when I plan and schedule projects. It's hard to explain because it is more a feeling than it is a thought. Maybe it's the self-confidence that I can use a tool to do something. Maybe it's a feeling of mastery over a technology that seems so forbidding to other people.

The closest thing I can compare this type of feeling with would be the following:

The cabinet maker who looks at a broken door and knows instinctively how to fix it.

The baseball player who points to the location he plans to hit the next pitch.

The golfer who knows that his putt will drop the minute the ball is struck.

The surgeon who knows cutting into flesh can excise damaged tissue.

It's as though planning and anticipating becomes a part of rote memory, routine in scale, systematic in process.

What has it hurt? I have trouble remembering telephone numbers, dates, and details. They're all in my PDA. I am lost without it. It seems that once the data goes in, my brain releases the data. It's almost as though my brain has become the RAM and the PDA has become my hard drive.

Michael Koss has become his computer!

10. Enlighten Others!

Once you become computer proficient yourself, help others. The stronger we become as a community of computer users, the stronger the community of computer users will grow. As Intel's Andy Grove wrote in his book, the Internet gains its power through the collective work of millions of users, not from being exclusive to an inner core.

Grove writes:

How could such a complex network keep up with such unbridled growth? It could precisely because of the fact that this is a connection co-op. As each computer strengthens its own network it contributes to the strength of the overall network. As in any good co-op, people acting in their own self-interest act in the interest of the whole.

Remember, no one is born computer literate. As I've learned while writing this book, helping others discover the power of the computer is one of the most rewarding gifts we can give. After all, what good is knowledge if we don't pass it on?

We are all fellow travelers on the information highway, caught in the middle of an incredible revolution. Teach, travel, and, above all, trade: e-mail, files, software, information, and insights. In a world with millions and millions on-line, we need all of the friends we can get. Those you help today will likely help you tomorrow. Take it from a former cyberphobe: they'll never forget your kindness.

CHAPTER TEN

Turn It On!

He was afraid.

Cyberphobic, computer idiot, technologically illiterate—these were all applicable terms. There was just something about the computer that turned him off, although he never knew what. To him the PC was a Pandora's box, a crucible of all his fears and insecurities, just another problem when what he desperately needed were solutions.

He was stuck in a rut, a typical nine-to-five job with all of the heartbreaks: confined to a cubicle, lorded over by a demanding troll of a boss, relegated to dead-end duties for a barely-making-ends-meet salary with the reward of a two-week vacation that passed in the blink of an eye. He was just another cog in the lumbering machinery of bureaucrats and bureaucracy, lost in the lie of middle-management fulfillment.

His personal life had become a joke. Where did all his time go? His days and nights each began with an hour-long commute to and from downtown. He and his wife were becoming strangers. He could never spend enough time with his kids. Forget about leisure. Weekends were gone in an instant, leaving him stuck in a state of perpetual smolder.

Initial frustration led to disillusionment and, eventually, surrender. He became desperate to find a way out, a way back to some nebulous "before," back to a time when he wasn't caught on a treadmill but was on the path to achieving his dreams. He vaguely remembered such a time. But that period was buried deep in his memory; it was a place to which he couldn't find his way back.

Then the new world introduced itself in the very window of his fears. A computer beckoned. It sat on the desk of a persistent friend, who had nagged him for years that the computer was the answer to his prayers instead of another problem.

One day, finally, he listened. He decided to face his fear and plug in to a power greater than his own. His friend showed him how to start the computer and how to operate a few programs and invited him to spend some time on the machine. He started with a simple word-processing program, and—miracles of miracles!—his words scrolled across the screen like battalions of disciplined soldiers. No matter how many mistakes he made, the computer didn't blow up! Soon he was typing with such speed and efficiency, the conventional typewriter seemed like a relic from the Stone Age.

Next he was on to computer games and, then, on-line networks like Prodigy, America Online, and CompuServe. Suddenly, with the click of a mouse and the speed of a modem, he joined a network of millions. He sent e-mail to friends and relatives around the world. He jumped on the Internet, entertaining and educating himself with dozens of incredible Web sites. He accessed his bank account, took part in forums, read the news, and even traded a few stocks—without ever leaving his friend's computer terminal. He kept repeating a single adjective: "Incredible!"

His wife and kids didn't see much of him during the several days he spent burrowed in his friend's office. When he emerged, his skin was a little pale from the fluorescent lights, but his mind was racing. His family listened as he told a tale straight out of Revelations. In the wildly changing world of technology, he now realized he had been standing still. But, by teaching himself in just a matter of days, he had become proficient in hardware, software, and the Internet. He could take his computer apart and put it together again. But it wasn't just the equipment that excited him, it was the *potential.* The world hadn't changed; he'd merely caught up with it.

"Fasten your seat belts," he said. "We're headed on-line."

He began spending so much time on the computer that his friend gently hinted that it might be time for him to buy one of his own. But he didn't rush out and buy anything. Not yet. Not until he knew *exactly* what he wanted to do with his life.

Back at work, he found his cubicle increasingly confining and the nine-to-five world excruciatingly slow. His boss seemed grouchier, his colleagues more pessimistic, the atmosphere more stifling. But now he didn't simply smolder. He acknowledged his dissatisfaction in his career and, in doing so, took a crucial first step toward freedom. Once he could assess himself and his situation clearly, he could begin to take action.

He kept hearing the phrase "home-based business," the $427 billion industry of millions and millions of people who have headed home from conventional corporations, keeping in constant contact with the real world through their computers. There would be fifteen million home-based business owners by the year 2002. Why couldn't he be one of them? Why did he have to chain his future to some corporate hierarchy whose power to lay him off, displace his family, and derail his future was not only its prerogative, but in light of tight economic times, almost certainly a possibility?

He employed a simple technique to define his dreams: he began with the end in mind. Where did he want to end up in his life? What occupation would best deliver him and his family to that desired destination? He wrote down his goals in the five most important areas of his life—relationship, finances, career, health, personal fulfillment—and narrowed his focus to fields that could satisfy these goals. What would be his perfect work? For guidance, he could choose from one of many home-based business books, available both on-line and in bookstores, including Paul and Sarah Edwards's *Working from Home with Your Computer,* which details seventy-five computer home businesses in the categories of sales, word processing, accounting, database, graphics, computer service, and communications.

But he knew what he wanted to do, although the calling had been hidden in the back of his brain for so long, he had forgotten it was there. Now it came back to him clearly, a passion emerging from a haze, as if he had just awakened from amnesia. For our purposes, it doesn't matter which occupation he decided to pursue. What matters is his *decision* to step out of his routine and dedicate himself totally to his dreams.

He returned to his friend's computer and, accessing one of the Internet's many search engines, typed in the words that best described his proposed home-based business. Pages of possibilities, advice, and encouragement scrolled across the screen. He determined that there was indeed a need for his services. He researched the field, asked questions of potential clients and colleagues, accessed information. Convinced that he was on a potentially rewarding path, he was ready to make the leap.

Mustering up courage and credit card, he marched into his neighborhood computer store. He asked questions and demanded replies in plain English, not cyberspeak. He sought out the proper software to accomplish his particular needs. He bought the best computer system, printer, modem, and accessories he could afford. He asked for precise directions to set up his new system and wrote them down carefully. Then, with the swipe of his credit card, he was in business. He took his bundles home and set up shop in a second bedroom, flipped the switch, and launched one more life on-line.

He quit his job and radically reinvented his existence. He set up his home-based business with specific rules and boundaries and vowed never to step over those self-imposed lines. He used his aggravation over his prior employment to propel him forward, never allowing that aggravation to slow him down. He found the new ways to do the old things in both his career and personal life. He risked failure, knowing that failure frequently teaches the greatest lessons. He trusted the Force at his fingertips and used it to surrender the superfluous, the accounting, scheduling, communications, and other processes that the computer can accomplish in mere seconds. He went portable, unleashing himself from his home office to work and play in the real world, where life is really happening.

When he looked up after the first year, he was not only succeeding financially, he was earning more of a far more precious currency: *time.* Time for his family. Time for his relationships. Time to learn, to explore, to grow, to contribute. Finally, he learned the importance of turning the computer off. He realized that life is not confined to what we can accomplish on-line, but is enhanced by the quality of our experience in the real world.

His life blossomed into a renaissance, instead of being stuck in a state of constant reversals. He and his family moved to a mountain town in the Rockies, far from the nameless skyscrapers, self-centered bosses, and noxious freeway fumes that once held him hostage. He now lives according to his own schedule, free of convention and corporation, a self-actualized citizen of the twenty-first century.

Who is this person, and how has he achieved such an incredible rebirth?

Well, he is also a she; it's you and it's me. The rebirth chronicled here is a portrait of a universal home-based business entrepreneur, a composite of all of us who first said "No," but later said "Yes" to the new computer technology. It is a portrait of someone who has harnessed the potential that exists, but all too frequently lies dormant, in us all. It is a reinvention of a life using the lessons in the nine previous chapters of this book, the journeys of the disparate individuals who have graciously passed along their inspiring testimonials of computer empowerment. Through this story, and those presented throughout this book, I hope you can see how the personal computer can become the vehicle for real and profound change in your life.

Someday soon, our collective stories will be one story, the story of an epoch when amazing new technology was first applied to the basics of human existence, an era of inspiration and enlightenment, an era when initial frustration led to eventual fulfillment. Like most revolutionary inventions—the electric light bulb, the telephone, the television, the air conditioner, the automobile, the airplane—the new invention always begins by serving the few before spreading to the multitudes. Once that happens with computer technology, the real story of millions upon millions of human beings who reshuffled their lives and achieved their dreams through the window that sat blinking on their desktops will be written in historical, not motivational, books.

That day is just around the corner. You have been afforded a rare and exciting opportunity to be part of that history, to write your own story on its pages. You cannot afford to wait another second before beginning. The first step is easy. The first step requires only a single word—"Yes!"

We are all on a technological journey. It can be the ride of your life, propelling you to heights unimagined, or it can pass you by just as dramatically. The technology is here, eagerly awaiting whatever you choose to bring to it. Bring a sense of wonder, exploration and possibility and the computer will enrich you with equal excitement and enlightenment. Look at it with fear, uncertainty, and dread and it, too, will close its eyes and remain mute.

Action is the force that leads to greatness. Say "Yes" to the new computer technology and then take the necessary actions to bring that technology into every part of your life.

Virtual power is at your fingertips.

Turn it on!

Index

Accidental Empires (Cringely), 32
accountants, 26
acting jobs, in CD-ROM games, 161–66
ACT program, 75
Adams, Scott, 157, 167, 168–69, 194
Advanced Research Projects Agency (ARPA), 83
Adventures of Batman and Robin, The, 162
advertising, 15, 16, 18
affirming one's goals, 168–72
age gap, in computer shopping, 58
aggravation, use of, 159–60
AIDS, 136
airplanes:
  networking on, 128
  notebook computers and, 192–93
Alderman, Lesley, 99
Alzheimer's disease, 136, 137
American Association of Home-Based Businesses, 54, 71
American Express, 115
America Online, 78, 134, 135, 136, 141, 143, 172, 224, 234
American Self-Help Clearinghouse, 156
Anasazi Indians, 190–91
Andreessen, Mark, 90–91
Andreessen World, 90
"Anglican Kids Association," 222
AOL, *see* America Online
Apple Computer, 29, 68, 118, 173
Apple IIe, 231
ARPA (Advanced Research Projects Agency), 83
ARPANET, 83
articles magazine, 52, 53
Asimov, Isaac, 94
Aspen, Colo., 201, 204
AT&T, 30, 87
Atlas Motorcycles, 98–107
attire, home-based businesses and, 217–20
Australian goats, 179
automobiles, 25, 26, 208–9

background noise, 73
bandwidth, 87
bar codes, electronic, 24
Bare Knuckles and Back Rooms (Rollins), 171
Barnes, Edwin C., 113, 115
Barry, Dave, 56, 58
Batman, 122
battery-powered notebook computers, 182–83
baud, 87
BBC, 185
BBN (Bolt, Beranek and Newman), 83
BBS (bulletin board systems), 224
Beaverhead River, 180
Beetlejuice, 122
Beginners Guides to Internet, 84–85
Bell Atlantic, 30, 207
Bell Canada, 208
Benetton, 127
BEV (Blacksburg Electronic Village), 207
Bill and Carole (on-line lovers), 142–49
Billings, Mont., 32
Black Pearl, 166
Blacksburg, Va., 206–7
Blacksburg Electronic Village (BEV), 207
blindness, 118–19
Bloomington, Ill., 124

Bobby (screenwriter), 151–52
Bolt, Beranek, and Newman (BBN), 83
books, computer, 62
Borland International, 29
Bosnia, 92
bosses, 157, 158, 159–60, 168
boundaries, home-based businesses and, 217–20
Bowen, Charles, 135
Braveheart, 182, 185–86
Breeze, 225, 226
British Telephony, 87
browsers, 78, 87, 88, 94
  see also Netscape
Buddhism, Zen, 223
Bunting, Kelly, 16, 18, 41, 72, 115, 116
Bunting, Kyle, 69–70
Bunting, Mark:
  cocktail-napkin bet of, 41, 43
  computer illiteracy of, 15–16
  computers discovered by, 17–18
  failures of, 108–15
  first notebook computer of, 191–92
  Manhattan move of, 129
  TV show of, 111–13, 114, 128–32
Bunting's Window, 130, 131, 211
Bunting's Window to the Net, 211
bureaucracy, 157, 158
business world, computers' effects on, 29–30

call management, 170–71
Calvin and Hobbes (Watterson), 169
Camus, Albert, 190
CancerNet, 189
career, traditional jobs and, 40
Carlyle, Thomas, 67
Carole and Bill (on-line lovers), 142–49
Carthage, Miss., 135
cartoonists, 168–70
cashmere, 178, 179
Cash Stud, 179–80
"Catholic Information Center on Internet," 222
Catholicism, 222
CB radios, 188, 189
CD-ROM drives, 69, 227
CD-ROM games, 162–66
cellular phones, 225, 226
central processing units (CPUs), 26, 65
chairs, 72–73
Channel 39, Houston, 111
"chat" rooms, 136, 142–49, 151
Chiatt, Jay, 183
Chiatt-Day Advertising, 183
Chicago *Tribune,* 99
Christian bookstores, 108–9
Churchill, Winston, 127
Clark, Jim, 90
Cleveland Free-Net, 137
Clinton, Bill, 81–82, 212–13
Clinton, Hillary Rodham, 177
clones, PC, 57
Clos la Chance Vineyard, 175–77
CNBC, 129, 130, 211
C/NET, 81, 90
Collector, 105
comic strips, 168–70
commuting, 28
Compaq Computer, 15, 70
Compaq Presario 850 PC, 225
competition, 50–51
Complete Idiot's Guide to Computers, The, 62
CompuServe, 78, 135, 136, 143, 202, *224, 234
Computer Broadcast Network, 211
Computer City Television, 211
Computer Howse Company, 19–20, 70, 73–75, 110
Computer Life, 229–30
Computer Man, The, 114, 128–32, 211
computer nerds, 15, 18, 26, 27, 37, 67, 112, 129, 232
computer revolution, ten ways to keep up with, 206–43
  become bionic, 234–37
  constantly reinvent yourself, 212–15
  constantly seek out enlightenment, 221–223
  enlighten others, 237–38
  establish yourself online, 227–30
  forever upgrade, 230–34
  go portable, 225–27
  keep ahead of the computer software curve, 223–25
  make your home a technological tabernacle, 217–20
  surrender the superfluous, 215–17
computers:
  addiction to, 17–18, 202
  capacities of, 22, 30
  children and, 201–2, 233–34
  communicative power of, 80
  crashing of, 66
  empowerment for, 23–24

in European and American households, 212
expandable, 69
as frontier, 32
illiteracy, 15–16, 140, 161, 195; *see also* cyberphobia
laptop, 30
newspapers vs., 184
Personal Secretary and, 170–71
portable, *see* portable computers
processors of, 16, 20
purchasing of, 56–75
relationships developed on, 135–56
selecting of, 37–38, 56
self-healing through, 139–41
support groups on, 139
Williams's fear of, 45
computer stores, 57, 61–62
"Computopia," 92
Condé Nast Traveler, 184–85
Conference on Goats, 181
consultants, computer, 58–59
Context MBA, 231
corporate takeovers, 33
cost of entry, 51
Covey, Stephen, 19
CPUs (central processing units), 26, 65
credit cards, 115
Cringely, Robert X., 32
"cubicles," 194
Curley (biker), 102
"cyberbars," 149
cyberphobia, 15–16, 23, 25–27, 161
cyberspace, 87–88
community on, 138–39
love and, 134–56
personas on, 147–48, 152–54
see also Internet
cyberspeak, 15–16, 20, 57–58, 62, 63
Internet, 87–90
Cycle World, 105

daily routine, work and, 27–30, 33
Dallas, Tex., 16, 186
Darby, R. U., 122–23
DARPA (Defense Advanced Research Projects Agency), 83
databases, 64, 66, 75
day care, 28
deafness, 118, 223–25
DeafNet, 225
Defense Data Network Information Center, 84
Defense Department, U.S., 83
Dell, 58, 70
Dell, Michael, 70, 110
Delphi, 234
Denver, Colo., 120
desktop publishing, 46
Dickens, Charles, 118
Dictaphones, 126, 127, 226
Digital Dungeon, 42, 214
Dilbert (Adams), 168–69
Dilbert Principle, The (Adams), 158, 169, 194
Diller, Barry, 227–28
Dillon, Mont., 178
discussion forums, 136
dissatisfaction, acknowledgment of, 36–37, 44, 159–60
Dolby, Thomas, 229
Dooling, Ann and Tom, 178–81
DOS, 26, 232
DOS-based computers, 57
DOS for Dummies, 62
downsizing, 21, 24, 33, 157, 168, 216
driving ranges, 77–79
drycleaning, 50–51
Duran, Alma, 92
Dutch John, Utah, 215
Dylan, Bob, 77

East Orange, N.J., 213
Ebert, Roger, 80–81
Ed (Alzheimer's sufferer), 137, 138
Edison, Thomas A., 113, 115
Edwards, Paul and Sarah, 241
Egghead Software, 224
electronic bar codes, 24
Electronic Village Mall Web page, 207
Elliott, Carter, 207
e-mail (electronic mail), 88–89, 106, 207, 229, 233
addresses, 176
notebook computers and, 192–93
on-line personal ads and, 134–35, 136
romance through, 134–35, 143–49
End of Work, The (Rifkin), 24
enlightenment, on Internet, 221–23
"Enlightenment On-Line—The Spiritual Search in Cyberspace," 221–22
Entertainment Weekly, 160
Episcopalianism, 222
Esquire, 228
ethernet PCMCIA, 233
E*TRADE, 203

Eva (bar frau), 102
Evans, Oliver, 25–26
eWorld, 151
Excel, 75, 232
Export Today, 105

failure, opportunity in, 108
Famous Monsters, 161
Far Side, The (Larson), 169
fat people, 59, 60–62
fear of technology, 15–16, 23, 25–27, 161
Federal Computer Week, 76
Ferrone, Michael, 114
fiber, 178–81
Fifty States in Fifty Weeks, 131–32
finances, traditional jobs and, 40
firing, 168
First in His Class (Maraniss), 212–13
First Person with Maria Shriver, 131
Fisher, Amy, 228
Five Rules for Dealing with Your Neighborhood Computer Salesperson, 64
flight simulators, 202
Forbes ASAP, 199
Ford, 29
Ford, Henry, 25, 26
Forth, Tex., 47
Fortune, 34
Fox Broadcasting, 227
frontier, in American history, 32
Frying Pan River, 204
"functionally unemployable," 218
furniture, 72
future, scenario of, 24–25
"Future of the Net" website, 81

Gabriel Knight, 162
Gary (TV station manager), 111
Gates, Bill, 77
Gateway, 58
Gemini Awards, 165
GEN (Global Entrepreneurs Network), 225
gender gap, in computer shopping, 58
Geological Survey Department, U.S., 200–201
Gerland's Grocery Store, 75
Gibson, Mel, 182
Gibson, William, 87
GlasNet, 228
goats, 179
going-out-of-business sales, 72
golf, 77–99
Gong Show, The, 131
Gonzales, Laurence, 23
Gore, Al, 228
Gottas, Linus, 137–38
Gottas, Ruth, 137–38
grapes, 173–74
graphic novels, 166
Grateful Dead, 43
Great American Cashmere sweaters, 181
Green, Brent, 120–21
Greene, Graham, 17
Green, Marvin, 208–9
Gretzky, Wayne, 126
Grove, Andy, 211–12, 237
Grove, Dick, 42, 195–200
Grove, Teresa, 199
GTE, 171
guerrilla marketing, 125
Gunter, Judy Slomovich, 223–25

Hall, Justin, 91–94
Hallmark Cards, 29
Hamill, Griffin, 165
Hamill, Mark, 160–68
Hannah, Daryl, 126
hard drives, 68, 232
Harleys, 101
Hart (journalist), 90–91
Hart, Mickey, 43
"Harvard-Radcliffe Catholic Student Association," 222
health, traditional jobs and, 40
Health Ride, 127
Henry, O., 117–18
Herrick, Jan, 59–67
Hewlett-Packard, 15, 29, 173
Hill, Napoleon, 111, 113, 116–17, 122–123, 127
Hoitsma, Tom, 128–29
Hollywood Squares, 131
home-based businesses, 23, 29–30
  computerizing processes and, 216–17
  defining one's passion and, 41–43
  dissatisfaction as step leading to, 36–37, 44
  empowerment through, 35–36
  failure and, 108–33
  fear and, 39
  front lines of, 132–33
  getting dressed and, 217–20
  Hall's views on, 92–94
  home pages and, 95

importance of separating work and home in, 71–72, 218–20
of John Koss, 230–31
questions to ask about, 50–51
sole proprietorships, 52
traditional jobs' capacity for fulfillment vs., 39–41
zoning and, 207–8
Home Office Computing, 157, 189–90
Homepage Creator System, 96
home pages, 90, 91–94, 172, 188
for communities, 207, 210
creation of, 95–97
financial gain and, 97–107
reasons for, 229–30
Home PC, 135
Home Shopping Network, 24, 25
Hope, Ark., 119
Houston, Tex., 17, 19
Howard, Peter, 209–10
"How to Create a Home Page," 95–97
HTML programming, 96
Hulk, The, 162
Hurricane Fran, 235
Hutchison, Kans., 195, 197–98

IBM, 15, 129, 130, 173
IBM 760cd, 233
IBM Thinkpad, 225, 227
ice skating, 124
Idol, Billy, 228
"ILC Glossary of Internet Terms," 87
Illinois, University of, at Urbana-Champaign, 90
illiteracy, computer, 140, 161, 195
inaction, 36, 49
INC., 225–27
Inc. Technology, 210
Industrial Revolution, 23
information retrieval, on Internet, 77
information revolution, 23
see also computer revolution, ten ways to keep up with
"in-line" skates, 124
Intel, 15, 129, 173, 273
Intel Pentium processors, 68
Intel ProShare Personal Conferencing Video System, 186, 187
International Data Corp., 77
Internet, 76–107
advertising on, 96
auctions on, 99
bottlenecks absent in, 91
capabilities of, 78–81
deafness and, 223–25
establishing oneself on, 227–30
financial security achieved on, 203–4
getting started on, 81–107
growth of, 84
guidelines for, 106
home pages on, 90, 91–94, 172, 175–177, 188, 207, 210, 229–30
marketing wine on, 175–77
neighborhood feel of, 92
on-line personal ads on, 134, 136
romance-based on-line chat rooms on, 142–49
size of, 82–83
spirituality and, 221–23
telephone system compared with, 86–87
television on, 91
terminology for, 87–90
truckers and, 188–89
X-rated sites on, 103, 221, 227
Internet for Dummies, The, 76
Internet service providers (on-line communication services), 89
see also specific carriers
Internetting Project, 83–84
Intervoice, 171
"Introduction to Internet by Professor Jimmy Lin," 82–84
inventory management, 174
ISDN lines, 187, 208, 210
"It's Not Just for Scientists Anymore," 94
ITT Night Mariner night-vision binoculars, 185

jargon, 15–16, 20, 57–58, 62, 63
Internet, 87–90
"Jason's Notes from Underground," 91–94
JOB (just over broke), 32, 131, 159
jobs:
career and, 40
downsizing of, 21, 24, 33, 157, 168, 216
finances and, 40
health and, 40
personal fulfillment and, 40–41
relationships and, 39–40
Jobs, Steven P., 25
jobseeking, on Internet, 173, 216, 217
Joffrey Ballet, 132
Johnson, Lyndon, 74
Jones, Jerry, 39

Judaism, 222
"Judaism.com," 222

Karen (legal secretary), 27–28
Keller, Helen, 118–19, 131
Kelly, Kevin, 80
Kennedy, John F., Jr., 126
Kinko's, 74
Koss, John, 230–31
Koss, Michael, 230–37
Koss Corp., 230

Landers, Ann, 155–56
languages, Web pages and, 103, 105
laptop computers, 30, 233
  see also portable computers
Larson, Gary, 169
Las Vegas, Nev., 139, 146–47
law enforcement, 32
law profession, 178–81
Lawrence, Kans., 199
layoffs, 21, 24, 33, 168, 218
learning, 18–20
Learning Channel, 211
legal secretaries, 27–28
leiomyosarcoma, 190
Letterman, David, 126
Lexis-Nexis, 217
librarians, 85–86
Library of Congress, 25
lifestyle, work and, 27–30, 33
Limbaugh, Rush, 136, 228
Lin, Jimmy, 82
Lincoln, Abraham, 120
Liquid Paper, 47
log cabin homes, 35
Los Angeles Times, 25
Lotus Notes, 234
Lotus 1-2-3, 231, 232
Love Handles, 60, 62
Love Thy Neighbor (Mason), 184
Lubavitchers, 228
Lucas, George, 163
Lucy@TheBuzz.com, 172
Lutz, William, 168
Lycos, 223
Lynx, 88

McCloskey, Paul, 76
machines, 23
Macintosh computers, 150
  Pentium-based computers vs., 67–68
Macintosh 270C, 102
Madonna, 228
Magellan, 222
Magnavox VGA monitors, 65
mail, electronic vs. "snail," 88–89
mail-order houses, 58
Maraniss, David, 212
Marconi, Guglielmo, 109
Marden, Orison Swett, 200
Marietta (transformed mother), 150–55
market research, 50
marriages, home-based offices and, 72
Mason, Jackie, 184
MCI, 87
MCI-Gallup surveys, 26
megabytes, 26
Men's Journal, 23
menu screens, touch-sensitive, 24
MessagePad, 185
Microsoft, 129, 131
Microsoft Access, 174
Microsoft Excel, 65, 232
Microsoft Word, 174, 232
Microtalk, 119
middle management, 236
Mobile, Ala., 134
Model T, 25
modems, 62, 68, 99, 134, 202, 225, 233
mom-and-pop clone shops, 57, 58
MONEY, 99
monitors, 68
Monster Board, 173, 216
Montgomery Village, Ont., 207–10
Mooneyham, Sandy, 118
"morphing," 132
Mosaic, 89, 94
Mosaic Communications, 90
motorcycles, 97–107
movie industry, 163
MS-DOS 3.3, 223
Multimate, 232
Murphy, Bill and Brenda, 173–77
music:
  background, 73
  production, 42, 214

National Association of Television Producers and Executives (NATPE), 114, 115, 130
National Center for Supercomputing Applications (NCSA), 89–90
National Information Infrastructure, 228
National Infrastructure Award, 138

National Science Foundation, 84
NBC, 228
nerds, computer, 15, 18, 26, 27, 37, 67, 112, 129, 232
Nesmith, Bette, 47
Netscape, 78–79, 81, 86, 88, 89–90, 99
Netscape Communications Corporation, 90
"Netscape Visionary Surfs to Fame and Fortune," 90–91
networking, 128
Neuromancer (Gibson), 87
New Doublespeak, The (Lutz), 168
Newsweek, 169
New York Times, 21
Ngemelis group, 185
Nike, 29
Nixon, 165
notebook computers, *see* portable computers
novels, graphic, 166
nursing homes, 137–38

Oakton, Va., 226
O'Donnell, Rosie, 228
Okidata OL-400 laser printers, 65
Olson, Scott, 42, 124–27
on-line communication services Internet services providers, 89, *see also specific providers*
Online Personals, 136
Only the Paranoid Survive (Grove), 211
Oregon Trail, The, 201–2
Orlandino, Jim, 99, 100, 105
Orlandino, Joe, 98–107
Out of Control (Kelly), 80
outsourcing, 173–74
"Overview of the World Wide Web, An," 94

Pacific Bell, 86–87, 168
PageMaker, 75
parole officers, 32
passion, defining of, 41–43
PC Anywhere, 226
PC Financial Network, 203
PC Gifts and Flowers, 226
PC Solution, 61, 65
PDAs (personal digital assistant), 233, 236, 237
pension plans, 33
Pentium-based computers, Macintoshes vs., 67–68
Penzias, Arno, 49
People Connection, 228
personal ads, on-line, 134, 136
Personal Connection, 148
personal days, 205
personal digital assistants (PDAs), 233, 236, 237
personal fulfillment, traditional jobs and, 40–41
Personal Secretary, 170–71
pest control, 213–14
pet store management, 43–44
Pickering, Philip, 188–89
Piscataway, N.J., 42
planning, 37–38, 50–51
player-coaches vs. coaches, 235–36
Polly, Jean Amour, 85–86
pornography, on Internet, 103, 221, 227
portable computers, 182–205
  computer revolution and, 225–27
  constraints of geography broken by, 186–88
  convention broken by, 188–89
  e-mail and, 192–94
  financial security and, 200–204
  loss broken by, 189–91
  Theroux's experience with, 184–85
  virtual workspaces and, 195–200
  workaholism and, 204–5
Potter, C., 26
Potter, Whit, 79
power strips, 73
"Prayer of a Cybernaut," 222
Presidents and Prime Ministers, 105
Prime Time Publicity and Media, 42, 195–200
probation counselors, 32
processes, time-intensive, 215–17
Prodigy, 17, 20, 79, 134, 135, 136, 142, 143, 148, 234

Quick Books, 75
Quicken, 174
Quick Mail, 196
QVC, 227

Raine's Real Estate, 207
RAM (random access memory), 26, 68
ranchers, 34
Reagan, Ronald, 171
relationships, on-line, 134–56
  "chat" rooms and, 143–49
  personal ads and, 134–35, 136

relationships, on-line (*cont.*)
self-help and, 139–41, 150–55
support through difficult situations and, 137–39
traditional jobs and, 39–40
Relcom, 228
religion, Internet and, 221–23
Rent-a-Husband Handyman Service, 54
Reston, Va., 201
Return of the Jedi, 160
reverse migration, 200
Rifkin, Jerry, 24
Roberts, Chris, 163, 164
Rock Islands, 185
rock music production, 214
Rockville, Md., 44, 71, 218
Rocky Mountain College, 34
Rollerblade,™ 42, 124–27
Rolling Stones, 165
Rollins, Ed, 171
ROM, 26
Romance Connection, 134, 136
Roosevelt, Eleanor, 107
Roosevelt, Franklin Delano, 42
Roosevelt, Theodore, 108
Roseburg, Oreg., 61, 66
Row Bike, 127
Royal Resources, 60, 62
Ruby, Dan, 81
Rundgren, Todd, 229
Russians, 228

sales personnel, 58, 63, 64
Sally (wife of Alzheimer's sufferer), 137, 138
S&L crisis, 33
Santa Clara, Calif., 59
Santa Rosa, Calif., 189
Sarajevo, 92
Saratoga, Calif., 173
Sattar, Sohail, 170–71
Saturn 20/40, 162
Sausalito, Calif., 195
Schaak, Dale, 34
Schaak, Maureen, 32–36
Scientific American, 228
screenwriting, 121–22, 163–64
Seal, Mark, 186, 187
self-direction, 36
self-help, computers as, 139–41
Senyak, Gene, 189–91
Senyak, Isaiah, 189–90, 191
Sharp, Susan, 71–72, 218–20
Shaw Cable TV, 208
Shock, 139–41
shotgun e-mailing, 106
Shriver, Maria, 22–23
significant others, 72
Silicon Investor, 203
Silicon Valley, 15, 16, 20
Sinbad, 229–30
Singles Bulletin Board, 148
Size Acceptance Movement, 60
Skaaren, Warren, 122
Skutchan, Larry, 119–20
Slatalla, Michelle, 137
"snail mail," 88
software, 62, 64, 65
constant development of, 223–25
staff vs., 178–81
see also specific programs
sole proprietorship, 52
spirituality, on Internet, 221–23
spouses, 72
Springsteen, Bruce, 126
Sprint, 87
"Spur That Drives to Riches, The" (Hill), 116–17
staff, software vs., 178–81,
Star Wars, 160, 161, 164, 166–67
stereo headphones and speakers, 230
Stewart, Martha, 114
Sting, 165
stock research, 203
stockbrokers, 183
Stone, Oliver, 165
stores, computer, 57, 61–62
"streaming," 211
Success, 199
support groups, 139
surge protectors, 73
Swarthmore College, 91

Talk Soup, 131
Taylor, Jeff, 216
technology:
adapting to, 21
communities and, 206–11
fear of, 15–16, 23, 25–27, 161
learning of, 18–20
movie industry and, 163
revolution in, 24–25, 26–27, 33
see also computer revolution, ten ways to keep up with; computers
Teen Chat, 228
Telefonos de Mexico, 87

telephone systems, 86–87
television:
as background noise, 73
computer sales through, 111–13, 114, 128–32
on Internet, 91
"10 times Force," 211–12
Texas Monthly, 122
Theroux, Paul, 184–85
Think and Grow Rich (Hill), 111, 113, 116–17
Thinkpad, IBM, 225, 227
This Old House, 113
ThrobNet, 228
Time, 90
time shifting, 234–35
TMP Interactive, 216
Tobin, Bill, 225
Today, 131
Top Gun, 122, 185
touch-sensitive menu screens, 24
Townsend, Ryan, 134–35
Townsend, Tracee, 134–35
trains, 26
Trimble Global Positioning System, 185
trucking, computer, 188–89

"Uncle Jimbo Gets Religion and It Gets Him," 222
United Airlines, 130
upgrading, importance of, 230–34
Upgrading and Repairing PCs, 62
URL (Uniform Resource Locator), 88, 100
USA Weekend, 206, 207

Vendredi Enterprises, 60
Ventura Publisher, 47
videoconferencing, 132, 148, 186–87, 208
video games, 59
video poker, 143–44
Vila, Bob, 113–14
Virginia Polytechnic Institute, 207
virtual power, secrets of, 157–81
affirm your way to success, 168–72
employ software, not staff, 178–81
find the new way to do the old thing, 172–77
never say no to the Force, 160–67
use aggravation, 159–60
virtual workspaces, 42
Visa, 115
Visicalc, 231
voice-activation technology, 22, 24
Voice of America, 185
voices, doing, 73–74

Waconia, Minn., 42
Walesa, Lech, 37
Wall Street Journal, 15, 18, 19, 20, 22, 39, 80
Watterson, Bill, 169
WealthWEB, 203
Welch, Stan, 63–64
White House, 177
"Whole Internet User's Guide and Catalogue, The," 86–90
Wigs, 201–4
Williams, Beverley, 43–50, 51–54, 71, 72
Williams, John, 53
Williams, Stacey, 214–15
Williams Associates Desk Top Publishers, 52
Windows 95, 68, 232
wine making, 173–77
Wine Spectator, 177
WinFax, 175
Wing Commander series, 163–66
Winnipeg Jets, 124
Winters, Doyle, 77–81, 84, 86, 87, 88, 90, 91, 94, 95, 97–98, 107, 139
Wired, 137, 183
wired communities, 206–11
women, corporate culture and, 59
Word for Windows, 174
Word Perfect, 45
workaholism, 204–5
Working from Home with Your Computer (Edwards and Edwards), 241
workplaces, traditional, 33, 93, 98
workspaces:
boundaries between home and, 71–72, 218–20
of Computer Howse, 69–73
virtual, 42, 183
World Trade, 105
World Wide Web, 77, 78, 91
Atlas Motorcycles home page on, 97–107
home pages on, 94, 95–97, 175–77, 188, 207, 210, 229–30
job placement and, 173, 216, 217
see also Internet
WorldWide TV.com, 211
Wright, Orville and Wilbur, 26

writers, 183
writing, 46–47
www.guytv.com, 230
www.headwaters.com, 208
www.Soulmusicfestival.com, 229

Xerox, 30

Yahoo, 84, 221–23
Yoffe, Emily, 122

Zap Records, 42
Zen Buddhism, 223
Zoppo, Richard "Zap," 42, 213–214

About the Author

Mark Bunting went from computer illiteracy to running his own multimillion-dollar computer television company in the span of twenty-two months. After conquering his fear of the keyboard, he became one of the first television personalities of the computer revolution, spreading the gospel of technology in an enjoyable, compelling, accessible style. As host and executive producer of the nationally syndicated television series *The Computer Man* Bunting demonstrates computer products to more than 44 million households each week. As host of *Bunting's Window . . . to the World of Computers,* which airs exclusively on United Airlines, he teaches viewers about the benefits of computer technology. He can also be seen on Computer City TV, airing in Computer City stores nationwide. Bunting lives with his wife, Kelly, and their two children in Dallas, Texas.